THE CLUE TO THE BRONTËS

THE REVD PATRICK BRONTË

THE CLUE
TO THE BRONTËS

by

G. ELSIE HARRISON

METHUEN & CO. LTD. LONDON
36 *Essex Street, Strand, W.C.*2

First published in 1948

CATALOGUE NO. 5090/U

THIS BOOK IS PRODUCED IN COM—
PLETE CONFORMITY WITH THE
AUTHORIZED ECONOMY STANDARDS

PRINTED IN GREAT BRITAIN

To the memory of my husband
Archibald Walter Harrison

PREFACE

It was the custom of our home to spend the last hour of each day in reading aloud. It was time won from lectures, sermons, committees and endless train journeys, and, for all its brevity, it was worth its weight in gold. In rich measure, it fulfilled the ministry of benediction. It was in this way that I was introduced to Mrs. Gaskell's *Life of Charlotte Brontë*, as my husband read it to me and as we both set our minds to work, in twinkling firelight, to puzzle out the meaning behind the drama of Haworth Parsonage.

We knew there must be a clue that no one else had stumbled upon and that Mrs. Gaskell had missed, for even she could not answer our questions of the why and the wherefore of the Brontë family. We believed we were like those two astronomers, Adams and Leverrier, who knew that there was another planet of our Solar System, which had not yet been discovered, because nothing else could account for the strange behaviour of Uranus, out on the edge of space. So with the science of history, instead of theirs of mathematics, we began to search for the hidden influence which had dictated the character of the Brontës.

The astronomers found Neptune, in unseen relationship with Uranus, and one day my husband came to me and put the clue to our problem into my hand. He bade me make of it what I could, but, before I had travelled far, he had himself outstripped me and gone forward into that world of light where no shadows remain with meaning to be guessed. He was the historian of Methodist origins, and, in his work, had discovered that the home of Thomas Tighe, who was Patrick Brontë's patron, was the Mecca, in that locality of Rathfryland, for Wesley's travelling preachers in Ireland.

That was the clue. It was the first link in the evidence which it was essential to find and to test, before the historian dare lean his weight on the chain of truth. That link has held good throughout the whole investigation and has had the virtue of joining all others to itself, so that the complete pattern is seen to be of one identity. Holding fast by my husband's discovery, I have found that the other scattered links of fact in the Brontë history have fitted, the one into the other, so easily as to experience not the least strain of manipulation.

This book is the fruit of that research. It is meant to enable the star-gazers, in the sky of English literature, to turn their mental telescopes towards the right quarter and there to see the incandescent flame of the Wesley portent behind the familiar constellation of the Brontës.

April, 1947   G.E.H.

ACKNOWLEDGMENT

THERE ARE many friends to whom I am indebted for help in the writing of this book, but the cloud of witness must be pegged down, here and there, with but few names. First, as always, my thanks are due to Canon Edwards, of Norwich, for his unfailing help in all my work. Next, I am indebted to Mr. Ellis Heaton, of Bradford, for his generous gift and loan of books and for his knowledge of Haworth. To Mr. Clifford Towlson, of Woodhouse Grove School, I am grateful for his help with its history and for the reproduction of Patrick Brontë's original signature and the engraving of Woodhouse Grove. To Mr. Frank Cole, of Belfast, and to Mr. John Hodgson, of Westminster College, I am indebted for their zeal in tracing Brontë footsteps in Ulster and in Yorkshire.

I want also to express my thanks to the Brontë Society for permission to reproduce valuable photographs to illustrate this book. To Mr. Alfred Arnold, of Belfast, I am grateful for all he did to secure pictures of Patrick Brontë's Irish haunts, and to Miss Winifred Waddington, of Luddenden, for her gift of Mr. A. E. Black's drawing of her hills of home. To Miss Molly Ingle, of Cambridge, I am indebted for her long-suffering help with many references. Also to Miss Edith Drummond, of St. Albans, another long debt of gratitude is due in that she once made learning lyrical for me, amidst the chimneys of Manchester. But it is to my children that I owe my chief debt of thanks, for it is they who have buttressed the wavering line of my present pilgrimage, at every point, with their glad fellowship.

CONTENTS

ILLUSTRATIONS

IRISH CABIN

It was in the year 1811, and the Rev. Patrick Brontë had been very busy getting his poems ready for publication. He had christened them his Cottage Poems, and was about to send them out into the world, a little defenceless and pathetic, like new boys at school, but impregnable in their rearward backing of parental pride. He had tried to protect them too, at the spearhead of their attack, by writing a preface to disarm criticism, but, for all his care, now that he was in bed, he felt apprehensive about their reception and was so excited that he could not sleep.

Patrick Brontë had been at the making of his hymn-like jingles from morning to noon and from noon to night, but now, in the darkness of his lonely bedroom, he was rallying his hopes against possible disappointment with this pious speech, that although "the delicate palate of criticism might be disgusted, yet his humble task was well pleasing in the sight of God, and might, by His blessing, be rendered useful to some poor soul who cared little about critical niceties, who lived unknowing and unknown, in some little cottage, and whom the author might neither see nor hear of till that day when the assembled universe shall stand before the Tribunal of the Eternal Judge."

This comforting reflection came to the poet at that notoriously difficult period for genius which he describes as "when night drew on and he retired to rest, ere he closed his eyes in sleep." Yet, for all those nocturnal pricks of discretion, no restraint of doubt could hold Patrick Brontë back for very long from the manufacture of rhymes which he supposed had upon them the approbation of the Eternal Judge. The parson's body might lie in a plain bedroom in a three-storeyed house in Birstall Parish, Yorkshire, but his soul was ascending to heavenly places. He told himself that this was the sort of pleasure he could wish to taste as long as life lasted. He was enjoying to the full the sensation of omnipotence, which might be an illusion held in common by most artists, but which was, for Patrick Brontë, made entirely convincing by its clerical dress.

He, Patrick Brontë, believed himself to be no other than an instrument in the hand of God Himself. He, Patrick Brontë, and his poems, were to be used by the Almighty for the souls' salvation of the labouring poor. In his mind's eye he saw crowds of poor

He called it the love of God and found it hidden in the heart of his friends. It had the quality of linking earth with heaven. Wesley could say quite simply: "Love is the beginning of eternal life; the same in substance with glory." And what of glory? There it was just above the tree tops eager to break through upon a desolate world. There it was in that light above the darkness of the Mourne Mountains and in the heart of a child. Here, to a little blind girl, who found her way, in eager sort, to his side, Wesley whispered: "Never mind, my dear, you will see in glory." The words went from mouth to mouth. John Wesley had said it. It must be as immutably true as any Vatican Edict. To his dying day Patrick Brontë would believe in the infallibility of what he called "Mr. Wesley's excellent little tracts." He would also believe in a life to come for which this weary world was but a preparation, for, by the side of the Mourne Mountains, in his youth, he had become the neofant of glory.

If we are to creep into the inner recesses of Patrick Brontë's mind we must begin where he began. However distasteful the discovery may be, that Irish Cabin of his must be made to yield up its secret. By what means and through what inspiration came Patrick Brontë to that alien Yorkshire bed? Why should he think in jingles when he was alone? However could he conceive the preposterous idea of saving the world by such poetry? A clue to the mystery surely lies in the significant fact that the memory of his Irish home floated up to consciousness borne on the words and couched in the metre of Wesley's hymns. The picture of Patrick's father, which he gives to us in his jingles, is that of a connoisseur of the Evangelical Revival of Religion. His son is back again, there in the Irish Cabin, seeing the tear of religious fervour drop even on to its earthen floor, and hearing his father consecrate the miserable herring and poverty stricken potato as though they were the very Bread of Heaven. He hears again the pilgrimage of life described as chiefly valuable in that it leads to the prize of death. He makes his old man in The Cabin say:

> "Then I with my children and wife
> Shall get a bright palace above,
> And endlessly clothed with life,
> Shall dwell in the Eden of love."

But what he really heard was his father singing Wesley's triumphal funeral hymn which runs:

"With joy let us follow his flight
　And mount with his spirit above,
Escaped to the mansions of light,
　And lodged in the Eden of love."

It is true that Patrick Brontë's verse tends to paraphrase Wesley rather than to reproduce him, but, to the initiate, the resemblance is unmistakeable. It seems quite idle to deny that Patrick's soliloquy

"That life as a dream
　Or fast-running stream
Glides swiftly away"

owes nothing to Wesley's

"Our life is a dream
　Our time as a stream
Glides swiftly away."

It is surely safe to conjecture that to that clerical ear, laid demurely on Yorkshire pillow, came the sound of old hymns and old tunes learned in a humble Irish home long ago. But what did they reveal to Patrick's inward eye? His jingles tell us all he saw in great detail and are invaluable in their revelation of the stuff of which Patrick Brontë's mind was made.

The Incumbent of Hartshead-cum-Clifton in the county of Yorkshire, in the year 1811, saw, from a horizontal position, the Mourne Mountains. He saw them covered with snow. He saw himself, as a fine upstanding youth, buffeting with the wind and struggling along the hill from Rathfryland. He saw his own old home, its welcoming light all dim with flying snow flakes. He saw its one chimney in the midst of its thatched roof. He noticed: "one window and one latched door." He thrilled again to the warmth and joy of his own home-coming, and, as clearly as though he were really there, he saw the family spring up to welcome him. Was it young Walsh who brought him to that three-legged stool and who stood by to admire this well groomed and highly respectable eldest brother? Patrick Brontë saw his mother with her spinning wheel and marvelled at the order and cleanliness of so poor a cot. He watched his father come in from the barn and hang up his flayle near the door. He saw him turn to welcome his son with that strange grace born only of the children of God. The style of that greeting went straight to Patrick's heart. In his "Cottage in the Wood" he calls it "That sweet Christian courtesy which springs from unfeigned love to God and his creatures."

His Irish Cabin might be poor but Patrick Brontë could swear that there was a grace about it. In memory, he thrilled to it again and gulped his emotion out in the lilt of Wesley's lines which bade him "Rejoice for a brother deceased." It was his father who took the centre of the stage. Here was a man often going hungry, often cold, but without a trace of bitterness. His only boast, his crown of glory was:—

> "We're all in the steep narrow road
> That leads to the city of rest."

Like any priest he dispensed his frugal hospitality. In the stark simplicity of that cottage meal Patrick Brontë realised that his father was doing the honours for The King of Kings. All life was sacramental, for, as the Methodists sang, "Thy Presence makes the feast."

The walls of Patrick's Yorkshire lodging seemed to dissolve, as the old beauty of home rushed again into the young man's soul. He was breathing Irish air. He was singing songs of Zion under an Irish heaven. But Irish poetry escaped him, for his frail barque of the muses was too overweighted with John Wesley and an axe to grind. It is impossible to get very far in verse with a preaching style and encumbered by Wesley's idiom of "a never dying soul to save and fit it for the sky." Or as Patrick would phrase it: "I write to fit you for the sky." Such verse has a propensity to founder in bathos. After all the emotion, Patrick's peak moment of departure from the Irish Cabin ends thus:

> "Now supper is o'er and we raise
> Our prayers to the Father of light,
> And joyfully hymning His praise,
> We lovingly bid a good-night.
> The ground's white, the sky's cloudless blue,
> The breeze flutters keen through the air,
> The stars twinkle bright on my view,
> As I to my mansion repair."

Yet it must all have sounded very good to Patrick Brontë as he turned the soft words on his Irish tongue. Tucked snugly up in bed, with his long, long thoughts, the Rev. Patrick Brontë was out of reach of the real world. He was preening his feathers now over that

last line and over what he was pleased to call "My mansion."
Bright palaces above might have their place in the plan of things,
but earthly mansions were not to be despised and these also Patrick
had enjoyed in Ireland. He knew that he had come into his true
kingdom when he entered the family circle of his patron the Rev.
Thomas Tighe of Drumballyroney. That man positively had a coat
of arms and his epitaph reads thus :—

"Sacred to the memory
of
The Rev. Thomas Tighe
late Rector of Drumgooland
and vicar of the united Parishes of
Drumgooland and Drumballyroney
who
during a resident incumbency
of more than 43 years discharged
the duties of the pastoral office
with zeal unabating, diligence unwearied
and love unfeigned.
Affectionately desirous of the
Temporal and eternal welfare
of his parishioners
They are his witnesses
how holily justly and unblamably
he walked before them
On the 25th day of August 1821 in the 78th year of his age
looking unto Jesus the Author and
Finisher of his faith
he closed his earthly pilgrimage."

That description of Patrick Brontë's patron fills in a little more
of those dreams of the pillow and gives dignity and purpose to the
son of the Irish Cabin. Here at Drumballyroney he got his chance
of "Temporal and eternal welfare" but it was still all of a piece
with the old background for Thomas Tighe himself was a friend
of Wesley. If Patrick Brontë could not cut such a figure as either
Wesley or Tighe in his own parish, yet he knew just how it should
be done. He is not above versifying Wesley's prose when he, in his
turn, would give advice to a young preacher. Wesley had said "Not
that I would advise to preach the law without the gospel any more
than the gospel without the law. Undoubtedly both should be

preached in their turns, yea both at once or both in one—according
to this model I should advise every preacher continually to preach
the law—the law grafted upon, tempered by and animated with
the spirit of the gospel. Upon this plan all the Methodists first set
out. This is the Scriptural way, the True way." Which good advice
Patrick Brontë whispered to his pillow thus:—

> "Divide the word of Truth aright,
> Show Jesus in a saving light,
> Proclaim to all they're dead outright
> Till grace restore them.
> The great Redeemer full in sight
> Keep still before them.
>
> Portray how God in thunder spoke
> His fiery law whilst curling smoke
> In Terror fierce from Sinai broke
> Midst raging flame!
> Then Jesus' milder blood invoke
> And preach His name.
>
> So God will own the labours done
> Approving see His Honoured Son
> And honoured Law, and numbers won
> Of souls immortal
> Though grace, will onward conquering run
> To Heaven's bright portal."

It all sounded so easy—lying down. But in real life the Rev.
Patrick Bronte was beginning to find this upward path to Heaven's
bright portal unconscionably steep. And it was lonely, too. Did
other memories come that night which were not so praiseworthy
as those of the Irish Cabin and the Irish Mansion? Thoughts,
glimpses, at the back of his eyes, of that first love of his? He had
never seen anything more beautiful than Mary Burder, of his first
curacy, with her sleeves rolled up to the elbow and her hands
buried in the glory of a pheasant's plumage. There and then,
regardless of the upward path to Heaven, he had been at her feet
in just one moment. Out it all had popped, how he thought her,
sure, as pretty as Spring Time. He had loved that girl only less
than he loved his own ambition. The hard facts of the case were
that she was the sort of girl who could draw the entrails from a
pheasant and that he lived in the boarding house of her aunt. Was

not his temporal and his eternal welfare rather linked with Tighe of the Coat of Arms?

But the poet of the jingles is nearly asleep. The music is becoming confused. He is not quite sure if the poor cottagers, whose souls he was after saving, are hymning his praises or those of his God. The long clerical body is relaxing in sleep. Duty has been done and conscience satisfied in a hostile world. The Rev. Patrick Brontë gathers up his dreams with his bed clothes and inserts them as a barrier between himself and reality. Mansions in the sky—mansions of Tighe? Love of God or love of Mary? Which was which and what was what? Patrick Brontë sleeps alone in Birstall parish in the year of grace 1811. He has just finished writing the "Advertisement" of his first volume of poems and that thrilling achievement has stirred up all the old memories.

CHAPTER II

IRISH MANSION

IN YEARS to come Patrick Brontë might wish to close the shutter over that one humble window of his Irish Cabin, but about his Irish mansion he need have no such reticence. When his children had brought him fame and Mrs. Gaskell asked him how it all began, he turned back unhesitatingly to that moment of his acceptance into the family of the Rev. Thomas Tighe of the united parishes of Drumgooland and Drumballyroney. He had then stepped into the main current of a great religious movement which swept him onwards, across the Irish Sea, to Cambridge and to Yorkshire. The friends of Wesley had seen to that. They were ever on the look out for earnest young men and their purses were always at the Lord's service.

John Wesley could count on the Tighe family. He and his preachers were welcome both at Thomas Tighe's Rectory and at his half-brother's mansion at Rosanna. In the plan of the Methodist preachers' itinerary here were their sheltering ports of call. They would pass from some humble earth-floored cottage to the splendour of Rosanna, there to be waited upon by liveried footmen. They would travel on again to the more modest Rectory at Drumgooland which still, to their eyes and to the eyes of Patrick Brontë, constituted a mansion. The Tighe family had a way of hospitality about it which was sweet to earnest young men under orders to save a sinful world.

On the last visit which Wesley paid to Ireland his home was at Rosanna. On the last night of his stay, under her hospitable roof, Mrs. Tighe creeps into his diary and brings a sense of foreboding and tears with her. Well the woman knew that, after all these long years of friendship, now at last, the end had come. She seems to linger in farewell, there in his private papers, and wastes his precious time without compunction. She managed to detain him for a little more than one immortal hour, before that final hopeless 9.45 p.m. for his bed time puts a stop to the record, like shears on the thread of fate. The Irish Conference had declared that its preachers must be in bed before 10 o'clock and what could a mere woman do against that horrible decree? She would fain have detained John Wesley for ever, but the very next day he sailed for

England on board the Princess Royal and his Irish friends saw his face no more. Wesley says :— "We parted in the same love that we met" and there was nothing for Mrs. Tighe to do but to return to her gracious good works of hospitality for his preachers and to her school for homeless girls which she had founded under his inspiration. John Wesley would never come to Ireland again, returning when the wild roses blossomed about Rosanna. But love remained, the same in substance with glory.

Methodism was no matter of church allegiance. It was a quality of life. To Wesley the charm of Patrick Brontë's home was the unanimity existing in his societies between Anglican, Presbyterian and Papist, for he says: "No striving amongst them except to enter in at the strait gate." So it came about that both the Presbyterian minister of Rathfryland and the Rector of Drumgooland were friends and followers of John Wesley. There was thus no sort of change in the loyalty of young Patrick Brontë when he passed from teaching school amongst the Presbyterians at Glaskermore to a place in the Rector's house in the same district. A mutual Methodism levelled all frontiers and John Wesley bridged all gulfs. He gives this description, in his Journal, of the hole in the pit whence Patrick Brontë was quarried: "The country was uncommon pleasant, running between two high ridges of mountains; but it was uphill and down all the way so that we did not reach Rathfryland till near noon. Mr. Barber the Presbyterian Minister (a princely personage I believe six feet and a half high) offering me his new spacious preaching-house the congregation quickly gathered together." That was in the month of June in 1787 and Patrick was ten years old. Was this princely personage his first patron, who rescued the boy from hand loom weaving and placed him temporarily in the Presbyterian school of Glasker and permanently in the school of Christ?

The constellations of Presbyter and Priest were in conjunction when Patrick Brontë first stepped out towards fame. The same hymns were sung in his cabin and in his mansion and in both Wesley was patron saint. It was Patrick's fate to belong to a generation which made no vows but vows were made for him that he should be a dedicated spirit—else sinning greatly. It was the Rev. Thomas Tighe who saw clearly what could be made of this young recruit to the Lord's service, and cheerfully he fanned the flame. He must go first to Cambridge and afterwards be propelled gently towards the ranks of the evangelical clergy. The choice of Cambridge fitted in to the plan as easily as all the rest, for it was all of a piece. Thomas Tighe knew that he was on safe ground there and that he could embark his protégé at Cambridge without fear for his soul. There Charles Simeon was at the height of his power and influencing the undergraduates of the university in a remarkable way. He had learned the art from Wesley's friend John Fletcher and what could be safer than one of whom Wesley could write: "I had the satisfaction of meeting Mr. Simeon, Fellow of King's College in Cambridge. He had spent some time with Mr. Fletcher at Madeley, two kindred souls much resembling each other both in fervour of spirit and in earnestness of their address. He gave me the pleasing information that there are three parish churches in Cambridge wherein true scriptural religion is preached and several young gentlemen who are happy partakers of it."

The importance of Charles Simeon lies in the fact that he was recruiting just such earnest people as Patrick Brontë to the ministry of the Church, and, by their means, was hoping to garner the great harvest of Wesley's sowing, and, at the same time, to build up a bulwark within the establishment itself against Lady Huntingdon's unofficial priesthood and Wesley's own vagabond preachers. Lady Huntingdon herself might have captured Patrick, for she had her feelers out in his Irish home and had managed to secure one of Thomas Tighe's curates, at least, for her schismatical chapel in Dublin. John Fletcher only just escaped her and fate was kind to Patrick Brontë also. The stars in their courses and Thomas Tighe fought for him. They linked his fortunes irrevocably to Wesley, Simeon and Fletcher and to just their brand of Methodism. To the end of his life Patrick Brontë abhorred the Calvinism of the great lady's patronage and clung through thick and thin to the Arminianism of John Wesley.

What's in a name? Perhaps the little Brontës of Haworth Parsonage could tell us what it was all about, for they imbibed the milk of that controversy even at their mother's breast. The names of Calvin and Arminius had been woven, deeply and indelibly, into their father's thought and speech. He had brought them with him from Ireland, for they hailed from beneath the roof of Thomas Tighe. They were eloquent of the Lord's controversy and they bore upon them the marks of blood. The battle had raged so furiously that it had separated Wesley and Whitefield for ever and caused grievous confusion amongst their disciples. The struggle assumed epic proportions. Ironical as it may seem the battle raged over love itself. Wesley and Arminius put no bounds to the saving power of the love of God, but Whitefield and Calvin must be allowed to damn a certain number of souls to vindicate His justice. Wesley believed that all could be saved and taught a vigorous gospel of hope and a joyful life of good deeds. Whitefield was certain that few could be saved, and, for these few Elect, they might dispense with good deeds altogether. And Thomas Tighe, the patron of Patrick Brontë, took sides with Wesley and must have talked divertingly, over many a good egg and bacon breakfast, of the horrible decrees of John Calvin and the pigheadedness of Whitefield and of his patroness, the Countess of Huntingdon.

In the background of all Brontë legend the great ones of the earth move about in a sort of nebulous manner, but they really had a foundation in fact. They were part of Patrick's past. The errors of Calvin became positively piquant when discussed with Thomas Tighe and when linked with Selina, Countess of Huntingdon, whose daughter had married Lord Moira of the next parish. Lady Huntingdon was of the House of Shirley and of Hastings and could boast, along with her evangelical enthusiasms, a whole cupboardful of aristocratic skeletons. It was William Shirley, the dark villain, who drew up that famous memorandum which separated the Methodists of Lady Huntingdon's Connexion from the Methodists of John Wesley's Society. His name storms down pages of musty print, throughout early Methodist history, as a veritable portent of doom. Yet, even William Shirley paled before his brother the famous Earl Ferrers. His character was a thing of shocked conjecture throughout Methodism, for he even startled Horace Walpole who was not so exacting in his standards.

The manner of Earl Ferrers's death gave Walpole a certain satisfaction and an uneasy wonder. He writes: "His own and his wife's relations had asserted that he would tremble at last. No such thing; he shamed heroes. With all his madness he was not mad enough to be struck with Lady Huntingdon's sermons. The Methodists have nothing to brag of his conversion though Whitefield prayed for him and preached about him." Whitefield, in fact, had roundly declared that my Lord Ferrers's heart was made of stone, and the biographer of The House of Shirley is inclined to agree with him in his statement: "The very hardened conduct of Lord Ferrers through every intricacy of this most horrid affair even to the last moment of his departure out of life but too well justified Mr. Whitefield."

Earl Ferrers had beaten a groom to death. He had almost murdered his wife and quite murdered his steward. He prayed to see his mistress just once before he was hanged, in a sort of exhalted passion of desperation which withered up Lady Huntingdon's horror of adultery as a thing of naught. He took pistols to bed for the edification of his legal wife and beat her up for his own relaxation. He was a very monster of a man. He drank and diced and was seldom sober. He shot his steward after ordering him to kneel before him and then from 3 p.m. until midnight tormented him to death. He tore the bandages from his wound, tore out his hair and essayed to beat the remaining spark of life out of his body. He went to hell with his eyes open, for, in the Tower, he wrote his infidel's challenge: "In doubt I lived—in doubt I die—Yet stand prepared the vast abyss to try—And undismayed expect eternity." The man positively flourished on brimstone, and the righteous trembled at such temerity. It illumined, in horrid sort, their own laborious ascent to Heaven by the steep and narrow way.

No one has enquired why the names of Shirley, Hastings and Huntingdon come so trippingly to the tongue of the Brontë family when it tries its prentice hand at literature. The children were shut away in a lonely parsonage on Haworth Moor, but they were shut in with Papa and his ancient inheritance. Patrick Brontë, equipped with the whole paraphernalia of the Shirley, Wesley, Whitefield controversy, could make the flesh creep on children's bones. He could produce the perfect villain in Earl Ferrers, as the foil to a heavy load of entire sanctification which must be swallowed ere the tale was fully told. It was nothing incongruous to the little Brontës that such villains and their less exciting saintly relations should find their way to Methodist chapels and take their seats in the gallery. In Papa's past such things did happen. A formidable galaxy of the nobility listened to Whitefield in Lady Huntingdon's chapels and Lady Margaret Hastings had actually married a member of Wesley's Holy Club. In Wesley's chapel in City Road London, a tablet commemorated Lady Mary Fitzgerald who was the friend of Thomas Tighe, John Fletcher and John Wesley. She in her turn was the high priestess of tragedy, living sadly separated from her profligate husband and set up with a family history teeming with murders, quarrels and imprisonments. Yet through it all she shone, a woman of "singular devotedness to God".

If we would hear Patrick Brontë talking of his Irish mansion, turn to his children's juvenile writings as they attempt the character drawing of a heroine. The woman of Charlotte's description might have risen up from the family table at Rosanna for: "Her aspect was benign—her voice was low and peaceful—her deportment very full of the grace of kindness. All this seemed very fascinating in one so young and so very lovely. You would have expected on being introduced to the fair and aristocratic Mrs. Percy to see some consciousness of rank—some air of peerless beauty—but she showed none. She looked kindly at you with her dark eyes and spoke kindly to you with her sweet voice, and moved with unostentatious though perfect grace—a fair young Christian lady. She was not gay—even in her smiles she seemed softly sad. She thought much and all her thoughts were tinged with a high religious melancholy. She really loved to ponder over the glories of a heavenly hereafter better than to play with the frivolities of the earthly present. This is was which seemed to free her so from the selfishness, the vanities, the pride of her station." The young scribe winds up this tale of virtues with a lament: "But she died and thousands were sorry for the untimely end of one so wholly beloved. She had no enemies even among the proud and profligate —for there did not breathe the man or woman on earth whom she by word, look or action had insulted."

This kind of writing does not come about by chance, nor is there chance in the naming of the heroine as Lady Mary. It is remembered description of a real Mary who was once the friend of Thomas Tighe and as Mary Fitzgerald carried such a weight of sorrow and gentility as to make the infant dwellers in Haworth Parsonage wonder. Their villains were chapel goers too, or how else account for this swashbuckling extract from their juvenile writings? How else explain this veritable hotch potch, save on the background of Papa's Terrible Tales:— "My readers are, I have no doubt, aware that on a Sunday evening I generally make a point of attending the ministry of Mr. Bromley at the Wesleyan chapel, Slug Street. Accordingly last Lord's day after tea Mr. Surena Ellrington and myself accompanied by Lord Macara Lofty who had called on us in the course of the afternoon, and whom in spite of his Voltaire sneers and insinuations we had easily persuaded to go with us, proceeded arm in arm to our accustomed place of worship. Being arrived and having taken possession of our usual pew in the gallery, each man after a private hiding of his face in his hands and a few internal groans sat quietly down. A devout set we must have looked seated in that long front pew which I forgot to say was also occupied by Mr. Timothy Steaton. Surena, who was suffering from a cold, in a great coat and a large spotted blue and white shawl enveloping his neck and chin, from which peered the most insignificant physiognomy mind can conceive, crowned by a peak of hair surmounting the low mean forehead and hungry eyes. Macara, whose delicate health likewise required care, in a cloak with a high stiff collar and black silk kerchief centrally adjusted over his bleak stock, forming an exquisite contrast to the ghastly rakish white of his physiognomy, in which all the lines of profligacy had been ploughed by courses of secret but delirious debauchery . . . Myself in a jauntily cut costume consisting of dark green frock coat, pale buff vest and nankeen pantaloons. My locks singularly light in their hue brushed smartly on one side, my dandy primrose gloves laid across over my hymn-book, on which rested my truly patrician hand decorated with a ring on the little finger, the habitual smirk of my face subdued to canting gravity and a preternatural groan every three minutes emitted from the bottom of my lungs. Mr. Bromley's short, broad, athletic figure having entered the pulpit and having delivered (end of line cut away. We would give much to know what hymn it was) with suitable power and pathos, all the congregation joined in singing it in strains of such melody as was fitted only for the ears of seraphs. While the last stave was being thundered forth, I noticed that a lady came gliding up the twenty-three gallery stairs, and as she stood still and seemed in doubt where to go, Lord Macara who sat at the end of our pew opened the door and signed her to approach. She advanced without hesitation bowing graciously to Lofty as she seated herself at his side. The sun being now set and the red glow it had left behind being greatly obscured by the oiled paper windows of the chapel through which it had to make its way I could discern only the outline of the lady's form, which was graceful and prepossessing enough. Amidst the increasing gloom the hymn ceased and Bromley knelt down to pray. As Macara and his companion inclined forward, I saw the former insinuate one of his sinister and revolting squints under her bonnet, and by the sudden biting of his under lip I judged he had made a discovery. I would have asked him what it was, but Bromley burst upon us in thunder. "O Lord! A more infernal pack of defiled, depraved, bemired, besotted, bloody, brutal wretches never knelt to worship in Thy Presence!" Loud, deep genuine and heartfelt rung the responding Amen as Bromley paused to breathe after this first clause of his vesper. He took his text without opening the Bible. "I came not to save but to destroy." A sermon followed, wandering and wild and terrible."

The young scribe exults in Bromley's native wit and uncouth enthusiasm, the prototype of so many of those ancient lay sermons, and goes on to state that the noticeable stir amongst the aristocratic sinners in the gallery was caused by the entrance of no less a person than Northangerland. That magic name is going to storm down the pages of Brontë literature in the same way as the name of Shirley rolls through old Methodist print. The critics have always had a blind eye here. What place has Northangerland in a schism-shop? What can the hero of Brontë children find congenial in Wesleyan chapels? Strangely enough that is the whole point of Northangerland, for he springs fully armed straight from schism. He is part and parcel of Patrick Brontë's ponderous legacy of both saints and sinners and comes from under the Methodist roof tree of Thomas Tighe. He is the offspring of Papa's cautionary tales and has become something more than mortal. He and his prototype of Shirley fame is the epic monster. He is, in children's ears, the dear antidote to an overdose of too much piety. He is the one bright compensation to set against long sessions of preaching and Papa's variations on the theme of Christian Perfection.

CHAPTER III

ALL SAINTS

A conspiracy of silence has well nigh obliterated all knowledge of that inheritance which made Patrick Brontë the man that he was. His biographer is obliged to work from the hint of names, from the internal evidence of Patrick's own slender literary remains, and from echoes of the parental past in his children's more voluminous writings. It is sure ground, if limited. The names of Tighe and Simeon indicate the nature of the road to which Patrick Brontë's feet were set. The names of Wilberforce and Thornton will presently confirm those footsteps upon that road, for help in his Cambridge journey, and Henry Martyn will enforce the same significant sequence. All the righteous of Wesley's circle knew those names of Wilberforce and Thornton in conjunction, for they had been responsible for paying that pension to Charles Wesley's widow which had so generously supplemented the money paid out to her from the copyright of her husband's hymns from the Methodist Book Room.

The name of Mrs. Fletcher of Madeley will assure Patrick Brontë's entrance later into Yorkshire and keep bright the golden chain which stretches across a dark sea of oblivion. The historian finds that significant series of names joined in a unity of purpose, and in a similarity of background, which provide his authentic clue to the Brontë mystery. The sober fact is that the advancement of Patrick Brontë, from Ireland to Yorkshire, was all at the hands of the friends of John Wesley. The kindly Presbyterians of Wesley's Journal discovered him. The Tighes of Wesley's fold nurtured him. The friends of Wesley, Wilberforce and Thornton paid his bills, for who could have resisted that description of the young Patrick which Henry Martyn, the great missionary, sent to Wilberforce to ask for his help? He writes:— "He will be an instrument of good to the Church, as a desire of usefulness in the ministry seems to have influenced him hitherto in no small degree."

With the coupling of the names of Patrick Brontë and Henry Martyn at Cambridge the old home atmosphere is consciously sustained. The great missionary was himself a trophy of that intensive discovery of the love of God which attended on Wesley's preaching. Martyn's father had lived at Gwenap. He was a Cornish

Above, to the east, and *below,* to the west, of Loughbrickland-Rathfryland Rd.

SITE OF PATRICK BRONTË'S IRISH CABIN

PATRICK BRONTË'S SCHOOL OF GLASKERMORE

miner and such were the apple of Wesley's eye. In all Methodist history no place takes precedence of Gwenap for its vast crowds and its discovery of the heights and depths of sovereign grace. Henry Martyn's sister, who exercised the strongest spiritual influence upon the motherless lad, was herself married to one of Wesley's preachers, but more important still the girl whom he loved—his world-famed Lydia—worshipped with the Methodists. After a brilliant career as Senior Wrangler and Smith's Prizeman at the University, Martyn became Charles Simeon's curate. Amongst the saints his name became one to conjure with. He was a sort of composite Cambridge Seven in himself. He did a great work amongst students and Patrick Brontë never forgot the thrill of having known such a hero. To those who knew him, the whole effect was heightened by the pageant of that bleeding heart which he carried with him to a lonely grave. God said "go to India." Lydia said "not to India, I." Both tug. The Devil looks up between the feet of Henry Martyn, but he goes to India alone and dies there. Angels may weep over that passionate sacrifice, for they could have been so happy, both of them, in Cambridge. Yet Lydia, in barren loneliness, declared she weighed every action as in the sight of God. She confided to her diary: " I reckon among my mercies the Lord's having enabled me to choose a single life and that my friend in India has been so well reconciled to my determination." But was he? In that burning climate, worn out by his own cruelly obsessional energy, he thought of her always. He called her still, from the midst of his boiling brain, "My own faithful Lydia." She lies buried in the churchyard at Breage and upon her grave is written "For a small moment have I forsaken thee but with great mercies will I gather thee." But Martyn lies alone in India.

Fate so conspired that it should be just this sort of hero who met Patrick Brontë on his storming of the gates of Cambridge University. That glory breaking behind his hills of home was ever the same, subdued and disciplined here, under a Cambridge heaven. He might drill with the volunteers who faced Napoleon's threatened invasion. He might love, to his dying day, the feel of carnal weapons. He might always keep in his heart that inch of reserve, knowing he should have been a soldier. But his place was fixed for ever here, in the army of the Lord. He had learned from Henry Martyn that such service could give points even to a soldier's loyalty. The die was cast and Patrick Brontë could do little else but obey. Meekly

c

he accepted his first curacy of Weathersfield in Essex, for it came,
also, relentlessly, straight from the hands of the friends of John
Wesley. It was in the gift of Trinity Hall, Cambridge, and the vicar
was one Joseph Jowett, Regius Professor of Civil Law in the
University. He, in his turn, was friend to Simeon and to Venn and
one with the evangelical clergy who followed Wesley's lead.

All the time that Patrick Brontë was in Essex he was agitating
to go farther still, by the help of his powerful friends. He must in
some way contrive to get to Yorkshire, for Simeon's friend Fletcher
had called it "The Goshen of our land." That meant preferment
for the evangelical clergyman and Patrick Brontë meant to get on.
He was distinctly nearer his goal when he reached Wellington and
the Madeley district, for there Mrs. Fletcher was still alive and still
active in advancing what she calls "my precious young men" to
good livings in the Church. Dreading a "carnal ministry", after her
sainted husband's death, she had found the powers-that-be gracious
in appointing men of her own choice. Mr. Gilpin worked with her
in full sympathy and to him Patrick Brontë penned one of his
poetical effusions of the pillow.

To have known Mrs. Fletcher was a liberal education. When
Patrick Brontë arrived at Wellington she was still living in Madeley
vicarage and still tottering about on the Lord's business. She was
dying of cancer but appeared undaunted. Her hope was anchored
within the veil. She was of the Thomas Walsh school of the
Methodists and when Patrick Brontë entered her orbit his fate was
doubly sealed. With her he was caught up to the very heart of
Wesley's works and ways. He saw now, at first hand, how a saint
must live and must die. The Methodist saint had to combine all the
virtues and all the religious orders in his one poor person. By turns
he must be Cistertian, Carthusian and Trappist, but there was no
retreat for him within sheltering monastery walls. He had to
sustain his sainthood in a real world which sweated and cursed and
blasphemed. His soul was ever in his hand. One nudge of Satan
at his elbow and he was undone. Even in high fever, or dying of
cancer, he must preserve the mind of Christ. So nearly had the
Fletchers attained to holiness that Voltaire could disprove the
divinity of Christ by pointing to a man, John Fletcher, who could
live in this world, in the 18th century, yet without sin. His story
was known everywhere and had even found its way to the French
Court. Fletcher had been stricken with spotted fever, after having
fought the plague single-handed by all the bedsides of his dying

parishioners in Madeley, but he had insisted on preaching and giving the Sacrament to a packed church ere he fainted and was carried home to die. His devoted wife had just to kneel in her pew and watch his crucifixion, for who was she to stay the execution of the Will of God? As his friends clustered round his death bed, they asked him a question, long after his power of speech was fled:— "Was Christ precious?" A hand thrown upwards was his soldier's salute of absolute, inarticulate loyalty.

To-day, in Charing Cross Road, the seekers after old books may pick up Fletcher's *Checks to Antinomianism* for a few pence, but they will be ignorant of their true value. This musty collection of volumes once cost human lives. It cost sixteen hours a day of work on two shillings a week for housekeeping expenses. Its author munched bread and cheese and went on writing. It cost, for Fletcher, the collapse of consumptive disease and an emigration from England, but it cost more than that. Far away in Yorkshire it cost a woman's breaking heart. The Fletchers laid on that altar the children who might have been for they paid for that musty work with their immortality. It was all to do with Calvin and Arminius and that dark villian Shirley. Fletcher undertook the work to defend John Wesley from the arrows of his Calvanistic foes, but it was a tribute also to his divine Master. The sacrifice was willingly made to vindicate the unrestricted love of God. The work was planned, along with so many of Charles Wesley's hymns, to show that God's will was for all men to be saved in contradistinction to the Elect only. It also insisted on holiness as a consequence of grace and trembled to think of the life of crime which the Elect might enjoy if they must be saved willy nilly.

In the midst of the turmoil of this polemic controversy there is one glimpse of a lonely woman, in Birstall Parish, Yorkshire, confiding to her diary the fact that she found great comfort that day in reading "Mr. Fletcher's *4th Check to Antinomianism*." And, even as she wrote, Mary Bosanquet could remember the little tender things of friendship which twenty years ago John Fletcher had done for her. They had both been caught up in that intensive phase of early Methodism when they had experienced together an outpouring of the Holy Spirit, under the ministry of Thomas Walsh, side by side in London. They had agonised together to enter in at the straight gate. Hardly did the young people know if they were in the body or out of the body, but older saints had a meddling hand in their raptures. More experienced folks had manipulated their loving hearts. Charles Wesley had speeded Fletcher to Madeley, bidding him to think no more of that beautiful girl of nineteen summers with that look of the soul's awakening in her sparkling eyes. By the help of the Lord, Fletcher wrote to his mentor, he had been able to accomplish the impossible. He had driven her picture away, from between his horse's ears, as he rode to Madeley, and had moreover banished it from its persistent endeavour to adorn his lonely vicarage.

It was a woman who had taken Mary Bosanquet in hand. For her sins, her epitaph shall be written as that "sickly, persecuted saint" Sally Ryan. She had carried off Mary Bosanquet, in her own possessive love, letting it be known that there was to be no hateful "mine or thine" between them. They were to have all things in common, which was a wonderfully astute working out of the will of God, seeing that Mary had all the money and Sally none at all. Together these two women, on Mary's fortune, built up famous orphan houses at Leytonstone and at Birstall, and during any moment of flagging on the part of Mary, Sally was ready to frighten her out of her wits with the bogey of the unholy chances of married life. And yet for all these human machinations the Fletchers persisted in attributing their long separation and their ultimate reunion only and entirely to the Lord. They acknowledged His hand again in the breaking of their tragically short marriage, for the words wail out, in Mary Fletcher's letter to John Wesley, thus: "Three years, nine months and two days I have possessed my heavenly minded husband but now the sun of my earthly joys is set for ever and my soul is filled with anguish which only finds its consolation in a total abandonment and resignation to the Will of God." Three years, nine months and two days! That is how saints count time when the Lord allows them so short a day of bliss.

It is essential to know more about these Fletchers, if we would understand Patrick Brontë and the way by which he entered Yorkshire. They belong, like the Tighes, to his mansion period, and were linked with his ambitious young soul in a strange intimacy. John de la Fléchère was born in Switzerland. He was the younger son of a nobleman's family and had thoughts of the army as a profession. But like St. Ignatius his plans went astray, for an illness prevented him from taking up his commission. In great disappointment of spirit Fletcher took a tutor's post in England with unlicked schoolboys in default of a sterner foe. It must have been a tough enough proposition for the young man seems to have been very unhappy. The family moved from Shropshire to London for the meeting of Parliament, and, whilst they dined at St. Albans, their young tutor sauntered out into the market place. He was nowhere to be found when his company moved on again towards London, so a saddle horse was left behind and a message to the strayed reveller that he must follow after. Where had he been? What kind of excuse could he offer for getting lost in St. Albans? When he told the truth the family split its sides with laughter. It really was too absurd, for this was Fletcher's story told in his own words: "I was walking through the market place and I heard a poor old woman talk so sweetly of Jesus Christ that I knew not how the time passed away." "Well I will be hanged" retorted his employer, "if our tutor does not turn Methodist by and by." "Methodist, Madam" said he "Pray what is that?" The lady replied "Why, the Methodists are a people that do nothing but pray. They are praying all day and all night." "Are they?" answered Fletcher. "Then, with the help of God, I will find them out if they be above ground." And find them out he did and Mary Bosanquet with them. Her experience had the same urgency behind it—to find out this People of God. When dancing in the fine 18th century ballroom at Bath and eddying upon the light fantastic toe, these were the thoughts going forward in her pretty head: "If I knew where to find the Methodists or any who would show me how to please God, I would tear off all my fine things and run through fire to them." And through fire she was allowed to go and she did find the Methodists and John Fletcher with them. But Divine love had to take precedence of human love for a long twenty-five years after that first dawn of joy.

The thrill of the story is in the reunion. Mary Bosanquet might read *Checks to Antinomianism* up in Yorkshire but she had not had a letter from Fletcher for fifteen years. She had lost Sarah Ryan. Several people had asked her to marry them. She was fettered with anxiety, loneliness and much work. She had spent all her fortune on the poor orphans, old women and cripples whom no man loved. And this was the proposition which she laid before the Lord, if perchance the great Shepherd of Souls should hear her prayer. She had just been told that Fletcher of Madeley was dying in Switzerland, worn out with all his pious labours. The blunt and communicative friend had casually remarked: "Mr. Fletcher is very bad; spits blood profusely and perspires profusely every night. Some have great hope that prayer will raise him up, but for my

part I believe he is a dying man as sure as he is now a living one."
And Mary Bosanquet crept away to her bedroom and prayed (1)
That Mr. Fletcher might be raised up. (2) That he might be
brought back to England. (3) That he would write to me on the
subject before he saw me though we had been so many years
asunder without so much as a message passing on any subject. (4)
That he would in that letter tell me——it had been the object of
his thoughts and prayers for some years. She adds "It came to my
mind further that should this occur in the end of the year 1781 it
would be a still greater confirmation, as Providence seemed to
point me to that season as a time of hope."

She was going to give the Lord two years of margin to fly to her
relief. During those slowly dragging years she heard a report that
Mr. Fletcher was to remain in Switzerland and felt cut off from all
hope. When the month of June arrived and the last date she had
fixed for her term of suffering came she was almost constrained to
say "Thou hast not delivered Thy people at all." But the diary
continues "The very next day, June the 8th, I received a letter from
Mr. Fletcher in which he told me that he had for twenty-five years
found a regard for me which was still as sincere as ever; and though
it might appear odd he should write on such a subject when just
returned from abroad and more so without seeing me first he could
only say that his mind was so strongly drawn to do it he believed
it to be the order of Providence."

Now who would have dreamed that after all *Checks to Antinomianism*
was a work of romance? The whole of twenty-five years! Well the
face of Mary Bosanquet must sometimes have looked up at the
lonely scholar in Madeley Vicarage between the lines of those
terrible decrees of John Calvin in spite of all the advice of the
saints. The God of John Fletcher and Arminius had conquered
after all. And victory remained with love. This kind of courtship
is surely the purest thing that ever happened, for it is dictated by
what the saint knows of the love of God. There is little of the flesh
about it. It partakes rather of the nature of heavenly fire taken
with tongs from off the altar. Still, it is good to picture the
throbbing heart and the strained eyes of Mary Bosanquet, watching
for the postman in Birstall Parish, Yorkshire, that first week of
June 1781—watching, more than men watch for the morning. If
Methodist love is untrammelled of the flesh, it is also true to say
that its very intensity may burn up almost the very soul. It was this
same Mary Bosanquet who wrote of her conversion at the side of

Thomas Walsh and John Fletcher: "It seemed most exquisite feelings were opened in my soul, such as I never knew before. If I saw or heard of the consequence of sin I was ready to die. For instance if in the street I saw a child ill-used or slighted by the person who seemed to have the care of it; or a poor person sweating under an uncommonly heavy burden; or if I saw a horse or a dog oppressed or wounded, it was more than I could bear. I seemed to groan and travail in birth as it were for the whole creation."

John Wesley was never tired of telling his preachers that they had nothing to do but save souls, but along with it and because of it went these exquisite feelings. In a cruel world they engendered philanthrophy and in a dull one, poetry. They set agog in England that strangest medley of orphan houses, of dumb friends' leagues, of trade unions, of poetry and of passion. In any study of the Brontë family the paramount fact to remember is that Patrick Brontë carried that flaming secret in his own heart. Patrick Brontë with his exquisite feelings, there on his poet's bed, was a very product of this same passionate thing called Methodism. He breathed the same spiritual atmosphere and he was one in its ecstatic circle of friendship. It was at once both a blessing and a bane.

It was so much to the good that, so far, Methodism had never let him down. It had materially assisted him in his onward march from the Irish Cabin. In Patrick Brontë's time its halcyon days might be over, but enough remained, safely locked away in his heart, to startle the world. That heart for ever retained that certain impression, that illusive style, that dream of the way of life which came to him in his inheritance. He was now coming to understand something more of its strange way of love. He liked to think that he too was following the Lord's will when he strode ambitiously forward into Yorkshire. In Weathersfield his human heart had almost betrayed him and that would never do. He must pass quickly over in his mind that part of his history in his first curacy. He did not like to remember that he also had left a breaking heart behind him there. If he had known it, that girl was as capable of passion and of suffering as was ever Mrs. Fletcher or the faithful Lydia. He had told her that he loved her and she had believed him. Where was she now? He was always inclined to be a little sorry for himself, in a real world, so he was ignorant of what he had made her suffer. It is certain that Patrick Brontë had awakened desires in a young girl's heart of which she was before quite ignorant. There had been walks. There had been talks. There had been a friendly aunt and a satisfactory distance between her house and the girl's home. There had been compliments and tales of a golden future. There had been chance touchings, a friendly hand at the stile, a strong arm for a steep hill. There were other dear tender little nothings, sweet in memory, but they had found it all out at home and, thinking Patrick Brontë had no honourable intentions, had packed Mary Burder off to a place of banishment. The mischief was however done for stone walls have a way of making no prison for young hearts. There remained memories and promises.

Patrick Brontë had told Mary Burder of his Yorkshire ambitions and how she must not hamper his progress there, until he had got firmly established among his grand friends. She drank it all in, and, not knowing that she was as pretty as paint, felt herself very small and useless and not at all on an equality with Patrick. It was a pity she had not been introduced to the Irish Cabin. She knew all about his brand of saints and of William Grimshaw in Yorkshire who was a burning and a shining light. Would Patrick make for himself an equally wonderful name? It was all too good to be true, but she went on hugging the thought of his love to her poor deluded young heart. Patrick Brontë, loving the shy modesty of the child, loving her beauty and her innocent hero-worship, yet knew that prudence forbade a more serious view of the situation. Henry Martyn had had to choose between his God and his Lydia. Patrick Brontë's choice might lie rather between vaulting ambition and a chit of a girl without prospects, but that choice could be made convincingly pious in the knowledge that Wesley's followers had views on marriage. For them a helpmeet must be found only after painful research, for it was no good standing in a golden kitchen and seeing celestial light in its copper pans or its cook's eyes, for the Lord never meant it to be as easy as that. What would have become of *Checks to Antinomianism* if the saintly Fletcher had not banished bright eyes and bare arms to their own place?

Yet, Patrick Brontë never forgot that young girl pulling the bright feathers from a pheasant in a kitchen and he had kept on writing to her aunt for many years. Now that correspondence had stopped, for Patrick Brontë had arrived in Yorkshire and Mrs. Fletcher could direct him there where truer joys were to be found. She had, in fact, prepared for him Yorkshire curacies, each with a tincture of Methodism, an inspectorship of a Methodist school, and a neat little Methodist wife with a neat little bank balance. The only difficulty was that Mary Burder had believed in Patrick

Brontë's love and in his integrity. She had silently taken upon herself the parts of the faithful Lydia and the patient Mary Bosanquet rolled into one. She too would wait, against all reason, for the Lord to be gracious.

CHAPTER IV

WOODHOUSE GROVE

PATRICK BRONTË's entrance into Yorkshire fixed the fetters of his past more firmly upon him, for he could not have come to any corner of England more deeply steeped in Wesley's legacy than was this parish of Birstall which the windows of his bachelor bedroom now commanded. The great John Nelson, second only to Wesley in his apostolic labours, had set his mark on the whole district. Here for fourteen years Mary Bosanquet had lived and done deeds of mercy as any Florence Nightingale. At Dewsbury had lived the saintly Heald who would presently have a descendant as priest of Birstall. It was to this elder Heald that John Wesley wrote: "Is it fit for *me* to ask a Methodist *twice* for anything in his power?" At Gomersal, up the hill above Birstall church, stood the Red House where Wesley was wont to stay with his friends the Taylors. There he enjoyed that keen atmosphere of bracing Yorkshire Methodism that lingered in that home even up to the time of Patrick Brontë's children's own welcome there.

The Taylors of the Red House might be sure of their own opinions but they were devoted to John Wesley. They were always ready to lend him a helping hand, as Wesley writes "I lodged in Joseph Taylor's house at Gomersal who labours for peace and would fain reconcile Christ and Beliel." There were always quarrels over trustees and meeting houses in Yorkshire and heated arguments in which the Taylors strove to find a way of peace. Methodism was the kind of yeasty thing that exactly suited Yorkshire for it was tense with emotion and informed with enthusiasm. Now, in Patrick Brontë's time, it was crashing ahead in its own boisterous way and causing minor earthquakes in all sorts of directions. It was only at the time of his advent into Yorkshire that the Methodists had decided to hold their services in church hours of worship and so at long last bring about that definite cleavage of the Society of the People called Methodists from their Mother Church. One Jabez Bunting, even now in this Yorkshire district, was busy pounding "The Old Body" into a corporate church, with chapels, schools, and ministry, quite separate from The Church of England. For this enterprise young men were needed, as in Wesley's day, when the wealthy and pious Methodists looked to Patrick Brontë and his

28

like to supply that need, in the bosom of the Church herself. Now, these hearty Methodists meant to fend for themselves. They would recruit their own ministers from amongst their own sons.

A new day was dawning, and it was Patrick Brontë's fate to be astride both movements for a time. So poised, he was likely to reap a crop of bewilderment in his own mind, but, for the present, he could make the best of both worlds. He had secured his Yorkshire curacy through Mrs. Fletcher's influence and had been appointed examiner to the new Wesleyan school at Woodhouse Grove also by her help. The Headmaster was the saintly Fletcher's god-son, and Crosse of Bradford was an influential friend to all Methodists within the Church of England. Mrs. Fletcher could always work that oracle on behalf of her "precious young men," of whom William Morgan was one and a friend, in his turn, to our climbing Patrick. But the school at Woodhouse Grove stood uncompromisingly for the propagation of young Methodists, and it speaks volumes for the quality of Patrick Brontë's inheritance that he was appointed as its first examiner. He must have brought with him all those hymns from the Irish Cabin, all the grace of Rosanna and Tighe, all that eager emotion and knowledge of the love of Christ which he would find again at Woodhouse Grove, even amongst the lambs of the flock.

No sooner had Patrick Brontë put his long nose inside the school than a revival of religion broke out amongst the boys. A letter written by John Fennell, the Headmaster, in that year of 1812, when Patrick Brontë became the school's examiner, says:— "I am happy to inform you that God has begun a most blessed work among the children. I preached yesterday from Proverbs IV 3, 4, ("For I was a son unto my father, tender and only beloved in the sight of my mother. And he taught me and said unto me 'Let thine heart retain my words. Keep my commandments and live.' ") In the evening many of them were deeply affected and sighs and tears were on all sides. To-day the work seems spreading among them and while I am now writing this, I hear the voice of prayer and praise in the higher part of the chapel, where several of them are assembled for that purpose. Blessed be God that out of the mouths of these babes, Woodhouse Grove is, this moment, resounding with His praise. In the morning at seven we assembled again and it would have gladdened your heart to have seen and heard what I then witnessed. The very grove echoed with the voice of praise and thanksgiving. Indeed to have heard the sweet warbling of the birds in the wood, and the melting strains of the boys in the chapel, uniting in one blessed, heavenly chorus to God, was enough to have moved a heart of stone. How often did we sing with hearts full of gratitude, and eyes full of tears,

> "Ye hills and ye dales, with praises abound,
> Ye rocks and ye vales continue the sound;
> Break forth into singing ye trees of the wood,
> For Jesus is bringing lost sinners to God!"

It is on just that note of Wesley's hymn for lovely places that the figures of a lover and his lass will take the stage. They will loiter in and out of the tall trees at Woodhouse Grove in just that old familiar setting, for it is here, with boys' voices singing Wesley's hymns, that the courtship of Patrick Brontë and Maria Branwell took place. Here was found the neat, pious, wife whom the Lord had prepared. Or was it friend Morgan that had done the preparing? He was about to marry John Fennell's daughter Jane, and Maria Branwell was her cousin and just now on a visit to her uncle's house. Morgan, with his heavy jokes and his too solid frame, must have fancied himself in the guise of cupid. He would indicate to Patrick Brontë a safe anchorage in troubled seas. He would suggest new confidence and new hope. Here would surely be an end to homesick verses from a poet's lonely bed. Once in the swing with these vigorous young Methodists there was no knowing where he might end, for the Fennell's Methodism was of the bluest blood and Miss Branwell's was from the Cornish vintage and positively tawny with age and respectability.

Methodism had conquered Cornwall more completely than any other county. There her sons now moved with a sense of importance and social grace and they led all civic affairs. Their chapels were the most imposing buildings on the horizon and they were filled with certain people of importance. Miss Branwell's own brother was mayor of Penzance and there was almost an air of sophistication about such Methodism. The fight for holiness was more decently veiled, for the soul no longer paraded in the awful publicity of the great White Throne, but, go below the surface, and the Methodist still remained, in a sensitive eager spirit and a desire to do and suffer the will of God. So Woodhouse Grove to Patrick Brontë's eyes must have looked like his old loved Irish Mansion restored in fairy guise. It was a beautiful place—fit cradle for romance. Warbling birds and warbling boys and love in an Irishman's heart—what more could the quality want?

Read the advertisement of the place in "The Morning Chronicle" for July 25th, 1811, and see if Patrick Brontë would not look on it all with joy when the time came for him to turn in at its imposing gateway. The advertisement reads:—"Yorkshire. Elegant Mansion House, Woodhouse Grove, delightfully situate in Aire Dale. To be sold or let, the elegant mansion called Woodhouse Grove, near Apperley Bridge, about eight miles from Leeds, four from Bradford, and five from Otley, adapted for the residence of a large genteel family. The house consists of drawing and dining rooms of large dimensions, with breakfast room, study, butler's pantry, house-keeper's room, servants' hall, kitchens and every other convenience on the ground floor, twelve lodging rooms, dressing room and accommodation for servants, wash-house, laundry, brew-house and other offices, fitted up in a complete manner. Out buildings comprise stabling for twelve horses, double coach-house, harness-room etc.: Conveniently detached is a farm-yard, with large barn, cow house, pigging house. The whole of the buildings are of free-stone, and in the best repair. The pleasure ground and gardens contain about seven acres, well planted, and laid out with much taste and beauty, with hothouse, greenhouse, an excellent bath, a fish pond well-stocked and supplied by a never-failing spring of soft water. The country for many miles round is beautifully ornamented by the seats of many families of distinction, and the picturesque scenery of this part of Aire Dale is equal to any in the country. In front of the house is eight acres of rich land, ornamented with large oaks, and other fine timbers. The river Aire winds in front and the stream affords fine trout fishing; the country also abounds in game that altogether renders this a complete residence for a gentleman."

But it was not for the use of a gentleman that the Methodist Conference had acquired this mansion. With its genius for knowing a good site it had obtained a bargain, but its financial resources would be strained to keep the place at all as a gentleman should. There would presently descend upon it that air of faded grandeur so well known amongst the saints with their potent dreams and their pinched pockets. Yet, it would fulfil its function as a nursery of Christians well enough, for, by the addition of this new academy of the north, the Methodists had decided to enlarge Wesley's own school at Kingswood, Bristol, for the education of his preachers'

sons. A glance at its mode of Sunday observance will indicate
its parentage and its inheritance. An artless letter, from one of its
first scholars, gives this time-table, as irrevocable truth, in the
year of grace 1812:— "Honoured Father, I received the parcel
which contained the cloth etc., on Wednesday last, and was very
happy to hear that you all were well, and to inform you that we
are the same. Thank God for every blessing. You required of
me when you were here, that when I wrote to you I would·inform
you how we spent our time, and to begin the Lord's Day. The
first, therefore, I will. We rise at six o'clock in the morning, and
to half-past, washing etc.; to seven, a public prayer meeting;
to eight, private prayer and reading; from eight to nine, family
prayer and breakfast; from nine to half-past ten, reading; from
half-past ten to twelve, preaching; from twelve to half-past one,
private bands, dinner; from half-past one to two, the chapter to
be read from which the morning's text has been taken and each
boy to remember a verse; from two to half-past four, preaching
and reading; from half-past four to six, public prayer meeting;
from six to eight, supper and family prayer and go to bed."

Woodhouse Grove, the mansion, with its ancient propensity
for hunting and fishing would hardly be able to recognise itself
with such monastic tenants. Nor would their fare do justice to
the farm and the kitchen, the brewhouse and the butler's pantry,
for a diet of bread and milk provided two out of their three meals
a day. Ministers' sons are a race apart, but the Methodists stressed
their singularity by segregating them in these schools where Wesley's
rules held good and where it was really believed that if a boy played
when a boy, he would play when a man. There were no Peter
Pans accepted for entrance here, for the preachers' sons were
embarked on a determined race to heaven.

The boys entered Woodhouse Grove School at the age of eight
and left at the age of fourteen. They came from Methodist manses
scattered over the country and travelled by various modes to their
appointed place. One came by sailing ship from Hull and then took
coach to Leeds. Many walked. Two brothers secured the circuit
horse and by the method of "ride and tie" covered the miles from
Huddersfield to Howden as knights of old. Their dress was uniform.
It consisted of a dark blue cloth jacket and corduroy trousers.
The cap was a hideous red and yellow contraption, flat, very heavy
and with slanting peak. The boys of Woodhouse Grove could be
easily identified on the roads of England and soon became well-

known both from their strange attire and from the fact that the
local Methodists on every stage of their journey turned out to wish
them a "God bless you" and to speed them on their way with a
slice of gingerbread. Their study, when once arrived at school,
was arduous and the discipline severe, as became saints inured
to flagellation. Says one of them "When I was a boy at the Grove
I was thrashed every day. I dare say I deserved it but it was too
much—it did no good." But there was no discharge in this holy
warfare and the school holidays amounted to one month only in
a campaign of eleven months of schooling. The Methodist was
not cruel by nature. Indeed, it was he who stressed kindness to
animals and the love of all fallen, lost things, but he was always
puzzled as to how to get his children's place secure amongst the
mansions in the sky. The spark of grace which he trimmed so
assiduously seemed so unequally matched with the sin in juvenile
hearts. The pious father would fly in alarm to the rod to save a
soul alive. Preachers' sons ran the risk of being doubly thrashed
for they were to be examples to the whole of the Methodist Society
and manly arms became braced with nervous energy over those
bent backs because the whole reputation of Methodism seemed
at stake in its erring children.

Perhaps the boys of Woodhouse Grove needed beating. They
had come by a singular inheritance. Hell yawned at their feet,
and it was so real to them that they could faint quite easily at
sermons which recounted their probable reception there. Seasons
of religious revival were warranted to flourish in such soil both
as light relief to the daily round and as an escape from a life of
hardship. Mr. Fennell's text seemed innocuous enough to arouse
such a storm of emotion, but it was the point that he was labouring,
about these boys being the sons of their fathers, that did the mischief.
The awful thing for them was that they knew themselves to be
preachers' sons and exhalted to heaven with privilege. If they,
of all the sinful world, fell short of holiness greater by far would
be their eternal doom. Boys can see visions on bread and milk.
They will find colour in Wesley's dazzling hymns, deprived of
all other colour in life apart from that fantastic creation of the
red and yellow cap of servitude. They will discover freedom in
prayer meetings when all other recreation is confined to a playground of stone for eleven months of the year. At least you can
tell God what you think of life, and believe that, if your father and
mother have so obviously forsaken you, the Lord will take you up.

The boys at Woodhouse Grove pleaded for a prayer meeting, in that year when Patrick Brontë came amongst them, with all the glee with which to-day children beg for a holiday.

Here is Mr. Fennell's letter: "After supper they gathered round me like bees, telling me how the Lord had been amongst them, and earnestly entreating that they might be permitted to spend a few hours more before bed-time in prayer. Love for their souls, and a desire to indulge them in anything that might do their souls good, on the one hand, and feeling the indispensable necessity of keeping all things in order and mixing prudence with piety on the other, caused such a struggle in my mind that I was at my wits' end while surrounded with the loud clamour of 'Do, Sir, do, Sir, let us, if it be but one hour.' And to the right-thinking Methodist there was nothing strange in such a demonstration. It was but the dawn of the day for which the school was founded. There was no better news than this to send to the Methodist Magazine under the heading of 'Religious and Missionary Intelligence,' for it meant that the new school at Woodhouse Grove, opened in January 1812, was by March of that year exhibiting the authentic signs, infallible proofs, of its parentage. All men could see that here was no bastard son. It was the news which the authorities expected to hear that these boys were "determined for Heaven' ".

It was to urge these embryo saints still further up the steep and narrow way that Patrick Brontë came to add his own pious efforts and to teach them the verb Amo and all other rudiments of a classical education. It is important to look more closely at his handful of scholars. There were about thirty of them at first, but soon these increased to seventy, and the one thing that saved them all from destruction was Methodism's own priceless gift of fellowship. Squeezed into those small desks, two at a time, and listening to Patrick Brontë, they will remember to their dying day the boy they sat by at The Grove. As grown men they will weep bitter tears when the school in 1883 will be thrown open to the sons of laymen and so cease to exist in its old entity. The love of their old school will go to the grave with every man jack of them.

Some of those original Grovites will become ministers of the gospel, some will be doctors, some tradesmen and some rebels, but the modest triumphs of each will be the glory of all. That little handful of boys, taken from the opening years of Woodhouse Grove School, will make a respectable contribution to English

WOODHOUSE GROVE WESLEYAN ACADEMY

From an engraving c. 1812

history. There is Rayner Stevens, the leader of the Chartists. There
is Atherton of the King's Counsel, who will die of a broken heart
as legal adviser to the Government during America's Civil War.
There is Morley with his discoveries of the properties of
strychnine and the application of his knowledge to the study of
crime. He will become the forerunner to Sir Bernard Spilsbury,
and, by means of his researches, the Rugeley murderer Palmer
will be brought to justice. There is MacDonald with the very
same background of Celtic Methodism as Patrick Brontë himself.
He will become the father, in his turn, of that family of girls who
married Poynter and Burne Jones and of those other two who
were the mothers of Rudyard Kipling and of Stanley Baldwin.
His only son will become a Methodist preacher. And some there
be that have no memorial. They will become just honest workmen
whom Woodhouse Grove had moulded and the humblest of them
will develop an inordinate sense of duty, a stirring in his heart
towards beauty, the inspiration of a charge to keep, and the reverence which springs from an over-mastering consciousness of the
reality of God.

It is not for nothing that Rudyard Kipling invoked the God
of his fathers in his famous hymn. When the world smiled at their
soldier poet, turned preacher, he replied quite honestly that he
really could not help it for he was "Methody on both sides."
And of course that was how it all began, with the boy striding
round his bedroom making jingles to the hymn tunes which
Miss MacDonald sang to keep his metre true.

It was on a threadbare Methodist circuit carpet that the Pre-
Raphaelites, Poynter and Burne Jones, had to kneel to the God
of MacDonald's fathers, ere they received the hands of his daughters
in a solemn contract of matrimonial engagement. It did not in
the least matter that no one had a penny with which to bless themselves, if only the proposed undertaking had upon it the blessing
of the God of John Wesley. The School of the Pre-Raphaelites
was made initiate there in that same glory which MacDonald of
the Grove, and Patrick Brontë, had first glimpsed from the narrow
door-way of an Irish Cabin. It was the glory, as of the Only Begotten
of the Father, full of grace and truth.

The fact that the courtship of Patrick Brontë and Maria Branwell
was conducted just here at Woodhouse Grove, in the old home
atmosphere and on the wings of religious revival, is not without
significance for the history of English literature. That the little

D

Brontës went into life with that legacy of vivid emotional Methodism, "on both sides," goes far to explain their meteoric flight across
the literary sky of England. Patrick Brontë has been blamed for
much, but the real nature of his sin has never been understood.
His chief crime was one over which he had no sort of control,
for it was this. He, and his wife, between them, contrived to be-
queath to their luckless children a soul-shattering enthusiasm
which the facts of life simply did not warrant.

CHAPTER V

MARIA BRANWELL

LITTLE Miss Branwell was seated in an upper room of the gentle-man's mansion at Woodhouse Grove. She was busy scribbling a letter to Patrick Brontë, for the honest old man who came for the post was almost due. Her eyes were bright. She had an eager air. Her fingers flew over the page. And yet there is a hint of sadness here. Can no one be found to warn her of the fate which is coming so surely upon her? Seen like this, there is something a little pathetic about this woman's maiden love. She really knew so little of life with her absolute reliance upon the Will of God.

Maria Branwell has always been called Patrick Brontë's poor little wife and has been dismissed, somewhat summarily, from the scene of action. In reality she was of the stuff of which heroes are made. Her literary remains are even more slender than Patrick's own and her biographer has little material save a bundle of old letters, written at Woodhouse Grove, and an essay intended for some pious magazine which never saw the light. Still, it is a living woman who moves amongst the old words and stirs the dust which has lain upon them so long. The essay itself is indicative of a tender conscience. It is entitled: "The advantages of poverty in religious concerns" and she must have believed it all when she wrote it. This was Maria Branwell's way of easing the intolerable burden of responsibility which Christians were beginning to feel for their poorer brethren. The Will of God must pay for all. If people starved to death because they had no work, and, when they had work, lived on starvation wages then compensation must be found for them in heavenly places. Patrick's poor cottagers must be avid for mansions in the sky and tighten mortal belts in hovels here below. Maria Branwell's brave poor things must be shown to be more sure of salvation than were the rich and profligate. They would win in the end. But, like Mary Fletcher of the exquisite feelings, the tender heart of Maria bled for the poor, the wounded and the outcast.

Now Patrick Brontë, lately aroused from his curate's bed, had assaulted that tender heart with all the impetuosity of his nature reinforced by thirty-five years of bachelorhood. Did he really mean all he said? That was the question to tease that tender yet

37

candid woman. Maria Branwell would hold on resolutely to what she knew of truth and to all she could command of her trembling heart. To her pride, too, for she declared she would never allow herself to love more than she was loved. And yet she distrusted that confession of Patrick's that he, a clergyman of the Church, was obsessed by one idea to the exclusion of every pious hope or heavenly endeavour. That could not be right. He must pray about that and not wreck the brightening future by an impious present. But it reads as a very gentle reproof: "Pardon me, my dear friend, if I again caution you against giving way to a weakness of which I have heard you complain. When you find your heart oppressed and your thoughts too much engrossed by one subject let prayer be your refuge—this you no doubt know by experience to be a sure remedy." Patrick Brontë was irresistible in just that mood whatever the restraint of tradition and the acknowledgment of God's supremacy. Maria Branwell could not really mistrust his kindness. She was almost ashamed to say how much she missed him. Nothing in that lovely Woodhouse Grove seemed the same without him. That wide view from her window of the fields of buttercups and daisies stretching down to the clear river bubbling over its white stones was now "insipid" to her eyes. There had passed away a glory from the earth along with the removal of Patrick's strong encircling arm. The hills seemed so steep without him and she missed him terribly as she toiled up them to visit a company of Yorkshire matrons who knew not the ways of an Irish lover.

Maria Branwell, for all that, was not going to yield up the keys of her heart without a struggle. She was nearly thirty years of age and had been for some time "perfectly my own mistress, subject to no control whatever." She had come from a very happy home. Her mother and sisters had always consulted her and taken her advice on all matters of importance. They had felt confidence in her judgment and her honesty which was ever informed with love. Life was full, bustling and important in far away Cornwall. Maria Branwell had her own circle of friends and took delight in writing to them and in receiving their letters. The Branwells were the centre of a charming social life and the leading people of Penzance where Methodism held the field in large chapels and in town business. There was a certain grace about the silk-clad figure of Miss Maria Branwell. Patrick Brontë himself paid her the compliment of feeling a little diffident in her society for here was a

different proposition altogether from Mary Burder. Suddenly he
had felt awkward and too conscious of his own Irish Cabin. It
worried him afterwards and he feared he had not been quite so
polite as that Fletcher, Fennell, Branwell company seemed to
demand. Had he spoiled his chances with the girl, when he was
just warming impetuously towards the idea of marriage? Her
answer to his nervous questioning perhaps gave him courage for
fresh advances. She says "The politeness of others can never make
me forget your kind attentions, neither can I walk our accustomed
rounds without thinking of you, and, why should I be ashamed
to add, wishing for your presence. If I know anything of myself
I am incapable of making an ungenerous return to the smallest
degree of kindness, much less to you whose attentions and conduct
have been so particularly obliging."

So far so good, but the letters soon betray a heart which is
nothing but clay in the hand of Patrick Brontë. Always before,
Maria Branwell had been able to cast her care upon the Lord.
Always before, she had been able to say: "By fervent application
to the Throne of Grace I have experienced that my heavenly
Father is able and willing to supply the place of every earthly
friend." But now she felt nearly desperate if the irresponsible
Patrick missed a post. "How could my dear friend so cruelly
disappoint me?" Now she could not sleep until she had written
to him to unburden her mind of its grievous anxiety. She will even
break the Sabbath to write to Patrick Brontë. The tender conscience was, oh so gracefully, eased as the Sunday letter wished
him well in his preaching and assured him of her prayers. To
await his letters became to Maria Branwell almost an agony of
suspense. What if they did not come? What if they showed a falling
off in affection? And then that ceaseless urge to write to him. How
could Maria cope with that insistence of desire amongst Aunt
Fennell's fine friends from Bradford? She confesses: "My thoughts
often strayed from the company and I would have gladly left them
to follow my present employment." And when she could escape
to her own quiet room above the hum of Woodhouse Grove and
its grand guests and poor scholars how the words tumble onto
the pages without any formality of introduction. Just this: "With
the sincerest pleasure do I retire from company to converse with
him whom I love beyond all others. Unless my love for you were
very great how could I so contentedly give up my home and all
my friends—a home I loved so much that I have often thought

nothing could bribe me to renounce it for any great length of time together, and friends with whom I have been so long accustomed to share all the vicissitudes of joy and sorrow? Yet these have lost their weight, and though I cannot always think of them without a sigh, yet the anticipation of sharing with you all the pleasures and pains, the cares and anxieties of life, of contributing to your comfort and becoming the companion of your pilgrimage, is more delightful to me than any other prospect which this world can possibly present."

Sometimes, as the pen flew over the paper Maria Branwell's conscience pricked her—was it right to feel so terribly the chances of lost posts and changing moods? Did the boys' voices reach her, in her retreat, singing of lost sinners, in that grove which echoed again with the birds' songs and the Wesley hymns? She rather wondered if she was losing heavenly ground in this absorbing passion of human love. How sweet to ask Patrick to pray for her in his hours of retirement for "I assure you I need every assistance to help me forward; I feel that my heart is more ready to attach itself to earth than heaven." And then of course, just as easily, the letters swing away to the intensity of religious emotion. Patrick's love had made all things new there also. Never so much as now had Maria's heart been so moved at the thought of her Saviour. The tender and half tearful heaven of forgiven sins mingled so sweetly with the joy of Patrick's love. In Calverley Church one of those experiences swept into the soul of Maria Branwell which perhaps only the Methodist can understand. Sudden, in a moment, a warmth about the heart, and Christ Himself is there. As Maria put it, shyly to her earthly lover: "I scarcely ever felt more charmed with His excellencies, more grateful for His condescension or more abased at my own unworthiness." Before her she saw the road of life stretching out in lines of ecstacy leading straight to glory. She saw Patrick Brontë and herself treading that road side by side. And at the end, as for all Wesley's followers, was that certain conviction that love led but to eternal life. It was the same in substance with glory. Maria Branwell exlaimed in the ear of her Patrick "Oh what sacred pleasure there is in the idea of spending an eternity together in perfect and uninterrupted bliss."

Perhaps it is always better for saints to contemplate union only in glory. Knowing all that was to come upon Maria Branwell there is something haunting in her pathetic trust in her Patrick and in his God. She writes, so confidently about it all: "I believe a kind providence has intended that I shall find in you every earthly friend united; nor do I fear to trust myself under your protection, or shrink from your control." And again "I think if our lives are spared twenty years hence I shall then pray for you with the same if not greater fervour and delight that I do now. I am pleased that you are so fully convinced of my candour, for to know that you suspected me of a deficiency in this virtue would grieve and mortify me beyond expression. I do not derive any merit from the possession of it, for in me it is constitutional. Yet I think where it is possessed it will rarely exist alone, and where it is wanted there is reason to doubt the existence of almost every other virtue."

That letter was written in November 1812, and twenty years by the side of Patrick Brontë then seemed nothing short of a prim-rosed path leading straight to heaven. In reality, the little scribe was allowed only ten years, in all, to pray for her Patrick and she would have been well advised to have kept her prayers only for herself. Her gracious, silk-clad figure will presently be dragged off stage in all the savage disarray of perpetual pregnancy. Can no one warn her before she leaves the shelter of Woodhouse Grove, with its tall trees and its singing birds? No, she insists on rushing on her fate. Here is her last letter before that fatal marriage day: "I am certain no one ever loved you with an affection more pure, constant, tender, and ardent than that which I feel. Surely this is not saying too much; it is the truth, and I trust you are worthy to know it." That was the crux of the matter. Was he worthy to know it? We wish we could forget Mary Burder. We wish we did not trace a falling off of ardour in his letters to his Maria, immediately after her confession: "I suppose you never expected to be much the richer for me, but I am sorry to inform you that I am still poorer than I thought myself." We wish a hundred, hopeless, useless wishes, but we know that nothing can now deliver Maria Branwell from the hands of Patrick Brontë. He is striding forward with a lusty new assurance. He is writing poems to a lady on her birthday and on Kirkstall Abbey by moonlight which is really rather a dashing performance for one accustomed to sing of children and wife climbing heavenly steeps, helped thereto by Wesley's psalmody.

So, from the Headmaster's house at Woodhouse Grove, two couples went out to Guiseley Church to be married, about Christmas time, in the year 1812. Stout Morgan secured John

Fennell's daughter and Patrick Brontë his niece, and perhaps those poor little urchins, the schoolboys, in their hideous caps, looked over the playground wall and wondered at so strange a double wedding. The boys of Woodhouse Grove were certainly on the premises as their one holiday fell due only in May each year. Did Uncle Fennell give them something better than bread and milk on that festive wedding-night, or did they have to be content with singing an appropriate hymn at Prayers and then going to bed hungry? The hymn would surely be the one for all Methodist weddings. It did equally well "For the Society Praying" and for the schoolboys themselves, for it ran:

> "Why hast Thou cast our lot
> In the same age and place,
> And why together brought
> To see each other's face,
> To join with loving sympathy
> And mix our friendly souls in Thee?"

Now that was delightful enough, but what of the co-mingling of bodies? English literature can answer a little of that question, but now it is hidden from our eyes. It is safe to say that the skull and cross bones of stark reality, now so decently veiled, would come to exact a heavy toll from one so spiritually minded as was Maria Branwell. It would all be much easier for Patrick. In his reasoning, every olive branch was a direct gift of God and his wife was fulfilling only her duty in her resignation—"Patient the appointed race to run." But, in a blaze of too much glory, Patrick Brontë was ignorant of the fact that the speed of that race was a trifle excessive. There were to be six little Brontës in eight years, with all that went to their creation and nurture, and to the training of their souls to fit them for the skies. Nature has her own charming way of making up for lost time.

CHAPTER VI

GAY GO UP MEANS GAY GO DOWN

PATRICK BRONTË at last knew that he had become that success
which he had always liked to think he really was. He positively
thrilled through all his tall clerical frame to know how easily
preferment came his way. He knew the right people. Linked as
he was to Mrs. Fletcher and to her friends Crosse of Bradford
and young Morgan, he was soon travelling gaily from Hartshead-cum-Clifton to Thornton and then to Haworth and to
an ever brightening future.

To Patrick Brontë was now vouchsafed one span of life which
was completely happy. It bears all the marks of vigorous enterprise
and eternal hope. The young father became sure of himself, as
never before, and found all life packed full with interest. He had
his national hero and could rejoice with Wellington at Waterloo
in 1815, as though he had done it all himself, for had he not joined
the volunteers in Cambridge in those dark days of threatened
invasion? He had his pistols still at the ready for any would-be
imitators of the French Revolution and he had been a doughty
champion of authority in his Birstall parish when the machine
breakers had threatened the god of private property in a vain
attempt to save themselves from the horrors of starvation. He would
never be tired of telling that story and of sensing the exquisite
excitement of the thing and the joy of his own prowess. Then,
his poetic muse was kind and clicked heels at his command,
for Patrick Brontë published his second volume of verse amidst
the budding and blossoming of his first begotten children, Maria
and Elizabeth. He rejoiced to know his star was in the ascendant
and dreamed comfortable, happy dreams of radiant authorship
and of a cashbox full of glittering gold, for at Thornton, Patrick
Brontë found the conditions of life which suited him. Here was the
friendly generous patron like unto those of his youth and here was
that brand of sanctity which he best understood. The Firths of
Kipping House were the great discovery and fulfilled the same
delicious role of protection and dignity which Patrick Brontë
had found so worthwhile under the roof of Thomas Tighe. They
had been Dissenters, with their roots right back in the great days
of Oliver Heywood, but they had entered the doors of Mother

43

Church, even as Patrick, by way of the Evangelical Revival of Religion. The description of the death of Mr. Firth, in his daughter's diary, is as to the manner born. Here is the artless tale: "My Papa complained of shivering. My Papa was very ill. My Papa worse. My Papa carried into the drawing-room. My Papa suffered great depression of mind. By God's blessing and Mr. Brontë's conversation became more happy. In holy ecstasies all day, blessed be God. My dear father's last words at half past eleven—All's well, all's happy."

When the saintly Fletcher married Mary Bosanquet he playfully told her that she must also espouse his parish. Mrs. Patrick Brontë achieved that feat and more. In this congenial haven of Thornton, with Miss Firth of Kipping House popping in and out of the parsonage on every page of her diary, four children were born to Patrick and Maria Brontë. Charlotte, Branwell, Emily and Anne all first saw the light in that house at Thornton, in the street above Kipping House. Whilst the proud father expands in affability, his little wife naturally fades into the background. Within that house there was work enough for her. She had brought her little Maria and Elizabeth with her from Hartshead-cum-Clifton and the addition of a sister or brother to them each year involved a strenuous organisation of domestic detail.

It is not difficult to see that the first-born child Maria would be pressed into the service at a tender age. Upon her would come the end of the ages. She would receive the full impact of her mother's epic struggle with fate and she would be old in experience and aware of man's need of a saviour long before her time. She herself had been the first fruits of the mating of her mother's piety and her father's passion and she was condemned to watch, at too close quarters, that uneasy contention. Like Patrick's poor cottagers and Maria Branwell's brave poor things, she came to build for herself future mansions in the sky to redress the balance of a highly uncomfortable present world. The child had received the full impact of that peculiar legacy which had been stored in the hearts of both her father and mother since Wesley spurred on his gospel way through the lanes of Cornwall and of County Down. She was an embryo saint ere ever she relinquished that speedily requisitioned cradle to the insistent claims of the next baby.

The two Marias, mother and daughter, like orphans of the storm, made what headway they could on this bleak journey, but, from the pages of Miss Firth's diary, comes a sense, an air, of a positively junketing Patrick. There are recorded tea parties. There are jaunts to Bradford. There is talk of good books. There is the grand excitement of the Radicals coming to slay all in their beds, but the equally glorious comfort of Mr. Brontë's pistols. Even the advent of all those children could not daunt so stout a heart. When they numbered six, Patrick could still call them "a sweet little family." There is the dear comfort, to a hero-worshipping schoolgirl like Miss Firth, of the help she herself could be to the valiant parson and his overburdened wife. She would take care of their children all day whilst Anne, the last of them, was getting herself born. And Miss Firth could help with the children's clothes and if she was inclined to be a little frivolous with her gift of bright things Patrick could always follow Wesley's advice and lay them quietly aside after a show of thanks.

When a man is beset by pressing domestic concerns he can find nothing more helpful than a bevy of admiring spinsters to help him over the hurdles of his wife's lying-in. Miss Outhwaite supported Miss Firth, and Mrs. Brontë's sister, Elizabeth Branwell, joined the happy band also. She came up from Cornwall for the birth of Charlotte Brontë and assisted at various christenings. She entered into the social gaiety of Kipping House with relish. She wept on Miss Firth's neck when at last she had to return to her southern home. Amidst the happy bustle shines Patrick with his services and his prayer meetings and his belief in himself, as the man marked out for promotion. Things went with a swing in Thornton long ago, for Patrick Brontë was just that pious, evangelical clergyman for whom there was always a wide welcome in Yorkshire.

It might not all be such fun for the parson's wife. She might come to question the justice of the bright young things jaunting off to Bradford whilst she toiled on at the mill at home. She might come to see that it was she, the girl of the golden future, who had lost all her youth even in a night. How if her nerve failed altogether at so terrible a working out of God's purposes in such a relentless surge of life? How could she cope with the birth of her fourth daughter but ten months after the birth of her only son? There was never time enough left her to enjoy one baby before the fear of the arrival of its successor was stabbing at her heart. Sick in mind and in body, a deterioration begins to make itself felt in the life of Maria Brontë. Nothing much at first perhaps, only a home-sickness and a wonder why she found herself so far from

Cornwall. A lost gaiety was inevitable and silent endurance had taken its place, but, after the birth of Anne, came the sure signs of unmistakable disease. Human body and immortal soul had been too severely overtaxed. Death began to wear a fairer face than life. Maria Brontë was soon to become so tired that she really did not care what happened to her, one way or another. How was the primrose path now? She did not much care where it led. The consolations of God Himself had become small with her.

It was just at this juncture that fate stepped once more out of that old background of Methodism to preside at the birth of Anne, at the promotion of Patrick, and to assist in the death of Maria Brontë. Morgan and the Vicar of Bradford were its agents, and they installed Patrick Brontë in a parish which was the acme of all Yorkshire Methodism—the last word in the ancient Wesley tradition—the home of Grimshaw of the Haworth Round. But first stout Morgan must baptise the latest arrival at the Thornton font and Maria must remain there for a month longer, before she dragged her weary body and her six little children up that steep hill to the new parsonage. Patrick Brontë was in the saddle and preaching at Haworth a month before Anne's birth on March 25th, 1820, but he did not collect all his family together under his new roof until April of that year.

His last little daughter had come to them amidst the anxiety and the excitement of all the "to be or not to be" of appointment to Grimshaw's parish. Patrick must have rubbed his hands with satisfaction to think that he had been thought fit to walk in the steps of William Grimshaw. It was more than an elevation from Log Cabin to White House and Thomas Tighe would have seen a miracle in it, for, through the length and breadth of the world of the Evangelical Revival, William Grimshaw was in Venn's famous phrase "a burning and a shining light." Wesley had chosen both the saintly Fletcher and William Grimshaw in turn to take the leadership of Methodism after his own death. Patrick Brontë was thus at the very nerve centre of this strange apostolic succession. He had more than Abraham for his father when he married the niece of John Fletcher's god-son and drank out of Grimshaw's flagons at a Haworth Communion Service. Familiar jingles ran riot over their old pewter sides and the place was instinct with ancient tradition.

The Church of Haworth was full of ghosts. Here Wesley had preached and there Whitefield's fiery eloquence had literally felled men to death as they stood in dense crowds to hear of Heaven and of Hell. Here the Countess of Huntingdon had worshipped, coming caparisoned as the Pope Joan of Methodism. Here in the golden light of a September evening Grace Murray had come— riding pillion behind John Wesley. Here Grimshaw had died in the Methodist style, for when death pointed "a javelin at his heart" he had looked into the face of the King of Terrors and seen but the face of an angel. "I have only to step out of my bed into Heaven" he had said. Was it possible for Patrick Brontë to become a second William Grimshaw? His sponsors must have thought highly of him when they proposed his name to the people of Haworth. But at the crest of the wave of success there is sometimes an unaccountable plunge into the very trough and Patrick Brontë was destined to take it. His ascent up that cobbled street of Haworth was the signal for his incipient decline. It began with his wife. Patrick no sooner got his little family safely housed in his fine new parsonage and began vigorously to see to the tidying up of his churchyard than Maria began to sicken with that hidden horror of cancerous growth.

Life had been a little hard on Patrick's wife since those days at Woodhouse Grove when she had boasted that she was "perfectly her own mistress." Now, it had come to pass that another should gird her and carry her wither she would not. The patter of little feet had been a shade too relentless, and perhaps she was always a little homesick in this strange Yorkshire. She used to raise herself to watch the blackleading of her sick-room grate because they did it just like that in Cornwall. She was uneasy too about her husband, for, by this time, she knew him only too well. Haworth was going to be a different charge for him and she was unable now to help him at all. She was sorry that he should have to suffer so much with that Irish temper of his, chastised by the fear of the Lord. The first flush of Patrick Brontë's meteoric rise to fame was over and he now had time to look round at his newest, greatest parish and to find it otherwise from the place in which he had dreamed that he might be a second Grimshaw.

In the old days Methodism had been Patrick Brontë's best friend, but now it was the very success of Methodism in Haworth that made his path more difficult. It had a way now of strengthening the tough Yorkshire sinews of independence. Grimshaw himself had built the Methodists a chapel in Haworth and chosen for it his own challenging motto: "For me to live is Christ." It was emblazoned also on the walls of his own parish church and so Jack was evidently as good as his master, way down at the Methody chapel as upon Parson's Hill. Of course Grimshaw had not meant it to work out like that. He had built the chapel for the saints who were considered "the purer part of the Church of England" and who might come to be persecuted for their faith should a ruler arise who knew not the Methodist Joseph. He had not dared to hope for so dutiful a son in the gospel as Patrick Brontë who was now trying to cope with the aftermath of history and with a dying wife at one and the same time.

To begin with, Patrick missed the backing of Kipping House. He felt himself a stranger in a strange land and in a domestic crisis there seemed nowhere he could turn for help. The people at Haworth were so different from those at Thornton, and, just at the moment when he sought consolation at home for his public anxieties, his wife had utterly failed him. Strong in his young vigour and safe in his home, Patrick Brontë believed that, up to the present, he had been successful in surmounting all difficulties, but now it dawned upon him that he would have to move with caution. The people of Haworth would need some managing, for they were democratic, self willed and proud of their ancient inheritance. It would never do to have them drive a donkey into church with a sweep aloft in protest against an infringement of their liberties as had happened before Patrick's arrival. The very thought made him turn faint at the desecration of Grimshaw's holy shrine. The very church, instead of being the Mecca of his dreams, assumed a sort of intimidation, for its high pulpit seemed full of the ghosts of abler and better men who had gone before him.

It was all very well for William Grimshaw to whip people into church but Patrick Brontë could not sustain that militant role. In his old parsonage, across the church-yard, at Sowden's Farm, William Grimshaw had looked into the face of death undaunted, but with the best will in the world Patrick Brontë, in his new parsonage, could not see the face of the King of Terrors as it were the face of an angel. Before him agonized reality on his wife's groaning death-bed and things did not seem to work out as they were once supposed to do. It had been easy on his lonely bed at Hartshead to sing of Christ and feel Him a sufficient Saviour. Patrick had proclaimed quite joyfully then: "His Presence from suffering does ease us," and that might have been true when Patrick lay alone, as a poor ambitious curate, feeling his genius rebuked under his more popular vicar, and taking comfort from the championship of God himself, but what now with the crucifixion of that woman he had made his own and enjoyed all the more potently because they loved in the Lord? There is evidence of a down-right collapse of nerve in Patrick's brand new parsonage. He describes it thus when writing to his old vicar at Dewsbury: "There were seasons when an affectionate, agonizing something sickened my whole frame and which is of such a nature as cannot be described and must be felt in order to be understood." Patrick Brontë would never be his own man again. His religion would from this time harden into a more professional form for it would be safer and better so. That old Methodism showed signs of wanting its wings of fancy clipped. It is Patrick's farewell to glory as he signs his letter to his old vicar to tell him of his wife's death, but, for all that, it betrays his knowledge of the way a soul should escape to life. He writes: "Death pursued her unrelentingly. Her constitution was enfeebled and her frame wasted daily, and after above seven months of more agonizing pain than I ever saw anyone endure she fell asleep in Jesus and her soul took its flight to the mansions of glory. During many years she had walked with God but the great enemy, envying her life of holiness, often disturbed her mind in the last conflict. Still, in general she had peace and joy in believing and died, if not triumphantly, at least calmly and with a holy yet humble confidence that Christ was her Saviour and Heaven her eternal home."

Words failed Patrick Brontë altogether when it came to a description of the storm that now broke on his own soul. His old past had stepped forward into his more sophisticated present and had him firmly by the throat. The women who attended upon his dying wife and knew something of her "capacity for feeling and loving" were shocked at his dry-eyed grief. But if he could have wept it would have been so much more easy for him. Now he was as one struck by a thunderbolt and wrought up to a despairing speechless questioning of the ways of God. Real life had come a shade too near. Patrick's mind was going round and round in barren circles. At his heart was a load like lead. Why had God sought thus to afflict him? Had he done something wrong? Was there some sin hidden away in the secret of his own heart that God would save him from, so as by fire?

The Methodists were cruel in their soul probings and in their teaching of the creature and the Creator. The Lord their God was a jealous God. Sometimes, in love, He must remove the idol, cut off the hand or foot, that the soul should not be lost for ever in torment. Mrs. Fletcher said that God sometimes set a hedge of thorns round a believer so that in the bristling difficulties there was only one way to look and that upwards. Wesley called affliction God's school and thought that it shut him more securely in with the love of God. It should instruct the afflicted one towards a time of prayer and fasting and bring about a new renunciation of all clogging clay.

What had the priest of Haworth done amiss? A tender conscience was calculated to rattle a host of skeletons in the cupboards of the mind. It was undeniable that his treading of the straight and narrow way had been greatly eased since his marriage and his preferment. Would Henry Martyn own him now as a good soldier of the cross? Perhaps the very bliss of wedded love might not be entirely in comformity with the Will of God? Was it a snare in itself, with its inevitable relaxation of the iron bands of restraint? In this awful Christian race of repressed human appetite it might have its dangers. Robbed of his wife, the man's nerves were in that terrible jangle of frustration which made the way of holiness intolerably steep and yet the more insistent in its claims. Denied all other relief, he was not even allowed to indulge in anger. Into his wild pistol shots at the church tower and his insane sawing off of chairbacks went that energy which anyone, with a different background, would have let rip in evil temper.

The little woman, lying upstairs, torn with that awful cancer of suffering, knew her husband and her Methodism only too well. She lay listening to those menacing, hopeless, staccato shots below her window and whispered with a wan smile: "Is it not wonderful that he never gave me an angry word?" The Methodist, brought up in the school of Thomas Walsh, must hold his tongue. That saint of God had beaten his whole body on the ground to hold back the complications of a young and lusty Irish nature, prone to hatred and to love in quick terrible spasms, yet sworn to holiness through the sacrifice of his Lord. Let no man take thy crown. Patrick Brontë was determined to keep his intact for the Judgment Day, but he must have been a little difficult to live with just then in Haworth.

There was undoubtedly with Patrick just now an all round speeding up of heavenly resolve, but it was only accomplished with

"Up that steep hill to
the new parsonage"

MAIN STREET, HAWORTH

great effort and with the Key of Promise going damnably hard. That burning hearthrug almost frightened the parson to death with its all too suggestive flames. He stuffed it recklessly up the chimney in spite of heat and stench, and the house was filled with smoke. Every true Methodist carries hidden in his soul a fear of fire. It has come down from John Wesley's own childhood when a great deal too much was made of the brand plucked from the burning, with Hell just on his heels.

In this flight of terror to the horrors of his own youth Patrick Brontë felt the souls of his own little family hang heavy upon him. His wife had taken all that load of anxiety off his vigorous shoulders, but now it weighed intolerably there. The very servants, for all their pains, seemed no better than fools to Patrick Brontë. They seemed to go out of their way to set the children's feet on the road to destruction and to implant in them a love of this vain world. Coming into the kitchen one day, Patrick saw with dismay that one of his henchwomen had actually rummaged out those gay bootees for the children which he and his wife had laid aside politely in the days at Thornton as an un-Methodist gift. Now, at Haworth, the much tried maid of all work, contending with six delicate children with wet feet, must have rejoiced to come across such treasure trove. There is just one twinkle of mellow happy light from a Yorkshire kitchen fire. There is just one glimpse of a young girl trying to do her best, in good Yorkshire fashion, for little feet on the rough moors of life, and then Patrick Brontë enters like an avenging deity. His brow is wrinkled with Methodist scruples. His heart is suffocating with a load of misery. At sight of those gay boots he could have bitten the girl's head off. Quick as lightning, six pairs of slippers feed the devouring flames. Patrick Brontë is after saving his own soul and those of his children by stern good works, now that the spring time of the soul's first love has been so rudely nipped.

To his biographers this bonfire of vanities has always seemed like the action of a madman, but then they have never taken the trouble to look at Patrick's background or to read the books in that lonely study of his. There was one especial volume which should solve the mystery, for it came to his help at any time of God's sudden visitation and it helped him to make his sermons in a crisis. It was the volume of Wesley's works with his sermon in it on the Cause and Cure of Earthquakes which Patrick Brontë found so useful when the bog moved, in sudden terror, on Haworth Moor.

E

It also contained Wesley's sermon on Fletcher of Madeley. But most of all there was within its sombre covers Wesley's advice to parents on the bringing up of their children. Had poor Patrick Brontë been reading that treatise in a desperate effort to take his wife's place, in the care of his children's souls, and then walked straight out of his study into that horror of the Whore of Babylon sitting on his own kitchen fender?

These are Wesley's words to the pious parent: "Next to self-will and pride the most fatal disease with which we are born is ' love of the world.' But how studiously do the generality of parents cherish this in its several branches° They cherish ' the desire of the flesh ', that is, by the tendency to seek happiness in pleasing the outward senses, by studying to enlarge the pleasure of tasting it in their children to the uttermost—yea, they provide them with comfits, gingerbread, raisins, and whatever fruit they have a mind to. They feed in them 'the desire of the eyes', the propensity to seek happiness in pleasing the imagination, by giving them pretty playthings, glittering toys, shining buckles or buttons, fine clothes, red shoes, laced hats, needless ornaments, as ribands, necklaces, ruffles; yea, and by proposing any of these as rewards for doing their duty, which is stamping a great value upon them. But herein a difficulty will arise which it will need much resolution to conquer. Your servants, who will not understand your plan, will be continually giving little things to your children and thereby undoing all your work. This you must prevent, if possible, by warning them when they first come into your house, and repeating the warning from time to time. If they will do it notwithstanding, you must turn them away. Better lose a good servant than spoil a good child."

The way of the devotee was hard, but Patrick Brontë, in great fear for his soul and in loneliness of heart, tried to carry out Wesley's advice to the letter. Mrs. Gaskell speaks of young servants discharged for wastefulness, but the victims, the Gars sisters, rose against her at that and told the world that Charlotte Brontë's biographer had got it all wrong—not waste at all, but perhaps too easy a tolerance and gingerbread for the asking. This was just where the significance of Tabitha Ackroyd, their successor, is seen. She came to rule in Patrick Brontë's kitchen as the patron saint of the old order. The souls of all the bairns were safe in her faithful hands. She was not above going to the Methodist Chapel herself and considered the downsitting and the uprising of the higher ecclesiasticism of a later day as rank idolatry. She could tell the children what William Grimshaw would have done to them for "laiking" on a Sunday. She could repeat his very words, remembered everywhere in Haworth, for he was given to what he called "market language" and he would exhort sinners in stentorian tones. He was accustomed to shout under the windows of dying and notorious reprobates: "If ye perish—ye shall at least perish with the sound of th' gospel in yer lugs." Tabby was the sort of woman not to give extra candles for the asking, just at bed-time. She would let Anne *look* at the cakes but not touch them. Thus far thou shalt come but no further. She was a part of all Patrick Brontë's past and knew every story worth telling about Parson Grimshaw. She also knew the Yorkshire manner of it.

The death of Mrs. Brontë left her husband and children like shipwrecked mariners "on a sea of distress, fast toiling to gain the blest shore." It had all sounded more pleasant when Patrick had made up that verse to match Wesley's and seen, in his mind's eye, his old father migrating to Heaven simultaneously with his wife and children. As he drummed it out at Hartshead, before he had a family of his own, it sounded a happy thing to do:

"Then I with my children and wife
Will get a bright mansion above."

But now Patrick Brontë had arrived at the hungry forties and instead of being clothed in light he found himself confronted with children who needed somebody to see that they had decent boots for their feet, let alone heavenly garments. His dead wife had once called him her "gay saucy Pat," but those days now could never know a resurrection. Instead, he saw the world as it were a wilderness and came to think and speak of it more and more as "this weary world." That also was a phrase out of Wesley's hymns, and the man was hardening into that old pattern and losing all gaiety or carefree poise in the furnace of affliction. The Patrick Brontë of Haworth is not the man who turned in at the fairy gates of Woodhouse Grove or swung down the streets of Thornton into Kipping House. He now has himself very much on his own mind and he begins to withdraw more and more within the sheltering walls of his parsonage.

It was difficult to keep the eyes of his parishioners fixed on Heaven when Patrick's own heart hung so heavy. He still had to go through his parish preaching and "exhorting", as he calls it, in true Methodist phrase. He still had to go on preaching and dividing the

word of truth aright, into law and gospel, for half an hour at a
time every Sunday. Moreover he had to contend with independent
people who talked openly of the iniquity of being made to pay
church rates when they were nothing better than non-comformists.
He had to run a Sunday school in competition with Baptists and
Methodists and feared to get the worst of it into the bargain. To
crown all, his children caught one infantile sickness after another
and his grand new parsonage, bereft of his wife, became nothing
better than a badly run children's hospital. What was to become
of the disciple of Henry Martyn and the protégé of Thomas Tighe
and the saintly Fletchers? In a hopeless collapse of nerve Patrick
Brontë believed life might be safer if he stayed altogether in his
study. His ancient shield of Methodism had become a little
tarnished and outmoded. He sometimes wondered, bemused and
bewildered, what could have become of the glory.

CHAPTER VII

MISS BRANWELL

THE ADVENT of Elizabeth Branwell into Patrick Brontë's parsonage served to stereotype the outer forms of Methodism without bringing any help towards the rejuvenation of its spirit. She came clad in her good silk dresses and her auburn front of hair and she came complete with regularity time-tables. She was severe with the children, but she was absolutely correct and kept Patrick Brontë from sinking altogether into sloth. As long as Miss Branwell lived, the house revolved with energy and purpose and Aunt was always the one to be reckoned with. She kept the girls at their sewing and their house work, and the people of Haworth said they could set their clocks by the regularity of the parsonage routine. There were no moments to be wasted in that Methodist household or Aunt would know the reason why.

Miss Branwell had come to Patrick's help at her sister's death, but she did not mean to stay. She was anxious to get back to the warm south and the social grace of Penzance. She detested Haworth. She used to click backwards and forwards over its stone floors on her pattens, and irritate Yorkshire nerves with her unamiable criticism of the true and tender north. Some of her dealings with the children might be laudatory but not always wise. There was an incident of a child locked up in a room where deathbed scenes still lingered. Perhaps some childish anger had put the infant soul in jeopardy, for the Methodists said that the scowl seen on a child's face was Satan looking out of its eyes. Death was ever a useful monitor to supply a cold shower bath to the heated tantrum but Miss Branwell reckoned without highly strung Irish nerves, fed on a background of Thomas Walsh. He had seen lights. So did this little sinner. He could do trances and so could she. Patrick Brontë's own kindly exhortations proved more beneficial, and Charlotte, at least, of his children never forgot them. Rather than Aunt's she liked to follow her father's advice, "Who from my childhood has counselled me."

But what was Patrick to do? He did not feel equal to managing his children himself and came to trust, almost against himself, in the efficacy of Miss Branwell's training. It was just what Wesley ordered in his advice to parents on the bringing up of children, but sometimes the yoke must have galled his son in the gospel. Sometimes the iron must have entered into Patrick's soul. Distressed in body and mind, he cast about for some way of escape, for if the spirit was willing the flesh was weak. There must be some more comfortable way to be found through this weary world, without shunning the steep and narrow path altogether. One thing is certain. Patrick Brontë became more and more a hermit in his study. There he could not be tempted. There he was saved the anguish of seeing ignorant, yet well-meaning, people imperil his children's souls, or the pain of seeing them buffeted by too much righteousness. He could not sustain that terrible fury of burning up red shoes and sawing off chair backs for there would soon be nothing left in the house and anyway it gave him indigestion. Perhaps it would be better if he had his midday meal alone. Storms so easily brewed up at the family board and he did not like the divided mind under which he laboured when his conscience made him support Miss Branwell's discipline and his heart turned cold in his breast at one and the same time. Patrick Brontë came to despair of ever presiding at his own table as his father had done in his Irish Cabin. That idyllic picture became more and more poetic prose, and, low be it spoken, Patrick even began to take a little wine for his stomach's sake. But of course it was only done under rigid safeguards, for he obtained a medical certificate, first, to be absolutely on the safe side. That libation was also better celebrated entirely in the fastness of his own room.

Now, the sad truth was that the manna from above had begun to lose its efficacy and that Patrick Brontë must needs comfort himself with other than heavenly bounties. It was in that mood one day, when safely bestowed in his queer Trapist retreat of a study that he bethought him of his first love, that girl of eighteen summers, that Mary of Westerfield. Had Miss Branwell's militant Methodism rather irked him that day? Had a flash of pheasant's plumage and a girl's laughing face suddenly stolen into his room with the sunshine? At least it would provide a happy issue out of all Patrick Brontë's afflictions, and be a possible escape from Miss Branwell's auburn front and from her propensity for taking snuff. Anyway it was worth trying, and Patrick Brontë believed that Mary Burder would come for the asking for he could swear she had looked at him with love in her eyes.

So with "divine assistance" the lonely man betook himself to letter writing to friends in his first curacy, for he must first discover whether or not Mary Burder was still single. The joyful answer at last arrived, after a period of anxious waiting, and the time was now ripe for action as Patrick found out that Mary had not yet changed her name. What visions began to form behind those eyes from which the colours had begun to pass away! The only difficulty seems to have been Mary Burder herself, for the letters which passed between this strange pair have survived, so as by a miracle. The unregenerate rejoice to find that the lovely Mary has grown into a woman of some spirit, for it looks as though she really did love Patrick once, because she is so angry with him now. She carries the war right into the enemy's country and gives him just as much of the "divine assistance" as he gave her. She also could quote well known hymns as glibly as he, and she begs, surely with her tongue in her cheek, that Patrick Brontë will try to live up to Grimshaw's reputation for piety now that he is himself Priest of Haworth. That taunt pressed on a sore point with poor Patrick, but worse was to follow. The girl had been so misguided as to keep his letters of fifteen years ago and a woman never forgets. Mary Burder rakes up all his old lusty ambitions and his ancient dread lest she should be the cause which hindered his promotion. She swoops on her luckless prey with joy, to get her own back after all these years, and writes with pen dipped in vinegar: "Happily for me I have not been the ascribed cause of hindering your promotion, of preventing any brilliant alliance, nor have those great and affluent friends that you used to write and speak of witheld their patronage on my account." This sprightly young woman had also come into some money since her days of humble youth and she is not above rubbing that in too, in her glowing description of her present state of happiness when she feels that "my cup overfloweth." The grateful language of her heart, she says, for money, leisure and freedom is "What shall I render to the Lord for all His benefits?"

It made Patrick Brontë feel very small, sitting there in his study, with Miss Branwell's pattens clicking in the offing and that sorry letter held in his trembling hand. Nothing could tell the lonely widower of Haworth Parsonage more plainly that lovely Mary Burder thanked God that she had not fallen upon Maria Branwell's fate. His retaliation is very lame, for his pride is in ruins. He writes: "You may think and write as you please, but I have not the least doubt that if you had been mine you would have been happier than you now are or can be as one in single life. You would have had other and kindlier views and feelings. You would have had a second self—one who would have been continually kind, and whose great aim would have been to have promoted your happiness in *both* the worlds." Alas! The arrogance of men. Patrick Brontë is really sorry for himself and more shaken than ever, for until his wife's death the Lord's Will seemed to be the same thing as the will of Patrick Brontë. Now a horror of great darkness opens at his feet. He is ready to cry with vexation and a hint of melodrama peeps out in his letter as he condemns "the many keen sarcasms which I think might well have been spared, especially as you knew the pale countenance of death was still before my eyes and that I stood more in need of consolation than reproach."

Who can blame Mary Burder? Patrick's very speech betrays him. The young woman had got right under his guard with her winged words and her matchless memory. Rejoicing in her own integrity, she wants her victim to know that at last she has discovered his own lack of candour in those old sad days of heartbreak and desertion. She had gone on believing in him, and now, after all those years, he had the temerity to ask her to come to his rescue and that of his "sweet little family." With all romance in ruins, she had waited all these years for the Lord to be gracious and the Lord had heard her prayer, but she had been asking all the time for bread and He had given her now only a stone. A much married Patrick was not the stuff of which her dreams were made, for she had not so learned her John Fletcher and her Mary Bosanquet. Those letters dropping so innocently onto Patrick Bronte's breakfast table must have required, for their digestion, all the Divine Assistance of which he was capable.

The Rev. Patrick Brontë, gathering together the shreds of his dignity, would turn elsewhere for consolation. Tradition has it that he turned to Miss Firth. That charming young woman was about to marry a clergyman, J. C. Franks, so that Patrick came too late. It is unlikely, in any case, that he would have been successful in his suit, as the lady's memory would be retentive of that long day, in her youth, when she had looked after Patrick's babies when Anne was born. But Miss Firth was at least gracious and she was also resourceful. It must surely have been she who came forward with the bright suggestion of the right school to ease Patrick's burden. It was one way out of a difficult situation for Haworth Parsonage, and, for Miss Firth, it was a much less arduous solution than matrimony. She was even ready to pay money to escape from such a fate. With her friend Miss Outhwaite she would assist in the education of Patrick's children and was ready with both money and advice.

Patrick Brontë was always grateful to his Thornton friends for gifts which he told them would be also blessed to them—under God. But his little family may sometimes have wished that both father and friends had spent their money to better purpose. Of course they were hampered by old tradition and clogged by the perpetual presence of the steep and narrow way. The chosen school must be cut out for all of them according to the old pattern and this school existed at Cowan Bridge, or so they verily believed. It seemed as though it were the very replica of Mary Bosanquet's school in Yorkshire, for it had borrowed from that pioneer with both hands. Here was found Miss Bosanquet's uniform dress, here her very mode of punishment; here also was commended that very instance when the little girl, in her school, said that Miss Bosanquet beat her because she loved her. Carus Wilson, Evangelical clergyman and founder of Cowan Bridge, was so pleased with this tribute that he put it, without acknowledgment, into a tract for his own school and copied the story word for word from the *Life of Mrs. Fletcher*. The little Brontës would be safe here with such a background and with such teachers.

It seems to have been without a qualm that Patrick Brontë deposited Maria, Elizabeth, Charlotte and Emily at Cowan Bridge. They were scarcely over the whooping cough and Aunt Branwell had kept the elder girls in to sew instead of blowing their cobwebs away on Haworth Moor. She thought it "proper for them to do so." Those little distressful children were surely the most pathetic camp followers of the great Revival of Religion who ever took the Kingdom of Heaven by storm. They knew nothing "systematically". The elder girls, for all Aunt's pains, could not even sew very well. Emily could read prettily but had little knowledge of arithmetic. They were equipped generously with only that sort of knowledge which the pious would call other-worldly, and which, at Cowan Bridge, for all its background, would not carry any of them very far. But their sacrifice eased things greatly at Haworth Parsonage and Miss Branwell was able to enter upon a period of peace. She was left with one adorable small boy named Branwell and with a ready-made baby called Anne. To the maiden aunt these two seemed just what children ought to be, and, to the end, these two were her favourites. She believed that so sweet a child as Branwell was born for eternity and that he was almost too good to live. So early, as he himself said, he could read "his title clear to mansions in the sky." And it must have been Baby Anne who, at her prayers, presented that compelling picture of the Romanist and the Methodist rolled into one which her sister Charlotte remembered to the end of her life.

If Patrick Brontë was finding the upward path uncommonly steep, Miss Branwell now enjoyed a kind of St. Martin's summer. Almost it must have atoned to her for those years which the locust had eaten. But what was happening at Cowan Bridge? Schooling for girls was in its infancy and Charles Wesley was positively revolutionary in writing school hymns for girls as well as for boys, but the quality of those hymns will go a long way to explain the sort of education which the pious believed was suitable for its girls, in contradistinction to their brothers. They were all designed to batter the sin of pride from feminine hearts. The boys' hymns deal with the deadly hilarity of youth and deplore the propensity of children for dancing on the brink of hell, thus:

> "How wretched are the boys at school
> Who wickedly delight
> To mock, and call each other fool,
> And with each other fight."

But the girls are honoured with this gem:—

> "Ah, dire effect of female pride!
> How deep our mother's sin, and wide,
> Through all her daughters spread!
> Since first she plucked the mortal tree,
> Each woman would a goddess be
> In her Creator's stead.
>
> This fatal vanity of mind,
> A curse entail'd on all the kind
> Her legacy we feel;
> We neither can deny nor tame
> Out inbred eagerness for fame
> And stubbornness of will.
>
> The poison spreads throughout our veins,
> In all our sex the evil reigns,

The arrogant offence;
In vain we strive the plague to hide
Our fig leaves but betray our pride,
And loss of innocence.

Deeper we sink, and deeper still,
In pride instructed and self-will,
As custom leads the way:
The world their infant charge receive,
To pleasure our young hearts we give,
And bow to passion's sway.

By folly taught, by nature led,
In sensual delicacy bred,
In soft luxurious ease:
A feeble mind and body meet,
And pride and ignorance complete
Our total uselessness."

Let a man only believe all that and he can develop into the incredible Carus Wilson of Cowan Bridge. He really was something of a hero to embark at all on this perilous crusade of the education of Eve's daughters. He knew himself to be leading nothing but a forlorn hope, yet by dint of burned porridge, shorn locks and spartan discipline he hoped to curb the major sins of feminine pride. The girls should have been everlastingly grateful to him for seeking their most precarious salvation in both the worlds, and so thought Patrick Brontë. He really did believe he had found the right school and the solution for his many daughters when he took them in relays to Cowan Bridge. He confidently hoped that they would come to sing together the concluding verse of Charles Wesley's hymn for schoolgirls, with its assurance:

"How highly favoured then are we,
Snatched from a world of vanity,
And called in Jesu's name
To cultivate our tender mind
And peace and happiness to find
With the Atoning Lamb."

CHAPTER VIII

MARIA

THERE WAS one child at least over whose soul Patrick Brontë need have no misgiving. He says himself that before Maria's death she showed distinct signs as of one under a work of grace. He does not seem surprised. It was what all pious parents hoped for and knew that they themselves must have failed, in their duty, did they not manage to produce such heirs of salvation. It was the only way to save the legacy of the Irish Cabin. It was the only way to ensure a succession of souls who would cut out the pattern of their life according to the "good old plan." Both Wesley and Patrick Brontë used that phrase when they contemplated the superhuman task of steering fallen men and women through this too real a world. Now, had it not been for Maria Brontë, her small sisters and her brother might have considered that plan preposterous. As it was, the plan had worked and that in the bosom of their own family. The word of exhortation of Papa had been made flesh in the child Maria. The tone, the spirit, the deeds of the Methodist saint had become incarnate and they had seen, with their own eyes, that miracle.

The children might read in Haworth Parsonage of a hundred pious deathbeds in those old Methodist magazines in their racy though limited library, but, as they grew older, they must have seemed like idle tales without the fact of Maria. That was something like a thrill, to have had a pious deathbed in your own family and in your own recollection. Maria was an angel for certain, for they had seen her die. They would continue to see her, throughout their childhood, on those wonderful nights on Haworth Hill "that bring the thickest stars." Often as they looked out of lonely windows some bright fixed star would rivet their thoughts. Maria seemed to be speaking from those high heavens when they were especially in need of her dear protection. Often the moonlight, stealing gently in over the counterpanes of their young beds, would remind them of God and of Maria. When she was alive, in nights of just such glory, she would "put up" for them their own halting childish prayers. They could remember the very tone of her voice with its thrilling sense of the love of Christ. They could also remember her cough when she got too excited with her word pageantry. She had the Brontë power of telling a story, in a marked degree, but her tales

were all of heavenly mansions and the awful battlefields of sin.
Her epic theme was of mortal man who slew immortal God. So
dazzling did she make the Hero on His Cross that the children,
after her death, would wake themselves by crying out against that
glory of excess of light. She had the good Methodist sense to croon
her message of love in the lilt and music of the old Wesley hymns to
little boy or girl lying snugly in her warm embrace. It was all so
true to her. It was breath-taking, epoch-making to them. Those
hymns are piled line on line with marks of blood and compelling
heroism. They vibrate with passion and are filled full of daring
imagery, half human and half divine. Surely the old words must
have come to Branwell's ear something like this:—

> "The dear Tokens of His Passion
> Still His dazzling body bears ;
> Cause of endless exultation
> To His ransomed worshippers.
> With what rapture
> Gaze we on those glorious scars!"

The memory of such poignant teaching is at least as vivid to him
years later when as a boy of nineteen he recalls that bed-time story:—

> "A flaming cross—a beacon light
> To this world's universal night!
> It seemed to shine with such a glow
> And through my spirit piercing so
> That pantingly I strove to cry
> For her whom I thought slumbering by."

The influence of such a child is incalculable in such a family,
left motherless so soon. For years the season of her death would
bring a yearning sense of home-sickness to both Charlotte and
Branwell. It was a time in which they kept tryst with ancient glory
for it befell in May and the shy Yorkshire spring would help the
ecstacy. The tolling bell in their father's church tower would
awaken the muse. The strangely pitched voice of the parson at some
funeral in the graveyard nearby was enough to stimulate that
feeling of old unhappy far-off things. They could never hear those
opening sentences of the burial service without thinking of Maria
and the way she had tackled the King of Terrors. Branwell puts
it all into his poem of Caroline complete with mourners, brass plate,
lych gate and "The Resurrection and the Life." And with it all

went the sound of the old Wesley hymns, for Branwell would make
that quite clear had we ears to hear:—

> "So while I lay I heard again
> Her silver sounding tongue
> Rehearsing some remembered strain
> Of old times long agone."

Long agone they were and yet how terribly near. What Patrick
Brontë could never achieve for his children, with all his admonitions
and his wild bonfire of worldly sins, the child Maria achieved by
just living his old gospel before their very eyes. The quality of her
love reminded them of the love of God. It was so pure, so
spontaneous, so disinterested. It had a grace about it. They must
be friends to all animals because children served a God of mercy.
And to the flowers, those gentle heralds of His footsteps, they
should be kind also. After Maria's death Branwell would not pick
a rose growing by the window because she would have stayed his
rifling hands in life with only a look of love. She was the children's
first inspiration. She was very surely their proof of the reality of
heaven. She made the straight and narrow road a primrose path
for little feet. She brought into being, under their own roof tree, the
Methodist gospel in its purest form. She was so young when she
died that there was no time for disillusionment. Holiness then was
possible and holiness entered Heaven. It was not just so much
pious print in magazines a little foolish and hopelessly out of date,
but it was real and had happened on Haworth Hill. Maria had
looked into the face of the King of Terrors and had told her
watching family not to grieve for her because she was very happy.

Maria Brontë and her sister Elizabeth were lovely and pleasant
in their lives and in their deaths they were not divided. The younger
children could not have clearly remembered all the actual facts
of that dark time, but one thing they surely remembered for they
had seen a dead sister in her coffin. Only Branwell and Anne were
at home for the arrival of Saint Maria, mortally wounded, from
Cowan Bridge. The whole family was reunited for the death of
Elizabeth. Charlotte, all her life, in times of agitation, would
dream that she held a dead child in her arms. Branwell remembered
being lifted up to peep into that long narrow box beside the bed
where Maria had once told him tales of glory. It was his most
poignant memory. It was his great experience and it stirred the

poetry in his young soul. He gets real feeling into his verses, as he lives over again that scene at the bed-side. He can even now show us, with a certain power, the frightened child calling to the sleeping sister to wake up and then burying its head on some capacious grown-up bosom in an agony of heartbreak. It was all the more alarming as the "stern eye" of his father actually dropped a tear and Branwell was always a little frightened of this solemn man, from his Irish Cabin, with whom he was condemned to sleep for most of the nights of his life on earth. Maria was very much more to his mind with her soft crooning and her gentle grace. And now she was dead and a world of harsh reality rushed in on a small boy very lonely and much afraid. The only hope was to make of her Heaven a place of bliss for all small boys on pilgrimage, in this Vale of Tears, with silent or volcanic fathers of terrifying aspect. In years to come Branwell so sees himself. He looks back and recaptures that imaginative small boy who knew the hymns that Maria had taught him about those "mansions in the sky!" When he comes to approach Wordsworth for his verdict on his poetry he chooses out that little boy of Maria's moulding and sets him fair and square among the lilt and the words of the Methodists' well-known hymn about "reading his title clear to mansions in the sky."

For Charlotte Brontë, too, the memory of those dead sisters never died. She would talk of them often to her friends with a strange enthusiasm. The sufferings of Maria reminded her of the sufferings of Christ. She would dream of them and be haunted in waking by her nightmare memory. Always when she felt she was about to meet them in the world of dreams she found them altered and no longer her wonderful sisters—once even she thought that they cared for fine clothes. Nothing more damning than that could be said of the plain Methodist. Charlotte could get a better glimpse of the lost sisters, as Branwell did, amongst the stars. Christmas morning was a favourite time to catch sight of Maria's cloud-capped heavenly home. Charlotte was not so confident of her own acceptance there, nor of her ability to force a passage to the skies, as was Branwell. With Charlotte the creature would always be too dear and she was apt to shun paternal advice there and lose sight of the Creator. She says herself that such love could step between herself and her "hope of heaven." And as she says it she is using Maria's hymns and remembering Maria's

admonitions. The Methodiat child was wont to give thanks over
its humble bread and milk:—

> "For the blessings numberless
> Which Thou has already given,
> For my smallest spark of grace
> And for my hope of Heaven."

That grace was as familiar as the child's evening prayer to
the Gentle Jesus and Charlotte would teach that to little Papists
in Brussels later without any feeling of incongruity. So children
should pray, for so she had prayed herself and learned the words
surely from Maria and from Charles Wesley in one of his lighter
moods. At bed and at board—at those elemental things rooted deep
down in childhood's memory, Maria Brontë, being dead, yet spoke.

To have taken such a child as Maria and to have put her to
school under the roof of the Evangelical Revival of Religion looks
like a sly trick of fate. What would Cowan Bridge make of a living
exponent of its gospel? As Charlotte viewed the contest it was
nothing short of tragedy. The rules and the form of Mrs. Fletcher's
school were there but the spirit had fled. It is difficult to sustain a
part at second hand for an understudy has not the flair of the master.
Methodism may run for years. It has indeed lasted even unto the
present day, but it demands saints to run it. That gay figure of
Wesley with the alert knee breeches and the brisk coat tails had
disappeared. Its place had been taken by a thousand marble
busts of the man—some black, some white, all saintly or grotesque
but not things of flesh and blood. In Cowan Bridge the same painful
metamorphosis had taken place. To Charlotte Brontë's young
mind a "black marble clergyman" now seemed to be grinding
them to powder under his cruel and unimaginative heel. How
different here did Mrs. Fletcher's uniform dress appear when
the visiting Principal decked out his own family in frills and fur-
belows. Mrs. Fletcher and her staff had worn exactly the same
simple dress of dark cotton as the children.

Here at Cowan Bridge were her rules for the correction of the
sinner but the spirit had fled. What she termed a family conclave
had now become a veritable police court where there appeared
a certain satisfaction in having run the culprit to earth. In Mrs.
Fletcher's soul was anguish as she corrected the culprit for she
only desired their "eternal happiness." She must surely have been

HAWORTH CHURCH IN THE TIME OF THE BRONTËS
Only the tower of this building now remains

COWAN BRIDGE
"A house or houses–for the building spread far–with many windows"
Jane Eyre at Lowood

the first of all the educational experts to say that it hurt her more than it hurt the victim to administer punishment. Here is the way that Mrs. Fletcher went about school keeping. "We continually impressed on the minds of the children that the only way to be happy was to be like God; to love what He loved, and to hate what He hated; but that was not their present state. They were now like the Devil and loved what he loved; if they were injured they loved to revenge—when angry they would cry and sob and be almost choked. But when did they find themselves so affected in thinking about the Lord Jesus? Did His love and sufferings come again and again to their minds so that they could not forget them? And when did they cry and sob because they had sinned against so good a God? It was plain therefore they were as yet the Devil's children and their minds and affections obeyed him only. We therefore declared that whenever we saw these marks of the Devil's power on their hearts we would tell them of it; and that if they would still obey him rather than God we would then add unto our words correction; making them feel pain that the impression might be strong and lasting. These corrections we told them they must never resent or resist as we were more pained in giving than they could be in receiving them. They must, on the contrary, take each correction not only with patience but with thankfulness; seeing that their own interest no less than our duty required its administration, and that we should make it a point of conscience never to punish or even to contradict them without consideration and prayer, having always that lesson before our eyes :—

> That mercy I to others show
> That mercy show to me.

These observations were not altogether fruitless for I do not remember one child I ever had who, if we ordered her to receive correction by the rod (which was not often) would not lie down in silence, as a lamb, and afterwards, yea immediately after, come and kiss us."

This system assuredly needed saints to work it and by the time it reached Maria Brontë and her pathetic band of pilgrims it had become a pious outrage. The Rev. Carus Wilson might stick to the letter of the law and issue his tract of Mrs. Fletcher's beggar girl for his pupils' edification but it is more than probable that the moral missed fire. The wretched children at Cowan Bridge could read how they should behave, but it was cold comfort

F

without Mrs. Fletcher. You did not rush to kiss a black marble clergyman. The staggering thing about Maria Brontë was that she fulfilled her side of the bargain. She kept the rules of the game and broke her sister Charlotte's heart by the spectacle of her lamb-like patience. It made the blood boil in infant veins, for it was all very well for Wesley to sing "With lamb-like patience arm my breast" when Charlotte Brontë longed to add the safeguard of militant fists. It was all very well for Wesley to write to some young person "I am not content that anything should be wrong either with your temper or words or actions" but Christian Perfection was no joke when both sides would not keep the rules. It was all very well for Wesley to ask "Do you steadily endure as seeing Him who is invisible?" But did he know what it looked like to see Maria standing in a crowd of prim school-fellows, standing on the side of her shoe, with badly folded garments pinned all over her, and with that look of absorption upon her face. That look Charlotte could never forget. It was as if she gazed at something beyond her punishment, beyond her situation, not round or before her. Her eyes were fixed on the floor, but Charlotte knew that she did not see it for her sight seemed "Turned in, gone down into her heart." It was all very well for Wesley to say: "To refine religion is to spoil it. It is the most simple thing that can be conceived. It is only humble, gentle, patient love." Only, indeed! Rather, crucifixion and martyrdom when it entered Cowan Bridge and stood there, in the school-room, placarded before the eyes of groundlings.

Years afterwards, Charlotte Brontë's outraged love swept that picture of the martyred Maria into English literature for all the world to see. Mrs. Gaskell speaks of the Helen Burns of *Jane Eyre* as "an exact transcription of Maria Brontë." But Charlotte would say that the half was not told. It was really an understatement of fact, although the world might think that what was written was incredible. It had lain in a child's heart so long that when it got itself said in print, at last, the deeds, the words, and the faith of Maria came to life in vivid sharp reality. Maria rose from the grave in the person of Helen Burns, and she was still talking like the hymn book. Charlotte could never forget Maria's sung gospel. She contrives to make a transcript of it. Translated into prose it did well enough for the conversation of Helen Burns for it had the merit of being true, but, so transcribed, it reads most strangely. The dying girl, wasted away to a shadow, remarks "Debasement

and sin will fall from us with this cumbrous frame of flesh and
only the spark of the spirit will remain—the impalpable principle
of life and thought, pure as when it left the Creator to inspire
the creature. Whence it came it will return." This sounds like
Maria reciting a prose version of Vital Spark, that strange ditty
beloved of Methodist funerals. The chant itself has an ecstasy
about it with its triumphant smiting off of flesh from soul and its
"Oh the pain—the bliss of dying." Charlotte Brontë worshipped
truth and how could she make Maria talk truthfully, after all
the long years, if she did not do it in this way. For example, Helen
Burns was an Arminian in theology and shrank from Calvin's
terrible decrees. She says "I hold another creed. It extends hope
to all. It makes Eternity a rest—a mighty home and not a terror
and an abyss," which being translated into Maria's language
reads:—

> "Lord I believe a rest remains
> To all Thy people known
> A rest where pure enjoyment reigns
> And Thou art loved alone."

Charlotte had to make a little go a long way, but it seems certain
that one hymn especially was Maria's favourite, for it does duty
in prose for quite a large slice of Helen Burns' conversation.
Here is Maria and her hymn:—

> "Angels our servants are
> And keep in all our ways
> And in their watchful hands they bear
> The sacred sons of grace.
>
> Unto that heavenly bliss
> They all our steps attend;
> And God Himself our Father is,
> And Jesus is our Friend."

And here is Helen Burns speaking to Jane Eyre: "God is my
Father, God is my Friend." And of the angels she saith "Besides
the earth and besides the race of men there is an invisible world
and a kingdom of spirits: That world is round us for it is everywhere;
and those spirits watch us, for they are commissioned to guard us;
and if we were dying in pain and shame, if scorn smote us on all
sides and hatred crushed us, angels see our tortures, recognise
our innocence—and God waits only the separation of spirit from

flesh to crown us with a full reward. Why then should we ever
sink overwhelmed with distress when life is so soon over and death
is so certain an entrace to happiness—to glory?''

Maria Brontë had need of all the protection of the squadrons
of the sky when Miss Scatcherd of Loowood was in full cry after
her poor disorderly little person. This was the picture branded
for ever on Charlotte's memory. She saw the long low dormitory
of Cowan Bridge and Maria so ill that she could scarcely rise
from her bed. Her side had been blistered for her cough and it
was terribly sore. The girls told her not to rise and that they would
fetch the Headmistress, but Maria will make no truce with suffering.
So did all her saints tackle life with one foot in the grave and
the black worsted stockings had to be got into somehow. Charlotte
never forgot their grotesque black length and those thin white
legs. In great pain she struggled on, like any Fletcher at his communion in Madeley Church with death at his elbow, or like any
Thomas Walsh, alive but only just alive. She had not left her bed
but the stockings were nearly on—and that was the moment for
Miss Scatcherd's entrance. In hot rage she seized the child by
the arm, on the blistered side of her little body, and whirled her
into the middle of the room. Her strident tones of harsh vulgarity
filled the dormitory whilst she abused Maria for her dirty and
untidy habits like any fishwife. Charlotte remembered all her life
that little heap of misery which was Maria, flung amid the alien
beds, and it would always bring the blood to her cheeks in hot
indignation. Maria hardly spoke except to bid the angry girls
about her hold their peace. It was a veritable Father forgive her
to Miss Scatcherd but all the more terrible for that. Then
trembling, and very slowly, the little victim finished dressing and
went downstairs with staggering gait. Of course she was punished
for being late, but the lamb-like patience never deserted her poor
little breast. The child was content to die as her father's saints
before her had died—on her feet.

Charlotte Brontë is but quoting Maria's actual words when
she makes Helen Burns say: "By dying young, I shall escape great
suffering. I had not qualities or talents to make my way very well
in the world: I should have been constantly at fault." Undoubtedly
it was all to Maria Brontë's advantage to make haste to be gone.
Indeed she very soon stole silently away and the gate at the bottom
of the Parsonage garden was opened once more for a handful
of mourners and for a very small coffin in transit to glory.

CHAPTER IX

NURSERY OF GENIUS

THE MARTYRED Maria was but rising twelve when she gave up the struggle with life. The saints were wont to sing a plaintive ditty about "Into a world of ruffians sent, I walk on hostile ground." and that at least was true of the offspring of Patrick Brontë. At the first fierce onslaught of the real world two of the pilgrims from Haworth Parsonage fainted and died. The whole means of their begetting rendered them all the easy prey of ruffians, for their young eyes had been too early dazzled with gleams of glory.

At the time of Maria's death, Charlotte Brontë was nine years old, Branwell was eight, Emily was seven, and Anne five. The sad little company was now reduced to a quartette, but after the tears had been dried, the children entered upon a period of healing and setting. At home they were happy. There is a persistent and brightly glowing fire throughout Brontë literature which is surely a legacy from this good time. It is round the kitchen fire at Haworth that Charlotte describes them all as children in an atmosphere of happy comfort and at the manufacture of some glorious games. Here was their nursery of genius. Here was the warm friendliness of Yorkshire. Here was safety and the smell of honest home-made bread. Here were tea cakes and hash and dumplings and a scrupulous cleanliness and order. Here was the bracing stimulus of much lively effort and the ethos of a spotless hearth. In the safe paradise of Tabby's kitchen the children learned the sweet, sane things of home. Here all day long they heard Yorkshire as she should be spoken. They might themselves be compounded of Cornish and Irish blood but here they inherited Yorkshire. There was nothing forced or superimposed in the process, for the background of all was the same. Like some persistent and winged destiny the eager horseman of Rathfryland hill and Cornish lane had clattered up their cobbled Haworth street with his good news of the love of God. And Tabitha Ackroyd knew all about it. She could tell every tale there was to tell about Mr. Wesley and Parson Grimshaw and about all those peculiar retainers which Parson seemed to pick up from the gutter into the warm embrace of his large heart. Some were beggars, some orphans, some preachers tainted with Calvinism but down on their luck. It did not matter

71

to Grimshaw what they were or how oddly they mixed with his
own family under the roof of his old parsonage. The only thing
that mattered was that the grace of God should not pass them by.

As is the way with such legends they were repeated over and
over again. Day after day Tabby sounded in children's ears the
very words and accents of the heroes of old. Grimshaw to-day
seems still alive in Haworth, but in Tabby's day his spirit walked
abroad. He was almost the next door neighbour to the little Brontës
and his memory throve on the clatter of Tabby's pots and pans.
And this was something of the manner of the telling:—Such goings
on as there were in the churchyard with Mr. Wesley preaching
and people dropping down dead. And always there was Parson
urging the preacher on and never letting him stop whoever died
for "they were most part of them going to Hell with their eyes
open." Saved the precious souls should be if Parson had to whip
every one of them into the kingdom with his riding crop. And such
a man of prayer as he was—why they do say that he could not eat
his victuals for this praying of his. And then his trances, too, and
his visions—visions of torn flesh and the purple mark of the print
of the nails, forcing themselves gradually in through the ceiling
of his little room in the Clerk's house down the lane. What, just
down the children's little green lane close by? Why of course, almost
on their front doorstep!

Maria Brontë had lived before them the quieter, more mystic
side of Wesley's gospel. Tabby could rehearse the whole panoply
of its sons of thunder. That was the side which their father favoured
too when he was accustomed to kneel at his family altar with a
large pistol in his hip pocket. Patrick Brontë was inclined to stress
the terrible to young listeners, just setting out on pilgrimage, and
his bed-time stories would be strong meat for babes. He also told
his tales over and over again and it is clear that his small audience
drank them in. A young friend of Charlotte's said that it made
the flesh creep on her bones to listen to this parental recital. Surely
day by day the wicked Earl Ferrers took the centre of the stage
and called all heaven and earth to witness his hardened apostasy.
Surely the sins of Shirley and the sufferings of the saints were
unfolded in constant detail in childish ears. It must have been good
to Patrick Brontë to have such a docile congregation and one
which would stand in the old paths and grasp the niceties of Arminius and Calvin at a glance.

Antinomianism would have its place also in the story telling and sometimes Papa would unbend and come a little nearer earth with praise of his old hero the Duke of Wellington, who, of course, was also related to John Wesley. It is certain that the Rev. Patrick Brontë would tell the tale of Grimshaw and his relatives of Lockwood and Sutcliffe fame in a different way from Tabby. There was a good moral to be drawn from Grimshaw's drunken son and Patrick could set the children reading about him in those old Methodist magazines which the boys of his day at Woodhouse Grove had been encouraged to read. Did the father tumble his innocent children into his study and bid them find a letter all about those good people who lived in Grimshaw's old parsonage just across the churchyard there, amongst those wind swept trees? They would come upon the moral before they had gone very far, for the whole household had to be saved from hell or Grimshaw would know the reason why. The style of the letter would do infants much good too in their first steps forward in penmanship. It was written by Grimshaw to Wesley and reads thus:—"You will desire to know how I do. O dear Sir, hearty and happy in the Lord. And how my ministry or rather the present state of my parish. Blessed be God, flourishing still more and more—our societies are in general very lively in the Lord, and several others, though not yet joined in society, are nevertheless come to a sense of the pardoning love of God; others are under deep concern, or eagerly hungering and thirsting after our Redeemer. Two under my own roof are just now under true conviction, one a girl about 18 years old, and the other a boy about 14: and I hope my own little girl between 10 and 11 years old. It is near six months since she first began to show a serious concern for her final state." Now, whatever happened to that little girl in the end? Did she get to Heaven at last or did something awful happen? Young minds sprang easily forward into the writing of a sequel, with such a beginning. There was plenty of scope for tragedy on the road twixt Heaven and Hell and far more spice than in any fairy tale, and then the child had walked and talked only at the other end of the churchyard. Perhaps that was her little window just over the porch of Sowden's Farm? Anyway you knew how she felt because Papa and Tabby seemed related to William Grimshaw who was her father. There were not many children's story books in Haworth Parsonage and young minds had to make up their own tales from scanty material and eke them out with wonder. Wesley would have been surprised to know that this also was a manifestation of his gospel, but with its mingling of the tender and the terrible this is just what it contrived to do. The very enthusiasm of Methodism drove its devotees headlong towards a certain sort of literary effort.

The Methodist literature in Haworth Parsonage was read and re-read over and over again. Branwell said he must read for the same reason that he ate or slept, because it was "a real craving of nature." Looking back in after years, Charlotte could see that those books made strange provender for infant digestion. She calls them "mad Methodist magazines full of miracles and apparitions and preternatural warnings, ominous dreams, and frenzied fanaticisms." And yet they had a delicious home feeling after all. They were supposed to be good for children and they were certainly helped on by bits of poetry. Here did Cowper cast his spell on minds already prepared to expect such despair in a Calvinist. Here also children could read nice chatty letters to a little girl of seven years old from Wesley's friend Vicar Peronnet of Shoreham. Surely this was good enough for any children's books with its:—"Love all—Have no party spirit. Be always joined to the Methodists as this is the work of God now upon earth. Of all evils avoid Calvinism—this worst shaft of the Devil. Supply your mother's place amongst your family. Take the lowest place with yielding spirit. God deals with children as they are to their mothers and fathers. God requires you to receive the gift of parents as from Himself."

These old books with their salutary props for parents, their morals, their death beds and their burden of the Will of God became the staff of life to children starved of other entertainment. So did their father's old loyalty dictate the children's early reading and their first flights of fancy. It helped also to confirm the truth of Maria. She cast her benign spell over it all, so that, as the Brontës looked back, in after years, that time of tales and games and reading and Arminius and Calvin seemed like one long summer evening of peace and contentment. Charlotte, in memory, sees herself standing, as a child, at an open window, reading of that French nobleman whose piety, she supposed, would rival the saints of old, and, even as she describes that experience, the words are the words of Wesley's sermon on the death of the saintly Fletcher of Madeley long ago.

The concentrated essence of old Methodism was let loose on this quartette of children, for better or for worse, in Haworth

Parsonage, whether they kept company with Tabby in the kitchen or talked with Papa in the parlour. In such a household it is safe to suppose that there was no toy cupboard. Wesley had said if a boy played when he was a boy, he would play when he was a man. The commotion which that one box of wooden soldiers caused in the Parsonage is eloquent of the fact that there were few other toys there. The house shook when Papa brought them home one night after one of his rare excursions to Bradford. They were welcomed by the little Brontës as the Israelites in the wilderness welcomed their quails after a surfeit of heavenly manna. Branwell was first out of bed, shouting news of his treasure trove outside the girls' door. Charlotte and Emily sprang out in their nightgowns to behold the miracle. Everyone was grabbing wooden soldiers out of the box and giving them appropriate names, all in a moment of time and in a grand excitement, on the landing.

Upon that foundation of a box of toy soldiers was built the whole history of Angria with the Tale of the Islanders in support. It was just like children, trained as were the Brontës, to slip away from the reality of the wooden doll to the realm of pure imagination. Reality might begin the tale but it could never sustain it. There grew from those humble, much thumbed soldiers, whole colonies in revolt, exiled royal houses and heaps of slain. Wild pirates, sundering seas, fair ladies, glass towns, plots and counterplots all were found to lurk somewhere in that Pandora's box of wooden images. Charlotte and Branwell were close coadjutators in this delicious game and small Anne did her best with sister Emily, as her rock and defence, in Gondal legend, in a similar enterprise. It became an inspiration for magazine making, for novel writing and for poetical expression. The history of the ghostly army, to whom the wooden soldiers gave birth, was celebrated in minute script on much coveted scraps of paper and remains to this day as a thorny problem over which devout Brontë enthusiasts still pick out their eyes.

The enterprise of Angria was an education in itself. It tended to pick up national events, Papa's conversation and the local history of Haworth and to incorporate all in itself as the plan unfolded. The Duke of Wellington and Branwell's own enthusiasms are all pressed into the service. It was the school in which Charlotte learned to draw character. She depicts her brother in his eager youth quite faithfully. She knows so well the zeal and the ambition in his heart and in those early days she could afford to chuckle as she spills the words onto the precious page. Here is her description of one Benjamin Wiggins whom all can recognise as Branwell Brontë :—"Striding fast and firm, there advanced a low slightly built man attired in a black coat and raven grey trousers, his hat placed nearly at the back of his head, revealing a bush of carroty hair so arranged that at the sides it projected almost like two spread hands, a pair of spectacles placed across a prominent Roman nose, black neckerchief adjusted with no great attention to precision, and, to complete the picture, a little black rattan flourished in the hand. His bearing as he walked was tolerably upright and marked with that indescribable swing always assumed by those who pride themselves on being good pedestrians." Charlotte asks this apparition if he is going to the end of the world, to which he replies "Not *quite* to the end of the world, that is not altogether— now sir, what do you say to a man's walking sixty-five miles in a day?" To which statement Charlotte adds "as I knew Wiggins' style of exaggeration I made no answer." It might be all amusing enough in childhood but Branwell's powers of exaggeration were to become, in manhood, nothing better than actual falsehood. Charlotte pictures him amongst her beloved Angrians swaggering to a public house and boasting of brandy and beef steak and of his powers of carrying such fare when all the time she has seen him ask the landlady most timidly for "a ha'penny'orth of milk." She also saw him pull from his pocket a handful of silver and offer it "with an air" to the landlady, saying "Pay yourself out of that, ma'am, just take what you will, I never call a reckoning." So in this early school of genius that unstable theatrical figure of the boy emerges which later is to develop too surely along the lines that his sister has here forecast in a whirl of fun.

And what lovely names those children created! Northangerland and Zamorna and Tree of Glass Town roll across the minute pages in a rattle of enthusiasm. Charlotte is strong on Biblical quotation and the softer scenes of love and despair. Branwell delights in heaps of slain and the standard of revolt. By the time the lad is fourteen he has done a crediable little play in verse on Caractacus and has used his historical material so as to make it march upon the stage. The theme suited the cast of his mind with its hero's vicarious suffering and a Judas betrayal. He wrote it in two days not counting Sunday "which came between." In that household on Sunday of course all such everyday employment as authorship must be put tidily away for the Bible, and the learning of hymns with services at Church and Sunday School would fill up that delightful day. It would be cold meat too all round, as true Methodists, for as Charlotte says:—"No unnecessary cooking on the Sabbath." Miss Branwell knew those ancient ropes only too well and her Methodism consisted in method. Much of the sparkle might have gone from her soul's experience of its love, but she reverenced the machinery which was supposed to keep it bright.

The little Brontës pursued the fortunes of their dream kingdoms against an uncompromising orderliness of domestic life. There was the diurnal bed-making, the tidying of rooms, the lessons and the morning walk. In the afternoon the inevitable sewing, of all pious households, obtained until tea time. Charlotte might not love Aunt Branwell but she very well knew how much she owed her for the early inculcation of an untiring routine. It was ultimately this blessed method of Methodism which was to prove a veritable sheet anchor in the head winds of young womanhood for these precariously poised daughters of Eve. Well for the Brontë girls and for literature that, like Dorothy Wordsworth before them, they explored the toils of an Evangelical home. The girls of that period had their reward in a disciplined life and in one of enforced meditation.

Dorothy Wordsworth had known that endless disciplined sewing with shadows playing hide and seek on the hills outside the parlour window. To get out. To escape. But no. Head down to seam and eyes glued on gusset. She also was of the William Wilberforce dispensation and had obeyed his wish and taught in Sunday School. She had also distributed his gift of £10 to the poor of her uncle's Evangelical parish. It wrought Dorothy Wordsworth into the woman to steady her brother William and would have done the same for Charlotte Brontë and her Branwell had not these two bosom comrades of glad early days drifted apart. Circling round these girls' hearts, in both homes, was an inspiration drawn from that gospel which had taught love for the poor, love for flowers even, love, which had spilt glory in the cart ruts of human life. Those girls of the Evangelical Revival of Religion were wont to sew with their souls in their eyes. It is highly probable that Miss Branwell, whilst keeping the letter of the law, was wholly ignorant of those visions which rose and faded and formed again in the demure bent heads of her sewing nieces. Dorothy Wordsworth, quoting from Mrs. Flecther, called them "exquisite feelings." Emily Brontë confessed that the potency of her own brew was

like to kill her with desire. Charles Wesley's "inward ear" and
Dorothy Wordsworth's "inward eye" were both alert at those
sessions of domesticity even in the threading of a needle and the
snapping of a thread.

Patrick Brontë seems to have been ignorant of all that was going
forward under his own roof. His habits were so regular and his
life so lonely that it was easy for quick witted young people to
carry on their various avocations uninterrupted. The study door
tended to open less and less. It worried him to have first hand
dealings with this growing family of his, save for his sessions of
worship at the family altar. He could besiege the throne of grace
more confidently because his eyes were shut and because this
exercise was now the only shred of omnipotence which remained
from old glory. He had become nervously hesitant about taking
the wrong turning, and yet was it right to leave that household of
children quite undisturbed? Like all nervous people Patrick Brontë
worked himself up to make periodic excursions into the family
history, but he could never sustain a comprehensive plan for its
erring fortunes. Every time he emerged he invariably found that
it would have been much better if he had left things alone. Yet,
one of these fatal seasons of resurrection was again upon him and
lay about him he surely would and that to some purpose. It was
Patrick Brontë who strode in on this happy period of the children's
life and performed the uncomfortable task of the eagle stirring
up its nest.

Now the time had come for Branwell to go out into the world.
In some unexplained way the boy was to plunge straight from the
daubing of pictures at Haworth into the bosom of the Royal
Academy in London. The girls were again to try the experiment
of going to school. In Patrick Brontë's philosophy all things were
possible to God, and, although the boy never recovered from the
disillusionment of that first awful onset of reality, and Emily and
Anne nearly died in the contest, Papa's eyes saw nothing but the
Will of God and rejoiced in being an instrument in its relentless
fulfilment. There is a complacency about Patrick Brontë's letter
to Mrs. Franks that is irritating were it not for a familiarity
with the wretched man's background. He writes:—"It is my
design to send my son, for whom as you may remember my kind and
true friends Mr. Firth and Mrs. Firth were sponsors, to the Royal
Academy for Artists in London. Amidst all the chances, changes
and trials of this mortal life we have still the glorious conviction

on our minds that we may have our hope immovably anchored in heaven, by the throne of God in whom there is no variableness neither shadow of turning. And I trust this blessed consideration will be a never failing source of comfort to you during the remainder of your journey through life, and especially at that last hour when you will step out of time into eternity."

CHAPTER X

CHARLOTTE

IT WAS all very well for Patrick Brontë, secure in his study at Haworth, to talk of no shadow cast by turning in God's plans, but to small people, suddenly thrust out into a bleak world, shadows of any kind have a way of being intimidating. Much was to follow from Papa's descent from Olympus, as the understudy of Almighty Jove, for much profitable heartbreak was still in store for that little quartette of children whom Maria had moulded. For them there was to be no escape to her heavenly mansions for some time to come and they must now assay the fortunes of their earthly warfare, quite alone.

It was a queer little lonely figure that the carrier's cart deposited at Miss Wooler's school for young ladies in Birstall at the beginning of the new year of 1832. Charlotte Brontë's dress was cut according to the pattern shown to Miss Branwell in the Mount. It was calculated to conquer all pride in the female breast, and, to the clustering schoolgirls in those large windows, it looked remarkably old fashioned. But what of the poor child inside those odd Methodist garments? The first memory of Charlotte Bronte which her girl friends came to cherish was that of a forlorn scrap of humanity, crying quietly, as Wesley had bidden, in the long shadows of an alien school-room.

Charlotte was terribly homesick. Cruelly she felt the uprooting from that delightful Haworth fellowship of Tabby's kitchen and Branwell's eager companionship. It acted like a shower of cold water on the flights of her poetic fancy, for, just as she would linger by herself in the schoolroom to invoke the shade of Northangerland, Miss Wooler would bounce in with a plate of butter in her hand and scatter reverie. The sound of the bells of Huddersfield Church would tear her heart in tatters. A letter from Branwell full of Zamorna and of the old dream kingdom would devastate her with that nostalgic longing which her father was wont to call indescribable anguish—a sickening, agonising, affectionate "something." But the sending of Charlotte to school brought her the gift of friendship and helped in great measure to make her the woman she became. It gave her confidence and it stimulated ambition. She discovered that she could travel to the top of any class in an

80

almost predestined way, so constant did the practice become. It filled her mind with new tales and new scenery, but all safely enclosed and explained by the old background of Patrick Brontë's past. That was the fatal difference between Branwell's plunge into a world of ruffians and Charlotte's timid entrance there. Wesley had not claimed the Royal Academy as his parish but he had practically owned Birstall, in a spiritual sense.

Here, in Miss Wooler's school, were the grandchildren of the men whom John Wesley had looked upon as the men of his right hand. The Nusseys had helped to sustain that chapel in Birstall which John Nelson had built and their names are there in the old records of a heretical past. The Taylors still lived in the Red House at Gomersall where Wesley had delighted to stay. In the town itself the Church parson was a descendant of that Heald of Dewsbury to whom Wesley had written about an urgent subscription—"Is it fitting for me to ask a Methodist twice for anything." And in Miss Wooler herself was the perfect preceptress for she throve on Simeon's sermons and lent them to Patrick Brontë. It was the same atmosphere as at Haworth Parsonage but so as with one important difference.

The friendship of Mary Taylor was in the nature of a new revelation to Charlotte Brontë. It opened up new fields of thought into which Wesley's gospel was now forcing its way. Radical reform was the stringent quality of the air which Mary Taylor instructed Charlotte Brontë to breathe into her conservative lungs. In Mary's home John Wesley was reverenced because he was himself a rebel. Once, in this very district, Patrick Brontë, as Church parson, and Jabez Bunting, as Methodist preacher, had both been on the same side against the Luddites and their revolutionary ideas of social reform. They had supported the mill owners in that fierce claim of the working man to resist the introduction of machinery and the unemployment which it brought in its train. Now Charlotte Brontë was to meet Methodists who hated all black coated Tories were they found in Church or State or Methodist Conference.

Jabez Bunting had welded Methodism into a corporate whole, but oh! so decorously and with an eye of reverence all the time on the Church of England. Mr. Taylor had gone one better than Jabez Bunting by helping to foment the first rebellion in the ranks of Methodists themselves. One Alexander Kilham had demanded more lay control in the councils of Methodism and had promptly been cast forth neck and crop from amongst his brethren.

It was the cause of these dispossessed liberal Kilhamites that the Taylors of the Red House espoused, and for whom they built a little chapel just across the road from their home. This was the place where Charlotte Brontë heard the singing of those riotous Methodist hymns "to which even the veriest Quaker might have been compelled to dance." It still stands to-day by the roadside and must be sought for, as those jaunty strains have now quite died away, but its very silence belies the sound and fury of its begetting and its modest proportions mask the scope of its influence. In the visits that Charlotte made to the Red House she was really presiding at the birth of the Labour Party. From those rebels, deeply imbued with Wesley's gospel of mercy, was to spring the great Trade Union movement. The first Labour members of an Empire's Parliament were to be drawn from the ranks of the lay preachers of that newer Methodism.

Charlotte Brontë was fascinated by Mr. Taylor's conversation, as she sat on a footstool at his side, in that lovely room of his with its stained glass windows, but she was bursting to contradict him. Instinctively she mistrusted so dangerous a gospel of liberty as he was wont to propound. She was of that older school of Methodism which once flourished inside the Church of England where it rightfully belonged and she was no friend of this new militant thing that went boldly into politics and seemed ready to tear everything, ordered of the Will of God, into pieces. It must have been some little comfort to her that the Taylors still went to church in the mornings as all good Methodists, who remembered John Wesley, always did. If the day was wet the children would have to be quiet at home with large doses of Wesley's sermons to keep them humble. At night the heat and the noise and the strange preaching of the Kilhamite chapel would bring the Sabbath to a stormy close. The decorum of Haworth Parsonage must have been as something seen down the wrong end of a telescope to a small schoolgirl perched on the hard back benches of such a sanctuary. It appeared to have receded into space. So this too was Methodism? Charlotte Brontë was shrewd enough to see that this new freedom did not always work out rightly, for the Taylor boys were a case in point. One of them had so fiery a temper that no one was allowed to contradict or anger him. Wesley had advised that a child's will must always be well and truly broken, but Mr. Taylor was feeling his way towards a more liberal philosophy of life and was exploring the possibilities of self expression. The logical eye of young Charlotte, trained on the Thomas Walsh brand of hero, saw the flaw in that line of reasoning quite clearly. This new freedom must inevitably breed a tyrant in the very bosom of a liberal household, but in the education of the Taylor girls Charlotte had to confess that the theory worked out better. They were encouraged to think of a career and were warned against the idea of marrying either for money or independence. They were sent abroad to study French and German and later Mary Taylor so well learned her lesson that she took the bit between her young teeth and emigrated to New Zealand and set up in business for herself.

The spirit of revolt was planted young in this new friend of Charlotte Brontë and her influence upon her was as Socrates and the gad-fly. Mary Taylor made Charlotte restless and spurred her on towards the activity of achievement, almost against her will. Into that safe home atmosphere of Haworth Parsonage this girl, Mary Taylor, burst with commiseration and jeers. She likened its once happy inmates to "potatoes growing in a dark cellar." She advocated a healthy worldly-mindedness—get wisdom, yes, but with all thy getting—get money. Money meant power and freedom for a woman and a woman had every bit as much right to develop her personality as ever a man had. She would have made John Wesley open his eyes in wonder to hear that Women's Rights were also an implication of his gospel, yet here it was, at Miss Wooler's evangelical academy, glowing in Mary Taylor's eye and leaping to her tongue. True, Wesley had advocated women preachers and sent them out with a sense of vocation. He had praised their school keeping and their deeds of mercy, but when it came to his own wife he was the perfect child of his age. He tells her plainly: "Do not any longer contend for mastery, for power, money or praise. Be content to be a private, insignificant person, known and loved by God and me. Attempt no more to abridge me of the liberty which I claim by the laws of God and man. Leave *me* to be governed by God and my own conscience, then shall I govern *you* with gentle sway."

The mischief was that Wesley could not restrain the widening circle of his gospel of God's mercy. It was bound to pick up in its embrace dogs, horses, children, slaves and women. The time would surely come when Wesley's own superb organising gifts would be utilised, in masterly style, by one of his own followers and on behalf of women in revolt. The time would come when the

G

lilt of Methodist hymns would whisper hope in the ears of a
suffragette, in Holloway Prison, who fought for Votes for Women
as for a holy cause. It was the wooing note which Mrs. Pethick
Lawrence employed at Caxton Hall which constrained that vast
audience to sally forth to the siege of the House of Commons. And
where had she learned it but in the bosom of her own family and
from the habit which the Methodists adopted of pleading with
repentant sinners? Most startlingly it savoured of that immemorial
rite of all Methodist Sunday evenings, in all stuffy heretic chapels,
when, after the sound and fury of the sermon, the preacher invited
his congregation to save its soul alive in a hushed, hypnotic silence
and with a whole world of meaning in that one word "Come". But
the time was not yet. It was surely somewhat nearer when Mary
Taylor and Charlotte Brontë joined forces and Charlotte could
write: "Each human being has his share of rights. I suspect it
would conduce to the happiness and welfare of all if each knew
his allotment and held to it as tenaciously as the martyr to his
creed."

The friendship of Charlotte with Ellen Nussey provided quite
other stimulus from this fierce liberalism of Mary Taylor. Ellen
fitted much better into the old Haworth background. Mr. Brontë
and Miss Branwell approved Miss Nussey warmly and Tabby was
loud in her praise. She was the right sort of friend for Charlotte for
she stood in the old paths whilst Mary Taylor was inclined to
laugh at Charlotte's portentious inheritance. She always marvelled
that she knew so much and could care so keenly about "isms".
There was something ludicrously out of proportion to Mary in
Charlotte's denunciation of Calvinism and Socinianism—who cared
anyway? But Ellen Nussey could understand. She might not be
able to enter into Charlotte's doubts and fears but she could
always grasp the fact that Calvin must always be Public Enemy
No. 1 to people taught of Wesley and of Fletcher. It was to Ellen
that Charlotte wrote of religion. To Mary Taylor the letters were
of politics and books and people, for that young lady was shaking
herself free from "isms" of any kind and reaching out towards
liberty.

On Charlotte's return to Roe Head as governess and later at
Heald House, Dewsbury Moor, Ellen Nussey was made the confi-
dant of her soul. It was a time of great religious depression and
almost Charlotte's faith was overwhelmed, but Ellen was always the
steadying influence. It was Ellen who could admonish and advise

her. It was Ellen who would fix a trysting hour of ten o'clock wherein friends may meet in spirit at the Mercy Seat. It was Ellen who thought they should learn a verse of a Psalm every day. It was Ellen who, in loyalty to her friend, asked her the old questions about her soul and begged Charlotte also to tell any faults she might see in her friend quite fearlessly. The old words of perfection and holiness come rumbling over the pages of schoolgirl letters in a quaint setting of string bags and lost umbrellas. The atmosphere of Ellen's home and of that solemn brother of hers were identical with Patrick Brontë's of the ancient past. Henry Nussey goes about getting a wife as Wesley would have advised him so to do, for he knew by heart that scriptural maxim of being unequally yoked with unbelievers. We have one peep of the young man at something very like a Methodist class meeting when we read in the diary of his youth: "This evening at a full meeting Mr. Heald exhorted from 2 Corinthians VI. 14 on the action of a member having married a worldly-minded man." That has the authentic ring about it, for the familiarity of the language and the word member in that setting convey at once to the initiate the membership of the Methodist Society within the Church of England. Again his speech betrayeth Henry Nussey when asked to partake of too worldly hospitality for this is the comment: "Stayed to supper, never asked to take family prayers nor to say grace. Much hurt that they did not see the propriety and feel the necessity of this line of conduct."

In the old days the saints would have taken upon themselves to remedy these omissions, but in Henry Nussey's day things were a little toned down and he might salve his conscience by committing the sins to the secrecy of his diary. The result is that we find instead of a saint—a stick; and when he asked Charlotte to marry him, on the recommendation of Miss Nussey, that must have been the light in which she viewed him. There was romance about the courtship of saints, but there was nothing lovely about the wooing of a prig. She answers quite simply that she had not the attachment to him "which would make me willing to die for him; and if ever I marry it must be in that light of adoration that I will regard my husband." Charlotte was prepared to take a leaf out of Mrs. Fletcher's life on this question of love, but she found the way of holiness uncommonly steep. Her mind seems crushed with this burden of old religion and she broods and broods and despairs of acceptance in Heaven. "Ellen," she writes, "Religion has indeed elevated your character—

I will no longer shrink from your questions. I do wish to be better than I am. I pray fervently sometimes to be made so. I have stings of conscience—visitings of remorse—glimpses of Holy, inexpressible things which formerly I used to be a stranger to. It may all die away, I may be in utter midnight, but I implore a Merciful Redeemer that if this be the dawn of the gospel it may still brighten to perfect day. Do not mistake me, Ellen, do not think I am good, I only wish to be so, I only hate my former flippancy and forwardness. O I am no better than I ever was. I am in a state of horrid, gloomy uncertainty, that at this moment I would submit to be old grey haired to have passed all my youthful days of enjoyment and be tottering on the verge of the grave, if I could only thereby ensure the prospect of reconcilement to God and redemption through His Son's merits. I never was exactly careless of these matters but I have always taken a clouded and repulsive view of them; and now if possible the clouds are gathering darker and a more oppressive despondency weighs continually on my spirits. You have cheered me, my darling, for one moment, for an atom of time, I thought I might call you my own sister, in the spirit, but the excitement is past, and I am now as wretched and hopeless as ever. This very night I will pray as you wish me. May the Almighty hear me compassionately! And I humbly trust He will—for you will strengthen my polluted petition with your own pure requests."

The comfortable thought of Ellen, with the kind placid face and the dark hair and the brown eyes, was like the shadow of a rock to Charlotte as she toiled on at uncongenial teaching and felt her soul lacerated with feelings which she was at a loss to explain. It was too difficult to pursue the life of religion in this everyday world. If she could only escape she might do better. It was a possibility which stood just at the elbow of the Brontë clan always, to escape, to get away from harsh reality. Even now at school Charlotte conjures up a dream picture of great comfort by the side of her friend Ellen. She writes: "If I could always live with you and daily read the Bible with you, if your lips and mine could at the same time drink the same draught from the same pure fountain of mercy, I hope, I trust, I might one day become better, far better, than my evil wandering thoughts, my corrupt heart, cold to the spirit and warm to the flesh will now permit me to be. I often plan the pleasant life which we might live together, strengthening each other in that power of self-denial, that hallowed and glowing devotion which the past saints of God often attained to. My eyes fill with tears when I contrast the bliss of such a state brightened by hopes of the future with the melancholy state I now live in uncertain that I have ever felt true contrition, wandering in thought and deed, longing for holiness which I shall *never never* attain— smitten at times to the heart with the conviction that ———'s ghastly Calvanistic doctrines are true—darkened in short by the very shadows of Spiritual Death! If Christian perfection be necessary to salvation I shall never be saved, my heart is a real hot-bed for sinful thoughts and as to practice, when I decide on an action, I scarcely remember to look to my Redeemer for direction."

The peril with the Methodists was that Wesley had taught them to *feel* their religion. Consequently, when jaded in body or mind they felt unable to rise to that ecstacy, they habitually thought that it was all over with them and that they were damned for good and all. These "feelings" run to and fro through the pages of their lierature and become a positive menace. Mary Taylor would recall how Charlotte could extemporise verse beginning on just that note—"Come thou high and holy feeling." And Charlotte herself gives us a glimpse of how the magic worked suddenly in great disappointment thus:—"Why are we to be divided? Surely Ellen it must be because we are in danger of loving each other too well—of losing sight of the Creator in idolatory of the creature. At first I could not say "Thy will be done." I felt rebellious; but I know it was wrong to feel so. Being left a moment alone this morning I prayed fervently to be enabled to resign myself to every decree of God's will—though it should be dealt with a far severer hand than the present disappointment. Since then I have felt calmer and humbler—and consequently happier? Last Sunday I took up my Bible in a gloomy frame of mind. I began to read; a feeling stole over me such as I have not known for many long years—a sweet placid sensation like those that I remember used to visit me when I was a little child, and on Sunday evenings in summer stood by the open window reading the life of a certain French nobleman who attained a purer and higher degree of sanctity than has been known since the days of the early martyrs. I thought of my own Ellen—I wished she had been near me that I might have told her how happy I was, how bright and glorious the pages of God's holy word seemed to me. But the 'foretaste' passed away and earth and sin returned."

That memory of childhood of the open window and the little girl contemplating the life of the saintly nobleman is a picture of Charlotte intent on the sermon of Wesley on the saintly Fletcher, but now, as she writes to the grown-up Ellen, she disguises the homely source of her juvenile inspiration in that characteristic twist of the nameless aristocrat whom she thinks, in that setting, cannot easily be recognised. She does not see how near her words lie to Wesley's in her description of "the purer and higher degree of sanctity than has been known since the days of the holy martyrs." It is a trick of memory, for Wesley had written thus of the nobleman de la Fléchère.

Charlotte Brontë was becoming a little ashamed of her father's ancient library which had once delighted her young heart, for Ellen Nussey, for all her family's past, was now an escaped Methodist only and a devout churchwoman. Her influence upon Charlotte was that of an anchor on drifting ships, for, although she confesses that she cannot help the gloomy thoughts that rose like a miasma on the old battle-ground of religion, Charlotte is now content to throw in her allegiance with Mother Church and stay her defiant hands. She came to conform, more or less, to the pattern of a parson's daughter, although she must always first possess the creature before getting the Creator at all into focus. Charlotte's creed in a lonely world was ever this, that she must "take to someone" or die, and, if not to the Captain of her salvation, then assuredly to one of His servants whom she could regard in "that light of adoration."

CHAPTER XI

BRANWELL

THE ONLY boy in Haworth Parsonage made a place for himself quite out of proportion to his size, and, for a long time now, Branwell had held the centre of the stage. Charlotte says truthfully "My father naturally thought more of his one son than of his daughters," and the girls themselves loved him unfeignedly. In that quiet and feminine household he provided their joy of living—by proxy. He was their most vital link with the outside world. Branwell was also the light of Miss Branwell's eyes and had done much to reconcile her to her long exile in the north of England. As a little boy she had thought him too good to live and had given him to understand that God had bestowed upon him a preferential issue of talents. With such backing it should be easy for him to storm a triumphant way through life. He came to take it for granted that both God and his family were tremendously interested in his welfare.

One of Papa's heroes, named Adam Clarke, had said that God would stop in His making of new worlds if He caught so much as a whisper from His old world of a sinner crying out "Son of David have mercy upon me." Now this sort of teaching, accepted as gospel truth, would tend to blur the sharp lines of reality and accustom the lad to rose-tinted spectacles. Where small Anne would say "Believe not those who say the upward path is smooth" that heady draft of God's favour went straight to Branwell's head. He saw no obstacles at all in his upward flight. Charlotte, still laughing, sketches the path of advance which her brother had mapped out for himself. In her portrait of Wiggins she makes the lad say: "My mind was always looking above my station. I was not satisfied with being a sign-painter at Howard as Charlotte and them things were with being sempstresses. I set before me the grand plain of Africa, and I traced a path for my own feet through it, which terminated at the door of a splendid palace situated on Cock-Hill, whose portal bore inscribed "Residence of the Duke of Thorncliffe", and beyond that a tomb under the oaks of my own park, showing to the passenger such words as these "Erected to the memory of Patrick Benjamin Wiggins, Duke of Thorncliffe and Viscount Howard. As a musician he was greater than Bach, as a poet he surpassed Byron, as a painter Claude Loraine yeilded to him, as a rebel he

snatched the palm from Alexander Rogue having earned all this
meed of renown—this summum bonus of human grandeur was at
length rapt to Heaven in a fiery chariot."

Charlotte loves to pile it on and whirl the boy off to the skies
at last, well used to just that sort of exit. This rushing enthusiasm
was native to them for they must all have enjoyed, in youth, that
captivating jingle of Charles Wesley's:

> "My soul mounted higher
> In a chariot of fire
> And the moon—it was under my feet."

In a solemn age it could give points to:

> "Hey diddle diddle
> The cat and the fiddle
> The cow jumped over the moon."

And all pious children believed the teaching of Wesley's birthday
hymn:

> "From Jehovah I came
> For His glory I am
> And to Him I with singing return."

There is always this air of intense excitement and of quick movement
about Branwell Brontë. His superfluous energy worked itself off
in voracious reading and endless writing. He spilt words on to
paper with lightning speed. He marched his imaginary soldiers
over the plains of Angria at the double. He tossed his pirates onto
the Atlantic wave with headlong effervescence. He got the map of
London by heart. He dashed to Leeds and back to Haworth to hear
snatches of Handel's Messiah—King of Kings and Lord of Lords.
He insisted on painting all his family. He talked and acted to all the
village worthies or unworthies. People loved to hear him talk and,
for such as he, danger lurks in secret places.

Most emphatically Branwell should have been sent to school,
had not the Rev. Patrick Brontë known so much better. He had a
wholesome dread of the slow stain of this too real world and would
not risk an only son in its ensnaring toils. He had taught other boys
before him and had been tutor to Thomas Tighe's sons, so that he
could well manage his own, and it thus came about that Branwell
had to learn his Latin at his father's side and paint his pictures in
the sanctuary of the parson's study. Mr. Fennell, with the light of
enthusiasm in his eyes, might write letters of boys singing hymns
in chapel like warbling seraphs, but Patrick Brontë was shrewd
enough to suppose that even the denizens of such an Eden might

sometimes hug Satan to their bosoms. His son should be taught to
cross swords only with his Satanic Majesty. It was thus the
concentrated essence of the old school that was instilled into the
whirling brain of this growing boy and it is very likely that the
only thing that did remain real to him in the end was that decorous
figure of his father—spectacles on nose, high cravated throat and
pistol at the ready. By day and by night the youthful Branwell had
to endure Thomas Walsh, Lady Huntingdon, Grimshaw and all
the saintly Fletchers. By night and day he canvassed the fortunes
of Calvinism, Arminianism, Socinianism and Antinomianism,
Methodism and Baptism. Religion filled up the measure of his days.
His cup overflowed. Not now Maria's brand of humble, gentle,
patient love, but words, words, words to make the head spin. He
must have missed Charlotte cruelly when she was thrust forth
into the real world of her Birstall school. He kept writing to her
about the pageant of Northangerland and made her very homesick.
He walked miles to see her and made her very anxious for he
looked so utterly weary, yet stoutly declared that he was not in
the least tired. Had not the family told him that he was a good
walker, like his father, and so all things were possible? Reality
must not dispel an illusion as easily as all that, and, besides, the
saintly Fletcher had even climbed the pulpit stairs in the article of
death.

There is one glimpse of a boy's escapade which is refreshing, but
almost too terrible to yield unmixed delight. Branwell went to
Keighley Fair and for one blissful evening tried to draw into his
rarified lungs the air a worldling breathes. He knew that he sinned
in going, for the pious ladies of his father's poems called all merry-
go-rounds "The engines of Satan." Dancing, acting booths, and
lotteries were no less than Vanity Fair for all Methodists for many
generations. Branwell was but one in a long succession of evangelical
youth condemned to the tent flap for the performance of Maria
Marten of the Red Barn, or to a precarious window sill for anything
so dangerous as the opera according to Gilbert and Sullivan. But
let it be said for their hardihood that in the breast of all was a
determination to go if they burned in hell for it later. And Branwell
went.

A friend has given the description of that expedition as though
he found himself attached to a comet in space and had lost his
breath in trying to keep pace with Branwell's enthusiasm. The
lights twinkled. The horns hooted. The engines whirred. The boys

went into absolutely every tent. The fat woman must have been a
welcome release from the checks of the saintly Fletcher, for Branwell,
for the first time in his life, was having a fling at Antinomianism
himself and he found it extraordinarily exciting and enjoyable.
The swing-boats yielded the peak moment of excitement. When
Branwell shot up above the dust and lights and bustle of the Fair
only to plunge again into unholy depths and as quickly to rise
again, he abandoned himself to a terrible bliss. Every time that he
left his stomach behind at the top of the dive downwards, he
shouted at the top of his voice: "Oh! my nerves." And not subdued
even then, and finding life so wonderful, he offered to fight his
companion on their way home. A pitched battle ensued, by a
cottage near the roadside, and it was not until both boys were
tired out that reality peeped over Branwell's shoulder. Why did
the lights of Haworth look so befogged? The awful truth dawned
at last that he must have lost his spectacles. He stood transfixed by
fear, for his father would now, most certainly, find out. The
Olympians always seemed to have divine assistance to discover
children's sins, for they shared with God the power of the all-seeing
eye. Branwell's friend was a young man of resource and of a more
liberal education. He promised that he would look for the glasses
next morning, and, if successful, would come within safe distance
of the Parsonage to restore them to their owner. The gods were
kind. The spectacles were found. They were delivered safely to a
miserable, white-faced boy hanging about in the graveyard at a
preposterously early hour, for it was the morning after the night
before. Did Branwell get his first glimpse then of the way small
boys might hoodwink the Almighty—given average luck? He must
have gazed very thoughtfully at his porridge that morning through
his restored spectacles. He knew that he had ridden on the engines
of Satan and had not been consumed, but it had been a near
thing. He must have seen the Hand of God in that smiting of the
glasses from his own patrician nose, yet there comes a wonderful
sense of self importance to a sinner who gets away with it.

There might be more in life than Calvin and Arminius and the
Will of God for there was certainly Keighley Fair. Even the fields
around his home began to look different, for Branwell says rather
sadly, in his poems, that he discovered that what were once fields
for children to run in were known to be battle grounds and Roman
roads. The intolerable age of things began to tease his heart. To
the scholar of Greece and Roman, what was Methodism? Haworth

Parsonage itself was but a mote tossed up for one brief moment in an age-long beam of light, spun off from one of a myriad worlds. The God of Maria's radiant cross was retreating a great way off into the light of setting suns.

The danger of Branwell's intense religious training was the abyss that was likely to open suddenly at a young man's feet. To the boy who had received the whole impact of Wesley's vivid gospel the shock of apostacy meant a desolation of the spirit. The warm nucleus of life was swept suddenly out onto a wide sea of doubt. At the back of the mind of a quondam believer is the passionate desire to believe, if only he could. He assumes a jauntiness of agnosticism which is itself spurious, but helps him to go on living with Calvin and Arminius and a doting Cornish aunt. Branwell had to contend with all this and with the great eyes of two younger sisters, fixed questioningly upon him and his god-like observations. At the core of Branwell's heart developed a void which the world could never fill. He might try to camouflage it with his man-about-town pose, but it remained a canker of the soul. Even as early as 1834 when the boy was only seventeen there is a cry of real heartbreak in Branwell's lament amongst his Angrians, for all their Jolly Roger atmosphere. In the mouth of Percy, an Angrian outcast, Branwell speaks the sorrow of his own heart:

> "Well, when I first launched from Eternity
> Upon this undiscovered sea,
> Hope shone forth with glorious ray
> Blazing round my dawning day;
> Expectation's eager gale
> Swelled and sounded in my sail;
> Ambition's ever rousing power
> Urged me on in morning's hour;
> And when I saw the expanse before me
> When I saw the glory o'er me,
> Oh how little did I dream Heaven and glory all a dream.
>
> Life alone with its midnight sea
> Howled on me in stern reality.
> Sleeper awake! Thy dream hath gone;
> Now thou art on ocean all alone."

The difficulty with Branwell was to fix reality in its right perspective. He would keep escaping into his dream world and then awaking with a start. That visionary region of imagination had a way of appearing reality to him as a child, and in early manhood it appeared a glorious dream from which the sleeper found it difficult to extricate himself. To Branwell the real and the unreal began to get confused. Those sharp lines of truth which Charlotte worshipped as a God began to be blurred and distorted, for the day came when Charlotte could not believe the tales he told, although it all seemed true enough to him. He told a friend of his rather sadly how he would fain have prayed with a dying Sunday-school scholar but that when he told his sister she cut him short in disgust, saying "I will go to her." Now would he have prayed? Could he? Anyway he could see himself enacting the Grimshaw death-bed scene and making a success of it too. There was just that something of the actor in Branwell which may be found in a certain type of popular preacher who can be carried away and weep at his own eloquence. The one thing Branwell might have made was a preacher but he was born too late. Rather bitterly he says that his only qualification for that office would be hypocrisy, for so much water had flowed under the bridge since Thomas Walsh clung all heaven by the hems.

There had been a great confusing of the issues since Wesley rode into Rathfryland. One could not now saddle horse and contest the kingdoms for Christ. As Charlotte said, she dreaded that if she made any profession of holiness she would be dubbed a wild enthusiast and in all probability a Methodist—this when she was trying to keep Ellen Nussey's importunity at arm's length. She had a horror of the idea of becoming "one of a certain set." She felt irksome disgust at the idea of using "a single phrase that sounds like religious cant." Too much had the well-worn phrases entered into the children's souls. Papa and his solemnities, at least to Charlotte and Branwell, began to appear just something of an anachronism. He always talked like his ancient Methodist magazines, if the style of his letters can be taken as the gauge of his habitual marshalling of the English language. It is always with him "This land of probation", "This weary world" or "This delusive and ensnaring world." His hope was ever "immovably anchored in Heaven." It was only through "A gracious Providence" that in great weakness he was able to discharge his ministerial duties. He had always need of "Divine Aid" and well the children knew it.

It must be remembered that it was Branwell alone who saw this paragon of virtue in its night-shirt. It is difficult to keep on talking like a book in the privacy of one's own bedroom. What were the thoughts going forward in the boy's head as he let his gaze rest on that sleeping clergyman who would ever have his family know that in his waking moments his face was Zionwards? A kind of imp of mischief was born in the lad and he seems to delight in making fun of solemnities. He can make as grotesque a sermon for the mouth of a great preacher as ever Charlotte can. It was a species of retaliation for all that he had been called upon to suffer from a too near acquaintance with the saints. Yet the reaction was not altogether healthy, for it was a little feverish and nonsensical. Always there lurked a nervous fear that perhaps London was really only another name for Babylon and that the flames of Hell were more tangible than the leaping fires of the blast furnaces of the north.

Branwell's whole background and upbringing incapacitated him from the grasping of any nettle not hedged round with Divine Assistance. His one excursion to London ended in pitiable collapse. Indeed, he never seems to have recovered from the shock of that disappointment. It was to have been his crowning mercy when he stepped forth "under God" to take the Royal Academy by storm. It turned out to be the abomination of desolation—standing where it ought not. He gives one glimpse only of that devastating experience, when he launched out into the ensnaring world, and the tragedy lies here that, in reality, London had no spells with which to bind him.

There is a little bit of prose writing tucked away amidst the boy's History of Angria and no one can doubt that it is a transcript from personal experience and that Branwell is feeling his way here towards the psychological novel, long before the time of Meredith. Why, he asks, should the mental contrast of the bustling streets of alien London with the "Far off summer loneliness" of Haworth have made him know, in the instant, what shadows we are and what shadows we pursue. The boy is only nineteen years old and is at the moment in his life when he should take the tide of fortune and realise the aching ambitions of lonely Haworth, and this is how he writes: "Then, on a sudden, the tears came starting into his eyes, and a feeling like a wind seemed to pass across his spirits, because now he felt that not even the flashes of glory which these streets and buildings had struck from his soul, not even these feelings which he had reckoned on as something to supply years of dullness, could preserve his thoughts from aimless depression. From his mind being overstrained the relapse was as strong as a spring, yet it was long ere he quitted the spot, and then he turned, passing through many noble streets without hardly turning his eyes to look on them. He entered his hotel, stretched himself on a sofa, and listlessly dreamed away his time till dark."

Branwell Brontë had fled from reality. He could enjoy London and fame better in a recumbent position and in dreams of the mind. So his father before him had felt stronger in bed when the weight of the salvation of those most awkward Yorkshire parishioners had wearied his conscience at Hartshead-cum-Clifton, long ago. The boy is shrewd enough to see his weakness, which for the father had been covered from his sight in the poor rhymes and the plagiarisms of his cottage verses. Branwell, from the safety of his hotel sofa, thinks of London ships as though they sailed from Charlotte's and his own old dream-kingdom of Stump's Land. He sees the people hurrying to buy the newspapers and pretends that they were full of news of war amongst the Angrian population. He sees himself rushing in to the help of the Duke of Wellington—their ancient hero—but characteristically he also sees himself leaning against a railing to make his mind up which side he will espouse as he "ran over the misfortunes of Zamorna, the righteousness of Fidena, the cant of Reform and the mysteries of Northangerland." "But to think" he adds "Africa in the flames of war! However, farewell peace and welcome glory!" All so tingling and lovely from the small of one's back on a hired sofa but all rather boyish and a little foolish at nineteen years of age.

Yet the lad had good stuff in him, after all, because he can rise to self criticism in the person of Wentworth, whom he pictures gazing at Apsley House and kissing the steps which Wellington's feet had pressed. Branwell writes "Now Wentworth was in a manner a creature of impulses. He hurried and thirsted after impulses. So now he had got one that impelled him to come nearer to the glorious regions one of whose portals he had been contemplating that day. But at midnight there came upon his mind the word—Anticipation! And he remembered all his present feelings were those of anticipation. How anxious and impatient and incomplete was his present pleasure, and was it all that was to be? For those who possessed what he thought about, in reality, were they happy? At morning, he arose cast down and melancholy with these and such like reflections. Again the world looked futile and he spent that day without an aim till late in the afternoon."

No one knows the full story of this expedition to London, but that it formed an epoch in the boy's life is certain. He confided once to a friend that he had never recovered from his disappointment over the Royal Academy. No one knows if he ever went there at all or if he simply, of his own weakness, failed to grasp the opportunity. He makes Wentworth wander about the city aimlessly with his letters of introduction fearfully locked away in his room at the hotel. They would set too many complications afoot, and, for Branwell, too, a devastating paralysis of nerve seems to have marked this taking of the city by storm. There is illumination in his description of his visit to St. Paul's Cathedral. They had always dreamed of the marvel up there on Haworth Hill and now he was to see it with his own eyes. The boy is almost transfixed by fear as he passes backwards and forwards before that great west entrance and he has to take himself firmly, as it were by both hands, and get himself forcibly up those stone steps, or, as he says, "He dashed through the dread." And what was he afraid of? Simply of reality. Could anything be better than this bit of self analysis in Branwell's description of that experience: "Wentworth wandered in front of the Western Towers long before he dared trust himself to enter the mighty Temple, but after he had asked himself the reason of his hesitation and found it proceeded from instinctive fear of ending his pleasure by approaching reality, he dashed through the dread, walked up the grand flight of steps, and soon found himself with hat in hand pacing the marble pavement in the still, shadowy coolness beneath the vast expanding roof and glorious dome."

Once John Wesley had come to this same St. Paul's at the very crisis of his fate. All the strength of his mechanised religion had collapsed beneath him. He was a failure and he knew it. He had fled by night from Georgia and he had crossed the seas in despair. Now the organ of St. Paul's wailed above him "Out of the depths I have cried unto Thee oh Lord," and he knew that it spoke his own heart's language. But salvation for him was round the next corner, for that very evening that frozen heart was "warmed" so "strangely". It was at a quarter before nine at a little meeting in Aldersgate Street that Wesley made his startling discovery that "To refine religion is to spoil it. It is the most simple thing that can be conceived—it is only humble, gentle, patient love." His message ran like fire through England and to the ends of the earth. There was a place for every lost and broken soul of man at the very heart of God Himself. Love is and was my Lord and King. But whereas Wesley fell back gratefully from his titanic good works upon a religion of feeling, Branwell Brontë took up the tale when the whole bent of the religious revival had become too concentrated upon feeling itself. Wesley insisted that his congregation must both hear and feel, and, although his message worked wonders and gave England a new heart in the sophistication and irreligion of the Eighteenth Century, for some of his more artistic disciples this feeling itself, cutting too large a figure upon Wesley's stage, robbed them of vigour and melted the iron of good works in salt tears. Branwell Brontë at nineteen knew it all too well, and of his London experience he writes with wisdom above his years: "Next day found him still unknown and unvisited without participating in the splendours of wealth, no more than if he had not a pound in his pocket. Nor was he bent studiously on ransacking the great libraries or studying in the picture galleries. He was restlessly, aimlessly, and with the same anxious face, feeding his feeling with 'little squibs of rums', as he called them to himself, since he was perfectly aware that they would only the more depress him afterwards."

What Branwell Brontë told them at home of that fatal visit no man knows. Perhaps it was Aunt Branwell who came to the rescue and packed him off on a visit to Leeds to paint that mountain of reality William Morgan. The little family at Haworth had always dreaded that man's visits and his tales had been of that brand of dullness that makes seraphs nod. He had inherited in his own person all the provokingly professional jargon of piety and he had the temerity to catechise children over their pitiable porridge bowls. Little Anne was terrified, for she never had an answer ready, and he was so big and so alarming an inquisitor. She must have suffered under those pointed Methodist questions "What does a child like you most want?" for the answer was not a doll or a sweetmeat but "age and experience". Emily had had easier questions on the punishment of an unruly brother, but then Emily always seemed able to rise to what was demanded of her. True she had nearly died at school from sheer homesickness, but she had been able to wrest beauty from that harsh experience and make of it poetry.

What teacher of English to-day would not welcome a pupil who, from a child's tortured heart, could achieve words like these:

> "Still as I mused, the naked room,
> The alien firelight died away;
> And from the midst of cheerless gloom,
> I passed to bright unclouded day.
>
> A little and a lone green lane
> That opened on a common wide;
> A distant, dreamy dim blue chain
> Of mountains circling every side.
>
> A heaven so clear, an earth so calm
> So sweet, so soft, so hushed an air;
> And deepening still the dreamlike charm
> Wild moor sheep feeding everywhere.
>
> That was the scene, I knew it well;
> I knew the turfy pathway's sweep,
> That winding o'er each billowy swell,
> Marked out the tracks of wandering sheep.
>
> Could I have lingered but an hour
> It well had paid a week of toil;
> But truth has banished Fancy's power:
> Restraint and heavy task recoil.
>
> Even as I stood with raptured eye,
> Absorbed in bliss so deep and dear,
> My hour of rest had fleeted by
> And back came labour, bondage, care."

The bitter cup of experience was drained so characteristically and so differently by Emily and Branwell. Emily would always drink to the dregs, where Branwell drew back instinctively when the awful fact of reality must be gulped. But Emily was more fortunate than her brother in that the family had never expected anything of her. Branwell's very impotence to realise his sisters' and his aunt's dreams for him drove him into a frantic state of spurious effort without getting him anywhere. Emily stuck to her books, her ironing and her baking, and, in her heart, shyly awoke the poet. If only Branwell could have known the sweet discipline of a maid of all work, the story might have been so different, for Emily, after all, owed him much for his startling effervescence. Silent herself, she was one who loved to hear him talk. She seemed to remember all he said in a strange pictorial way.

H

CHAPTER XII

MARVELLOUS BOYS

THE FAILURE of Branwell Brontë's dream of winning fame at
the Royal Academy marked an epoch in his life. His sister Anne
stated the stark tragedy thus: "Branwell has given up painting,"
but it is doubtful if she knew the full significance of the shock
which her brother sustained when so much went wrong with "divine
assistance." She could not have known that she was the chronicler
of the beginning of her brother's ruin, for, at least for that time,
Haworth Parsonage had escaped tangible tragedy. They might
all have been called upon to mourn the death of another Chatterton,
for these marvellous boys had followed much the same pathway
towards a fading heaven.

It is clear that for Chatterton also apostasy meant apostasy
from Methodism, for his honest boy's heart had risen in indignation
against that cad whom he names "Apostate Will." This man,
in Chatterton's jingles, is depicted as taking all that Wesley can
give him and then departing to the more profitable service of
a rival fold. The poet knows all about the little chapel in Broad-
mead, Bristol, for he pictures Wesley there, in his home, pressing
money upon this ungrateful wretch with all his well-known charm
of manner. The eager desire of Wesley always to help is there and
his own characteristic admonition: "Do not repine—the whole
collection shall be thine." Both these boys, nurtured on dreams
of Heaven and a stormy realisation of Hell, developed the same imp
of mischief as their horizons broadened. What could be better
than Chatterton's description of Whitefield's famous squint in
that gay phrase "the oblique lightning of his eye."

Those inevitable hymns were the birthright of each of these
children. Chatterton, with a wisdom beyond his years, speaks of
those Wesley compositions as "hymns which do sanctify the throat,"
for had he not watched the Methodists sing and never forgotten
that ecstacy? Seen from a boy's angle, amidst the crowd, the
glowing words appeared to melt, in pious mouths, as so much
butter. A gracious oil of sanctity seemed to trickle down holy
throats as they mouthed their dulcet strains and the singers looked
too good to be true. Was their piety only throat deep? That was
a question which also exercised Branwell Brontë, who from his
own boyhood's observations could remark: "As for the Church—

PATRICK
BRANWELL
BRONTË

*From a
Silhouette*

ANNE,
EMILY, AND
CHARLOTTE
BRONTË

*From a
Painting by
Patrick
Branwell
Brontë, c. 1835
now in the
National
Portrait
Gallery*

I have not one mental qualification, save perhaps hypocrisy, which would make me cut a figure in its pulpits."

Chatterton's head was crammed full of unreal Rowleys and the exploits of ancient warriors, as was Branwell's with dreams of Northangerland, all his life. The heart must mourn both dreamers for reality surely got them in the end and London served them both one of her scurviest of tricks. There is one glimpse of Chatterton swaggering there with eager editors who in reality neither paid up and perhaps never existed. There is one letter in which he promises to send his mother and sisters a lovely tea set, and then silence. Without a penny in his pocket, the marvellous boy poet of Bristol asked bread in a baker's shop in High Holborn and was refused, when on Redcliffe Hill they would have pressed gingerbread on him for nothing. And so to bed and to take his own life in an alien attic, by his own hand. But the significance lies here, that before he died he posted his hymn of Nunc dimittis to the editor of the oldest of all Methodist magazines. He was back just where he had started with all the ribaldry silenced and with only God and the sunrise in heavenly places at all real to him. For some time truth had been blurred to the boy, but now his dream kingdom was rounding again into the shape and colour of the Kingdom of Heaven, "which God my East, my Sun reveals."

In the case of Branwell, the Rev. Patrick Brontë was spared that working out of the inscrutable will of a gracious Providence, but he came to reap a harvest of bitterness in his only son. Branwell indeed escaped from the great city with his life, but he came home wounded and betrayed a new feverish sense of futility and the ravages of a mind unstrung. He writes impassioned letters to Words-worth and to the Editor of Blackwood's Magazine which read like the ravings of a caged animal fighting its way out of prison. The words boil over and wear their writer out with an inept rush of importunity. They created for Branwell himself the illusion that he was fit to enter, nay had already entered, that fair literary world of which he had always dreamed. He tells the Editor of Blackwood's Magazine just what his publication had meant to him as a boy when his sister died, for he can remember its very words and quotes them as he would quote the Bible. He is sure he can write as no one else can for the paper, because he loved much and cherished the magazine as a veritable passion in his childhood. He writes in great letters over this rhapsody: "Oh Sir, read at last."

It was the fate of Branwell Brontë always to thunder at locked doors. In his letter to Wordsworth he pleads: "But read it Sir; and as you would hold a light to one in utter darkness—as you value your own kind-heartedness—*return* me an answer, if but one word, telling me whether I should write on, or write no more. Forgive undue warmth because my feelings in this matter cannot be cool." And again there was none that answered, although the poet might have helped so much from his knowledge of a background which might be more than a little suspect as resembling Branwell's own. Had not the great William as a school-boy eked out his rhymes with Charles Wesley's metaphor of Thomas Walsh's soul clapping its glad wings to win the port of Heaven? In Wordsworth's school-boy composition wisdom claps her strong wings, and when as a grown man he talks of glory and its trailing clouds the poet means the same glory that Wesley meant and his same "native heaven."

The fluting treble of pious children in Wesley's:—

> "From Jehovah I came
> For His glory I am
> And to him
> I with singing return."

was Wordsworth's "Intimations of Immortality from Early Childhood" in a nutshell. Branwell in any case believed the poet as conversant with all that old legacy as he was himself when he quotes verses of those inevitable hymns amongst his own rhymes which he submitted to Wordsworth for his criticism. Shall he write more or leave it alone? He will not ever be able to make of his "mansions in the sky" all that Wordsworth made of them, but then his sinews had not been toughened by pulling on Words-worth's oars and the great Power had never arrested Branwell in a searching way. Aunt Branwell had seen to that when she thought he was already a little angel too good to live, whilst Wordsworth's mother had had a juster view of her son's hard entrance into Heaven with a knowledge of that stubborn temper of the boy. Life was too easy and too hard for Branwell Brontë, at one and the same time, and now Wordsworth, who might have helped him, seems only to have taken refuge in silence.

There was always something nebulous about Branwell's idea of truth. He would tell his friends of the many great people who thought well of his poetry and if he said it often enough he would come to believe it himself in the end. But what could they have made of his pitiable screeds? They are full of perpetual deathbeds and the burning chains of Hell and through the ambling verse comes cry after cry from the heart of a forsaken boy who once believed himself to be the darling of the gods. Death is always at his elbow and Cowper's Castaway is his uncomfortable yet constant bedfellow. He sobs out:—

> "Great God! To-night shall fires infernal
> Hold me down in hideous pains
> With devils bound in burning chains
> And fires and pains and chains eternal?
> Oh! Christ when thou were crucified
> Thou heardst the felon at thy side
> And in his bitterest agony
> Thou promised him a heaven with thee!
> But he repented and confessed
> Ere thou wouldst give his anguish rest;
> And Oh! In my last hour do I—
> Thus wretchedly afraid to die
> Dare I repent? Can I repent?
> When with my very life are blent
> The feelings that have made me sin."

It was too bad of Aunt Branwell to have told the boy those tales of his pious youth. He had thirsted then to die and go to heaven and he had longed after that translation when Maria died. Now it made this present horror of adolescent darkness more intolerable, and no one could help him in Haworth Parsonage. It remained for Branwell to pass it off as best he could in foolish bravado, but he is a very pitiable little Don Juan. From his first appointment as tutor in Broughton-in-Furness he wrote to John Brown, his friend, the sexton of Haworth, a letter which is supposed to show the depth of depravity to which he had fallen. It does nothing of the sort and was treasured for long by his older friends because it was just like the boy was wont to talk when he was all wound up and ready to discharge his most infectious nonsense. He told them all how drunk he had got and how he went to bed in his boots, when all the time they knew he had been Secretary of the Temperance Society and even in this letter admonishes John Brown to keep to his teetotalism. Branwell tells him it will mend his body. With this good advice he is more at home than at going to bed in his boots. He is much more at home when it comes to letting off

Grimshaw-like remarks such as "The tongs of hell" and "he whose eyes Satan looks out of as from windows." His friends could enjoy a good laugh over that knowing all the old background so well. It would be delightful to them to see small Branwell, in their mind's eye, trying to change himself into the robust figure of old Parson Grimshaw and hear him preaching to them of their sins.

It was in this brief period of tutorship that Branwell Brontë met Hartley Coleridge, who was so like himself in the stuff of which his dreams were made. In Hartley Coleridge was found again that type of marvellous boy conceived amidst the unsubstantial shadows of emotional religion. Listen to his father, Samuel Taylor Coleridge, and study his mode of address to his young wife on their honeymoon. Sarah Fricker is serenaded as "a meek daughter in the family of Christ." The whole poem smacks of conversion and connubial bliss. It incorporates a text from Micah VI. 8. for Coleridge himself was a preacher and could not let that kind of thing alone. Queer stuff indeed if we did not know that Coleridge was then proclaiming "Christ crucified" and launching into his subject as an eagle into the wind. That little cottage at Clevedon must have wondered at the lovers under its roof with their Eolian Harp stuck in its windows to represent the spirit of God. Here is Coleridge's love song:—

> "For never guiltless may I speak of Him,
> The Incomprehensible! Save when with awe
> I praise Him, and with faith that inly feels;
> Who with His saving mercies healed me,
> A sinful and most miserable man,
> Wildered and dark, and gave me to possess
> Peace, and this cot, and thee, dear honoured maid."

Watch Samuel Taylor Coleridge again when they tell him of the birth of this very Hartley. His first reaction was to fall on his knees. He seeks instinctively "the throne of grace", but was perplexed to find no answering heavenly visitation "inly felt." His mind was stunned and his thoughts confused. He confessed his heart full of shapeless feelings. The only thing to do was to have a good cry. Tears run helplessly down his cheeks and then, gathering up the stress of body, he manages to win through to the "Lover of souls." The carnal man had rushed forward in imagination to Sarah's bosom and the son hanging there, but at last after a struggle he can sublimate that emotion and pray as the saints were accustomed:

> "Oh Lord! To thee I bend,
> Lover of Souls! And groan for future grace,
> That ere my babe youth's perilous maze has trod,
> Thy overshadowing spirit may descend,
> And he be born again a child of God."

The Rev. Patrick Brontë would have sympathised with the poor man entirely, but whereas Coleridge professed a freedom from old bondage Patrick was inhibited with Wesley's own caution in this peculiar language of religious love which decreed that his brother Charles's great hymn of "Jesus, Lover of my soul" should find no place in his hymn book. This Wesley trick of to "inly feel the same" had its dangers, but it is significant that Coleridge "inly feels" without compunction in both effusions. So in a sort of mystic twilight of the gods was Hartley Coleridge sired and so was Branwell born. Behind both boys was the insistent, wistful parental desire that they should be born again, children of God. As a baby, Hartley had been rushed out into the night to see the moon in heaven and so stifle his too earthly cries, and as a little boy he had made pious remarks about the street lamps which had been taken up into the mansions in the sky and shone there as stars. He had been but a baby when his little brother had died and Coleridge had rejoiced and told his stricken mother that "There is no room for death." He had been fretted by sallies of this same mother's kisses as Wordsworth and Coleridge compared notes on his heavenly origin and speedy return to glory, but he came to shamble through real life like a tramp.

Hartley Coleridge and Branwell Brontë were handicapped from the start with their possession of fathers who were eager to bring up these pilgrims of eternity without contamination of a world of sin. These boys were of too exquisite a moulding for the sweat and the blood and tears of human birth, conceived as they were by edict from above and born on contemplation's wings. So it came about that Hartley Coleridge could not help Branwell Brontë although the boy implored his help, and it also happened that they both shuffled off into eternity in the same year and Hartley's epitaph, written by himself, would have done just as well for Branwell Brontë. It ran:—

> "Long time a child, and still a child, when years
> Had painted manhood on my cheeks was I,
> For yet I lived like one not born to die,

A thriftless prodigal of smiles and tears,
No hope I needed, and I knew no fears.
But sleep, though sweet, is only sleep and waking,
I asked to sleep no more, at once o'ertaking
The vanguard of my age, with all arrears
Of duty on my back. Nor child, nor man,
Nor youth, nor sage, I find my head is grey
For I have lost the race I never ran;
A rathe December blights my lagging May;
And still I am a child, though I be old,
Time is my debtor for my years untold."

Branwell Brontë was now busy about losing the race which he had never really run. He had already heaped up too much of failure upon his young shoulders, for, in every encounter with life, he had been defeated. His artistic ambitions were stone dead. His dreams of studio life had vanished in Bradford smoke. His genius had been rebuked under the sculptor Leyland who could do it all so much better that he made Branwell despair. He seems to have got as far as telling the great man about Maria but somehow that inspiration could achieve no marketable value. His one attempt on life in the guise of a tutor had also failed. It has left behind it only that one letter, full of nonsense, to show that it ever had been. Yet Branwell remained painfully conscious of that load upon his back of the arrears of duty. He did make one more effort to lead a life of action and say farewell to dreams, for he actually got a job on the Leeds and Manchester railway and marched off to his new work with a certain flourish. He would show them this time how it should be done. He could see success here just round the next corner for this was the age of railways. Branwell would lay hold on fortune with both hands and, as he swaggered off across the moors, he reminded Charlotte of a knight setting forth on some heroic exploit. His enthusiasm infects his sister's pen. It was typical of them both to feel that ecstasy of adventure and to embellish the all too pedestrain enterprise of life on a railroad track. Charlotte writes to Ellen Nussey with a proud flourish: "A distant relation of mine, one Patrick Boanerges, has set off to seek his fortune in the wild, wandering, adventurous, romantic, knight-errant capacity of clerk on the Leeds and Manchester railway."

The Son of Thunder's heart was probably failing him for fear, but he must still go on acting his part of hero under his sisters' wondering gaze and his aunt's proud belief in his genius. These brittle bright boys of the heavenly mansions are more sinned against than sinning, and station life at Luddenden Foot is surely not their most suitable destination. Yet as Branwell's friend Grundy reviewed the tragedy, in after years, he could not see what could have been altered. He remembered the boy riding freely on the railway with an abandonment of pleasure. He remembered him sunk in gloom. He knew something of his "gross carelessness." He chuckled over his pictures sprinkled in the margin of a station's ledgers, but he saw no sort of vice in the lad. His opinion is worth remembering, for Grundy wrote just what he saw without complications of God or Satan to confuse the issue. He says:—"Patrick Brontë was no domestic demon—he was just a man moving in a mist who lost his way."

Now, that was not a satisfactory picture of the son of the Rev. Patrick Brontë, the heir of all the inheritance of Tighe, Wesley, Fletcher, Shirley and Huntingdon. Such an one should never lose his way. The steep and narrow path had claimed him from the beginning. But times had changed. An age of rattling machinery was hard on the heels of the horseman of the Rathfryland road. Was eternity just above the tree-tops now? If a man die shall he live again? A hundred questions of which Maria never dreamed were being debated by the Grundys of England and her practical engineers. Branwell Brontë, trying to make friends with the new and yet keep faith with the old, became literally like a man lost in fog.

CHAPTER XIII

LUDDENDEN FOOT

BRANWELL BRONTË was not long in making the discovery that his new station life was monotonous. The only thing to stir his apathy became the thunder of the passing train which shook the ledger upon his desk. He would sit pensively decorating its margins with pictured faces and quaint devices. Then he would write a line or two of verse in his old notebook, look hopelessly for inspiration to the grimy windows of his railway shack and contemplate the wintry solitude of his little platform. He came, more and more, to leave all active business to a friendly porter, and, when he could get away he fled the station altogether. Often he walked up the hill to Luddenden itself, for there was refreshment at the Lord Nelson both for mind and body. There was here a good library of old books, until lately preserved, and here Branwell found life more to his taste than amongst his station duties. The books must have reminded him of his father, for here were gathered volumes of Whitefield's works which in that convivial atmosphere must have looked positively racy.

Branwell Brontë might be a young dare-devil in his own estimation and he might show off to his friends as a man about town, but he was really more at home amongst bookshelves lined with old magazines and musty volumes dealing with the Evangelical Revival of Religion of the Eighteenth Century. He was abundantly at home also in Luddenden Churchyard, for here lay all that was mortal of old Parson Grimshaw of Haworth. Here rushed the boisterous stream past the quiet grave where Grimshaw had come in death, having begged to lie as near his old first love as possible, in that hallowed place. Here the hill sloped up to the moor above with its tall trees and its memories. What thoughts must have swirled past in that water as Branwell leaned over the wall and watched the stream tumble over the rocks, there by the old church, for here were tales and pictures the boy had known all his life.

The faithful people of Haworth had brought the body of Grimshaw here, right across the moors, by the old stoops road, had they come, singing all the way. They had rejoiced, as Wesley had bidden them, "for a brother deceased." The echo of that old, well known, triumph song must have been tossed up to listening ears with its strange promise of hope for "A soul out of prison released and freed from its bodily chain." The rough old boisterous prophet lay so still now. Only the stream thundered. Branwell was back in memory with his friends of nursery days when Grimshaw kept company with him in Tabby's kitchen. She could imitate his "market language" to the life. She could tell of his methods with a dying sinner. It was no good telling Parson Grimshaw to go away as the patient needed rest. He would reply that he must be about his Father's business and if they would not let him in he would shout under the window:—"If you will perish you shall perish with the sound of the gospel in your lugs." Branwell could hear the dear home language of those his earliest tales of romance tossed up to him from the rushing water.

The Luddenden stream brought up to him murmurs and scents of the infinite sea, and, if he returned to his station, he was still with Grimshaw. There above his place of exile stood Ewood Hall in its glory, for that was Grimshaw's home and there on the terrace Wesley had preached. There the drunken son of Grimshaw had lived with that strange history of marriage and intermarriage and the names Lockwood, Grimshaw and Sutcliffe to ring the changes on. Here in that house of the painted staircase Wesley had made a note in his Journal: "I rode to Ewood to sister Lockwood's, formerly the wife of young Mr. Grimshaw, afterwards married to Mr. Lockwood and now again a widow. Her sister was with her, the relict of Mr. Sutcliffe." Now if Branwell had been at Wesley's elbow he might have told us all we want to know about so strange a household. He did his best with the material at his disposal and set his brains to the spinning of yarns in this place also. Too surely here again he looked out onto his own old dream kingdom. Sometimes he told his friends, Leyland and Grundy, all he saw and they confessed it seemed to them like stuff thrown out wildly from a diseased fancy. But he stirred them to interest. It was like a session with Kubla Khan and they remembered Branwell's Ewood Tales long afterwards. They were tales of a lost sister, of market language and a drunken son. Always it was a storming tale of fortune's wreck and love's disaster and the wind sighing through the desolation of great houses. It seemed as though the lad had but to lift up his eyes to Ewood House, above them, to be carried away in spirit across the moors and see swashbuckling Grimshaw with Tabby as interpreter.

In Branwell's heart there was a perfect passion for romance.
To make up a story, to tell it to someone, to have the moon and
the seven stars bow down in admiration before the wizard narrator,
that was life. But just as he drank the heady stuff the trains on the
Leeds and Manchester railway would thunder past and find
Branwell with lamp untrimmed and no tickets collected. He came
to hate the solid things of balanced ledgers and correct change, for
he felt his soul degraded by such carping reality. Hating the office
work and the tedium of the station routine, he would visit the
public house and there seek to revive the fainting heart of the poet.
Later, as he looked back on this part of his life Branwell called
it a season of cold debauchery. He saw himself as a man who walks
the plank over a lurking hell and wonders how far he can go and
retain his balance. He could never get any joy of abandonment
from his dissipation as he was set up with such a tender conscience
and with so lively an appreciation of final judgment. He was
pitiably lonely, for his stalwart friends were so different from
himself.

Grundy was that amiable type of young man with a merry face
and a habit of calling a spade a spade. He could enjoy himself and
know when to stop. He was no victim of a galling past. He had no
fear of Hell and considered that Branwell had been brought up
foolishly by that courtly old father of his on Haworth Hill. Grundy
was the kind of young man to enjoy falling out of a train and letting
it rattle over him as he lay on the ground between the rails. He
would get up, shake himself and make for home, but he would not
tease his wits with God's plan for his deliverance as Branwell would
have done. He had escaped the terrible demands of an Evangelical
conversion, for his people were of the Unitarian fold. Grundy
took life as it came and was at a loss to understand much of
Branwell's gloom. He believed in the efficacy of a glass of brandy
for morbid youth and could not understand the queer sensitiveness
of the boy who professed still to hear the voice of a dead sister
reminding him of Heaven. Branwell looked so strange at times
and talked so much and so strangely too. It was impossible to take
him seriously. If Grundy happened to miss a friendly word with
him at some party Branwell was in tears and seemed on the verge
of heartbreak. He had to fly to verse-making for relief and the
practical engineer, Grundy, was quite at a loss to understand such
a storm in a tea cup.

It is difficult to know what could have saved Branwell Brontë. The notebook of his poems which he carried home with him from Luddenden Foot reveals a turmoil of feeling. High endeavour is there. Despair is there also. Hope in God is there and again the hopeless prostration of fear before Him. A longing for home is there and yet a realisation of frustration when the wanderer returns. Sadly the boy writes this note against one of the Luddenden poems:—"The piece endeavours, I fear feebly enough, to describe the harsh contrast between the mind changed by long absence from home and the feelings kept flourishing in the hearts of those who have never wandered and who vainly expect to find the heart returning as fresh as when they had bidden it farewell." That dying freshness of a boy's heart becomes an obsession with him. At the age of 24 he feels himself an old man and, in a sad collapse of nerve, he feels his hand tremble and his foot falter. The colours have all passed away from his eyes. He must drink a little more to bring the inspiration back and yet he knows, in his heart of hearts, that there lies only despair on that road also. He turns in thought to his home, trying to revive its old enthusiasms and failing again, in pitiable weakness, to reap joy from memory. He fancies himself again in his bed-room at Haworth Parsonage. He can see the guns and the fishing rods and that picture of Wolfe at Quebec, all in their familiar places, on the plain walls. He used to enjoy it all so much but now he can see that the picture is faded and the heroics stone dead. He had thrilled once over those Heights of Abraham but now an apathy is drugging his mind.

What is this life anyway—a stage for fools rather than heroes? Branwell had once believed it to be the borderland of Heaven. He had once believed that God led him personally through its winding ways to the Promised Land. His youthful heart had known a passion of love for Christ and for His saving Cross. He had believed himself a child of God. He had wept in rapture at the glory of that whole divine epic and here he now was, in drizzling rain and howling wind, taking tickets from a lot of Yorkshire boors at Luddenden Foot station. It was a terrible humiliation. Walk that little platform to-day. Look out, as Branwell looked, at Grimshaw's house. Remember Grimshaw's grave. Ask what secret of frustration, what hidden flaw of character, what legacy from the past made shipwreck of the brother of the Brontës.

It breaks the heart to know that as Branwell paced that platform at Luddenden Foot—a grown man of 24—he was straining his ears to catch one note of the voice of the angel child Maria. One of his poems in the Luddenden Foot notebook would tell the plaintive fact quite plainly for all its pedestrain verse. So real a presence was that little lost sister, dead these 17 years, that Branwell could hear her calling:—"Remember me" above the rattle and roar of the Leeds, Manchester railway. He had always so heard her calling him, at his bed-room window or in moonlight at his father's door. Now he trembled to think that he might lose even that spiritual consolation in this lethargy which crept like a paralysis over his spirit. It seemed to Branwell, as he sat on his office stool scribbling verse in his notebook, that if Maria should be eclipsed, by the gloom of Luddenden Foot station, with her would go every shred of glory he had ever known. She seemed even now struggling to get through to him from a great distance. Yet he could hear her well known voice still gently reasoning with him. Maria seemed to know all about the failure of his ambitions, for he could hear her say:—

> "And though thy lot be widely cast
> From what thou picturest in the past
> Still deem me dear to thee,
> Since to thy soul my light was given
> To give thy earth some glow of heaven,
> And, if my beams from thee be driven,
> Dark, dark, thy night will be!"

Here is no trace of cold debauchery but rather evidence of the youth's hyper-sensitive appreciation of the height from which a child of God could fall. Here is a cry from the heart for a lost sister and her ancient heaven. So deeply miserable is Branwell that his strained nerves vibrate to an air-borne voice. Clearly Maria seems to call him, her little brother of whom she hoped so much. "Remember me" she calls across the years, now, to an abject youth on an office stool in the growing horror of failure. Of that ghostly admonition he writes:—

> "I when I heard it, sat amid
> The bustle of a town-like room.
> 'Neath skies with smoke-stained vapours hid—
> By windows made to show their gloom.

MIDGLEY ABOVE LUDDENDEN AND THE ROAD TO EWOOD

From a drawing by Albert Edward Black in the possession of the Author

The desk that held my ledger book
Beneath the thundering rattle shook
Of engines passing by;
The bustle of the approaching train
Was all I hoped to rouse the brain
Or startle apathy.
And yet, as on the billow swell
A Highland exile's last farewell
Is borne o'er Scotland's sea,
And solemn as a funeral knell
I heard that soft voice, known so well,
Cry—"Oh remember me!"

It is significant that the summons seems to come to Branwell in the notes of Haworth's passing-bell. He is transported back in memory to his happy childhood amidst the old loyalties of home. He sees himself again an eager boy lying in the sunshine reading "some noble page." Above him in the Parsonage garden the trees whispered words of "wondrous prospects meant for me." Again he sees the moors of home where fancy ever came to him. He is back with Northangerland and "adventures bold and scenes divine." Closer to him the vision came. It was the more heartbreaking for even now Branwell felt himself guided by Maria's little hand to the only playground her soul had ever known in this life—"The steep of Calvary."

It is highly unlikely that the station officials could guess what was going forward in the tousled head of their incompetent railway clerk. They found their accounts muddled, no entry for tickets sold or taken, and crude pictures scrawled in the margin of their ledgers. It could end only in one way. After an enquiry Branwell Brontë was dismissed in disgrace. In the heart of the Son of Thunder then burned shame, consternation and anger. How was he to face Haworth again? How was he to face life? This sort of treatment amounted to an insult to a gentleman, a philosopher and a poet. What sort of a world was this that demanded correct figures in careful columns? He had been led to believe this state of probation was other than that. Could not the officials of the Leeds and Manchester railway give a thought to the pageantry of God and the Devil in mortal combat? Could they not know that Branwell must be about the business of verse and story in this world of romance? Had not Maria called him from her heavenly home?

What meaning could there be in life apart from her gentle admonitions?

All Branwell knew was that he was uncommonly tired. He
dragged himself home to Haworth on the verge of a nervous
breakdown, down at heel, wild-eyed and hopeless. True to his
upbringing the only thing remaining real to him then was the
arbitrament of the Eye of God. Here is the lad's heart-broken
prayer and his farewell to Luddenden Foot:—

> "My body is oppressed with pain,
>   My mind is prostrate 'neath despair—
>   Nor mind, nor body may again
>   Do more than call Thy wrath to spare.
>
> Both void of power to fight or flee
>   To bear or to avert Thy eye,
>   With sunken heart, with suppliant knee,
>   Implore a peaceful hour to die."

CHAPTER XIV

WILLIAM WEIGHTMAN

THE Rev. Patrick Brontë was withdrawing more and more into the fastness of his study. He found it easier so to do. He was ready with a cast-iron excuse to himself and to his family—"My own health is generally but *very* delicate." He would perform his ministerial duties "through a gracious Providence and with great care," but the children knew that when they were discharged the Rev. Patrick would lock away all semblance of gaiety or vigour, with his hat and cane, in the hall press. Even these duties began to hang heavily now. It needed a younger man to go into people's houses and talk about their souls. This indigestion, too, became worse when Patrick Brontë had to do anything he did not like doing. And then the family became more difficult in these days. They seemed to refuse to settle into God's plan for their advancement. Charlotte had returned in a queer depressed mood from Dewsbury Moor and would do nothing but worry them all about the state of Anne's health. Emily was back from a teaching spell in a really good school near Halifax and seemed to have determined never to go on her travels again. Branwell had not stormed his way into the Royal Academy nor had he succeeded in making his way as a portrait painter in Bradford or Leeds. His one achievement had been to run up some alarming debts. It is true the boy had fondly hoped that Papa and Aunt would never find out these uncomfortable liabilities but they had taken the unfair advantage of a delayed action bomb and made their presence felt. Money, for Branwell, would always prove too unreal and too real at one and the same moment and it would always constitute one of the chief difficulties in his dealings with life.

What was the father of the family to do? He kept warning them all how delicate he was and how, when he died, they would be left defenceless in an unkind world. The time had clearly come for action. He would consult his medical adviser and think about finding a clerical assistant to ease him of the things he hated doing in his parish. He was not quite a second Grimshaw, but then times had changed and he was very delicate in spite of his famous walking powers. He became more and more dependent on Mr. Milligan's medicine and it did wonders for him. It came, it seems, not so much from a medicine bottle as from a larger, more festive looking container. No wonder Papa took his mid-day meal alone. He had to be careful in the bosom of his family over so wordly an aid to digestion. Still more it behoved him to be careful outside, for his parishioners so easily gossiped over any odour, not of sanctity, proceeding from their parson. His letter to his medical adviser speaks for itself. Patrick Brontë writes:—"I have frequently thought that you might have wondered why I was so particular in requiring your signature—the truth is—I wished to have *Medical Authority* for what I might do—in order that I might be able to counteract (under Providence) the groundless yet pernicious censures of the weak, wicked and wily—who are often on the alert to injure those who are wiser and better than themselves." Patrick Brontë, thus fortified, had pacified conscience and got something more tangible than his first excuse that the smell about his person was due to the eye ointment he was becoming more and more compelled to use for his weak eyes. That might satisfy Papa but it was more difficult to hoodwink some very bright young people of his own acquaintance. It became a kind of breathless, fearful family joke, at least between Branwell and Emily, that the pious needed "Divine aid" to digest their dinner.

Patrick's other effort towards relief had much happier consequences for his growing family. He became the means of introducing them to one of their most delightful experiences. Although the tale of William Weightman must come to tragedy in the end, he was lovely and pleasant in his life and as welcome as the flowers in May. That he came amongst them at all was due entirely to Patrick Brontë's old loyalties. He makes that quite clear as he takes pen in hand to write to his old friend Mr. Franks to ask for his advice in this matter of the appointment of a curate. He wants a man who is not a Calvinist. He must go the same way as Patrick "in our preaching and exhorting" and not fight against Arminius, either. Patrick Brontë writes:—"I could not feel comfortable with a coadjutor who would deem it his duty to preach the appalling doctrines of personal Election and Reprobation as I should consider these decidedly derogatory to the Attributes of God, so also I should be fearful of evil consequences to the hearers from the enforcement of final preservance as an essential article of belief. I am well aware that many clergymen, far wiser and better than I, do not accord with me here; but as I freely leave them to the possession of their views so I hope that they will kindly permit me to enjoy mine.

I want for this region a plain rather than an able preacher; a zealous but at the same time a judicious man—one not fond of innovation but desirous of proceeding on *the good old plan* which alas! has often been *mar'd* but never improved."

Patrick Brontë remained what he had always been, an Arminian in theology and a follower of John Wesley at heart. The Methodists, taught by Wesley and Fletcher, always held that that fatal belief in final preservance would open the door to antinomianism. Patrick Brontë wanted none of that school of theology corrupting the morals of his flock on Haworth Hill. He held to the old school in praise of "Mr. Wesley's tracts" and to Adam Clarke's Commentary—these were his stock in trade. These he applauded in his few prose ventures into print with praise of one Daniel Isaac, one of Wesley's quaintest preachers. The ease with which the names trip off the Rev. Patrick Brontë's tongue, as he crosses swords about Baptism with the authentic dissenting Baptists of his parish, show that to him they are household words. That unmistakable "Mr. Wesley" is a positive shibboleth. The inner circle always spoke of him so, never as Wesley or John Wesley but always with an implied bow of reverence in their "Mr. Wesley." Charlotte Brontë knew the difference well and when she entered the Taylors' revolutionary household at Gomersal she truthfully records its speech in their plain "John Wesley." That blunt appellation came as a sort of shock to ears trained only in Haworth Parsonage and to heirs of the older dispensation.

It is significant that all Patrick Brontë's worthies are of this old school and all enemies of Jabez Bunting and the newer Methodism, for the Brontë household had a more personal grievance against that great man than his work of separating the Methodists from the Church of England. He had been instrumental in dislodging Uncle Fennell from Woodhouse Grove, and had edged his own brother-in-law into the position of Headmaster there. Uncle John Fennell had betaken himself wholly to the bosom of Mother Church and he was now the vicar of Cross-Stones and cherished no illusions about the dictatorship of Jabez Bunting. But now at last the shades of all the Wesleys and the Fletchers had been kind and William Weightman stepped in amongst the Brontë household straight out of that oldest background. Here was something like an exponent of the good old plan.

Patrick Brontë regarded Weightman as his son in the gospel. Branwell and the girls loved him on sight. He was the gayest thing

that ever came up to the help of the Lord. He believed in the love
of God and was eager for all the world to believe it, too. His was no
formal religion of cant phrase and melodrama but was a quality
of his very life. It was with him when he brought the sunshine in
to Haworth Parsonage with a refreshing dose of nonsense. It was
there when he picked the primroses for Anne. It was present in
the little cottage where he nursed the old woman's cat as though
he loved it. And could not the man preach? Patrick Brontë lamented
that he preached above the people's heads and William Weightman
promised most humbly to do better, but the Parsonage pew must
have rejoiced that never could he mend his ways there. Papa's
own discourse was so simple that he who runs might read. Miss
Nussey said that he expounded a parable not once but twice and
in such a way that the meanest intelligence might grasp it. Young
Weightman, with the world before him, and a scholar's grasp of
the Classics, could paint a picture to delight a whole pewful of
Brontës. When he added to the humanities an adoring gaze at
Anne, who was as pretty as paint with her bright colouring and
adorable curls, the excitement of churchgoers ran high. Charlotte
believed that she positively heard Weightman sigh.

Every day brought some new thing of delight when William
Weightman was about. His visits to the Parsonage were frequent.
Once he showed them his Durham gown and they all tried it on.
Then they had a gay competition in drawing each other and
comparing notes on character and everything else under the sun.
Once there was a never to be forgotten expedition to Keighley and
a walk back at midnight. Weightman was escort and the Parsonage
girls were taken out for a lecture but it is not likely that they
remembered much about that. What they did remember was the
feel of those Yorkshire moors about them at night and the presence
of Weightman, beautiful as a young Apollo in their midst. Did
they link arms? Could young people do so then with propriety? In
any case it was a gloriously exciting expedition. They all
remembered the home-coming. There was a going in the tree tops
amongst the solemnities of Haworth Parsonage that night. Eager
young people are rushing in with their manly escort to drink all
Aunt's coffee and ask for more. Aunt has no more and Aunt's
temper is precariously poised. Aunt, in fact, can stand very little
of this sort of thing, but, for the young people, trifles have suddenly
become important and solemnities of no significance at all. When
William Weightman is your knight errant, eyes are bright and

cheeks aflame. A peal of laughter rings out from Haworth Parsonage and makes the heart leap in glad fellowship for it is like a tale of all our youth and so joyful in the telling. There is something particularly compelling about a debonair saint.

Charlotte Brontë and Ellen Nussey found the young man an interesting topic for their letter writing and their maiden meditations. They canvassed between them all his possible love affairs. Emily passed him before the bar of her judgment with approval. Anne fell in love with him, and William Weightman treated them all with a brother's impartiality. When it came to February 14th and he discovered that the girls had never received a valentine he walked a matter of ten miles to post them each one. He must have enjoyed that and they certainly did. They even composed a piece of poetry as a Roland for his Oliver. They must have made a pretty picture there in Haworth Parsonage putting the lines together with so much laughter and just a trace of solemnity. After all they could never quite escape from Papa's shadow and the ghost of the saintly Fletcher in the background. The verses read as though they were written from the heart of friends to a fair visitant from another world. They know that he must leave them soon for fresh conquests. Nothing so splendid as William Weightman could pass all his days on Haworth Hill. Their rhymes tell him that they believe he is signalled out for a great future:

> "Not always in these lonely hills
> Your humble lot shall lie,
> The oracle of fate foretells
> A worthier destiny.
> And never may a cloud come o'er
> The sunshine of your mind
> Kind friends, warm hearts and happy hours
> Thro' life we trust you'll find."

The words run backwards and forwards like a shuttle as each girl gives a word or an idea, approves or puts in some eager remonstrance. It is wholly as it should be that the jingle echoes the strangers and pilgrims of Wesley's hymn and Mrs. Fletcher's sermon on the anchor cast near the shore. But it is also significant that when Wesley wrote:

> "Strangers and pilgrims here below
> This earth we know is not our place"

the Brontë girls write with minds not now fixed on heaven. They say of William Weightman:

> "A stranger and a pilgrim here
> We know you sojourn now,
> But brighter hopes with brighter wreathes
> Are doomed to bind your brow."

The anchor of hope is also cast towards a land of earthly promise thus:

> "Then cast hope's anchor near the shore
> 'Twill hold your vessel fast
> And fear not for the tide's deep roar
> And dread not for the blast."

The younger generation is settling down to have a good look at this ensnaring world and perchance enjoy it before it goes hence and is no more seen. But was it Anne who insisted on "our earnest prayer to speed you on your way".

Anne Brontë was an intense young woman and although she passes silently across the Brontë stage she possessed a heart of flaming loyalty which would have surprised a mere modern. She suffered much under the family jokes of Weightman's numerous love affairs of which he wrote to Branwell and which Charlotte and Ellen Nussey discussed with the enthusiasm of all unattached spinsters. Anne liked to think, in her heart of hearts, that it was really only herself whom he sighed over. She beguiled many a pedestrian bit of life's journey with tales of his goodness and his love and was, in her own quiet way, happy with her mental son of consolation. Anne Brontë has never attracted much attention but she deserves more. Charlotte thought she went through life, as it were, under the protection of a nun's veil, but in reality she of all her family held down a job of work in an unkind world for four years. None of the other Brontës could have done that, and where Charlotte was a failure as governess Anne was a success. Her pupils loved her and came to appreciate the quality of her heart.

Anne Brontë, in a wilderness world, kept herself going with shy breezes from celestial hills and with little bed-time stories about William Weightman. So spiritual was the girl's make-up that it was quite enough to carry her through triumphant. She needed no love of the flesh, and when she came to die, she was buried where she had been happiest—on a cliff above Scarborough, dreaming of Weightman. She loved to hear all Haworth's gossip of the man's goodness and carry it away in her heart to make the hero of the tales she kept writing go and do likewise. She called the story

"Chapters in the Life of an Individual" and she would later re-christen it "Agnes Grey", so that Anne's pages give to the world William Weightman, walking and talking. When Charlotte visited the sick and the curate had been before her, she was wont to bring back the kind of tale which Anne would deck out to adorn the character of her Mr. Weston of the dreams of her pillow. It is reported speech which Charlotte sends to Ellen Nussey about this paragon of virtue when she writes: "He was always good to poor folk, and seemed to have a deal of feeling and kindheartedness about him." It is just so that Anne's characters speak of her hero, for how often had she heard it and rehearsed it all in her own silent head.

Upon Charlotte, Weightman had a different influence. She set herself to observe his character critically. She had had few opportunities of studying mankind apart from her brother and father and the Taylor household at Gomersal. Now she has something more festive to write about to Ellen Nussey than her soul struggles and childhood's memories of the saintly Fletcher. She has a real man of flesh and blood under her mental microscope. She sees him "handsome, cheery and good tempered" on a Sunday. She hears him in low spirits talking with her father on a Saturday, because death is abroad amongst the lambs of his fold. She knows him clever, and that he is able to take any examination he likes in his stride. She laughs at him when he paints his own name on the clouds traced there by the fingers of fame. She feels a little sorry for him and a little motherly—"his sanguine temperament bothers him grievously." She could almost forgive him for his sighs and his gentle flirtations for she feels a little superior and sees through the young man so easily. She warns Ellen not to lose her heart to him for the ground is strewn with his ancient loves and the man knows his own irresistibleness. Charlotte is heart whole and distant. She can write: "I am not at all surprised at all this—it is perfectly natural—a handsome—clean—prepossessing—good humoured young man—will never want troops of victims amongst young ladies." And then with a genuine smile of appreciation she adds: "God bless him! I wonder who with his advantages would be without his faults."

The sunshine of his mind was, after all, the great thing. He acted on them all as a tonic. And when that awful man William Morgan arrived to stay at the Parsonage then William Weightman was worth his weight in gold. Poor Aunt Branwell presiding at that table! Did she know the cross currents above and the gentle pressure of the curate's feet beneath, when Morgan prosed too long? Weightman's face was a study of patience and good temper and the girls loved him for the part he played, for he made even Morgan's dull solemnities seem gay, and, all the more so, because they could all laugh together later when Papa withdrew with his old friend to his study. Then William Weightman could throw himself down on the sofa, almost fainting, and declare that he was "done up by his long stories". Those hoary tales had wound their long way from Thomas Walsh and Ireland to the saintly Fletchers and on to Woodhouse Grove and all about the parishes of Bradford and Leeds. The Methodist has a devastating magazine of long stories at his finger ends and Morgan was soul brother to all the pilgrims of that ancient background. He knew everything there was to know about the Fletchers and the Shirleys and the Wesleys and it all had a way of seeming so fresh to him that he was remorseless in repetition and tedious in detail to a fainting audience. It was a wearing performance for Aunt even, who should have stood up to it better as it was her period. Charlotte, the observant, reports her as "precious cross" after the visit was over. Such a guest can tell an intolerable number of tales during three days and the old-time leisure of family meals. Weightman was a god-send and there was no denying that fact. It is likely that Aunt's nerves were in fiddle strings as the hash grew cold before that remorseless spate of words and Weightman's patience would but add to her irritability. She was getting more and more thankful in this household of grown-up Brontës to retire to her own bedroom and her own old treasures of memory and romance. The spinster aunt can not tolerate, for long periods, the laughter of bright young things.

Miss Branwell was beginning to feel her age. She could depend on Emily who never lingered over any job and who was invaluable in the house where Charlotte says "her usefulness and willingness make her indispensable". But Charlotte was a different proposition and her aunt and niece had never got on very well together. She never seemed to settle anywhere for long and if she ironed she burned the clothes. To the old lady Haworth Parsonage began to feel too full of people who, in spite of all her training in method, were not pulling their weight as they should. They seemed to find a great deal too much time for laughter. Miss Branwell felt that she had now reached a stage in the family fortunes when she must once more assert herself for peace. She enjoyed reading Blackwood's

Magazine to her brother-in-law and she enjoyed tilting her arguments against his at a quiet tea table, but she was beginning to feel that she was getting too old to contend with these unattached young women in a land of probation. It was time for a second school project to take shape in the minds of Aunt and Papa and now it was the girls who were to be the teachers. They should have a school of their own, in Bridlington perhaps, and were it a success it would be a pleasant change from Haworth for Miss Branwell herself when able to pay them a stately visit of inspection. Anne was a governess already and Aunt was prepared to sink some of her own money in preparing her other nieces to take their place in the scholastic world.

Miss Branwell lived long enough to embark Charlotte and Emily on their great adventure to Brussels, but the bubble of that peace which she had contrived for herself in Haworth Parsonage was so soon and so cruelly shattered. Death was becoming impatient to continue his unwelcome attentions and his next victim was none other than the young man Weightman. Branwell Brontë alone, of all those light-hearted churchgoers, was present to hear his father preach the funeral sermon. Branwell Brontë alone, wild-eyed and broken hearted, after a long attendance on Weightman's death bed! A nervous prostration must have held the youth as Papa elaborated the great White Throne. He was just back from Luddenden Foot in disgrace. How could he stand up to those piteous memories of his childhood inseparable from Patrick's painstaking discourse?

The sermon which the Rev. Patrick Brontë preached for William Weightman is saturated with the words and phrases of the old background. It must have been pregnant with memories of Maria. Branwell, in the pew, knew well that never for him could there now be the hope of a pious death bed, but how his soul hungered for one crumb of hope. Everyone who loved and understood him seemed to have gone and now he was shuddering before a glimpse of outer darkness. His father's voice went on relentlessly, making the points which his son knew so well. Why was life so difficult? It seemed blent with a riot of feeling, too strong for a weak will to control, and yet always witch-ridden by conscience and dogged by Satan with his Tongs of Hell.

Patrick Brontë's funeral sermon is good as funeral sermons go. It suited the ageing man to feel for once immortal with that stripling cherub of but twenty-five years of age already in his coffin at his feet. Also the Methodist is abundantly at home with death. It was wont to give the preacher his opportunity of launching, in a receptive atmosphere, a thundering exhortation. It provided a more hopeful conquest of sinners and a gratuitous comfort for the saints. The Methodist preacher liked to bring his congregation to the edge of eternity and to pin it down before the Judgment Throne. Here in Patrick's sermon he is to the manner born with the mingling of terror and pathos and with that note of appeal in his voice: "Yea, we must come after all our windings and subterfuges and seek out the strait gate and narrow way which is Christ, the Truth and the Life." There was absolutely no other way of escape. We must all die and after that the judgment when the wicked shall be turned into Hell. Heaven, as Patrick Brontë is at pains to point out, is peopled only by the redeemed. His sermon is built up round the idea that the sting of death is sin, but to the saint death is swallowed up in victory—thanks be to God.

It is not seemly in a funeral sermon to praise the departed one. With quiet dignity Patrick Brontë speaks a tempered eulogy of his young friend who even now had washed his earth-stained robes and made them white in the blood of the Lamb. Gently the older man acknowledges the charm of the younger, with his insistence on the love of God rather than the terror of the law. William Weightman had divided the word of truth aright but with the weight of the argument resting upon love. As Patrick said of him "He thought it better and more scriptural to make the love of God rather than the fear of Hell the ruling motive of obedience." This young man was one of the right sort and Arminian to the core for "His sermons, with the key of scripture, opened through Christ the door of salvation to all."

Branwell Brontë, in the pew, knew every twist and turn of that argument. He had thought about it so much that his tired mind sagged hopelessly under its weight of theology. Far too worn out to care either way, believing himself already numbered amongst "the fallen", he perhaps might dimly have wondered if after all it was all his own fault. His father was talking now about Weightman's home and the chance his parents had given him in sending him to school and to college, believing that "education was his best fortune". It must have seemed strange that Patrick had that piece of knowledge up his sleeve and yet had never lifted a finger to bestow that sort of fortune on his only son. But it is the prerogative of preachers to reck not their own reed. At the heart of

Branwell there was just a suspicion of bitterness—a realisation that somehow life at home had frustrated him, a knowledge as he says that "from the day of my birth I have lived among secluded hills where I could neither know what I was nor what I could do." But let that pass. His father is praising his friend now and Branwell is always generous. Tears cannot be far away then as the preacher draws the portrait of Weightman whose first introduction was "prepossessing", whose "character wore well", who was "constitutionally cheerful". Patrick would have all know that he and his winsome curate were as father and son for they were working "in the same glorious cause and under the superintendence of the same Master". Not that the young man was faultless. Patrick would never hold such "anti-scriptural views of human nature" as that, for all have sinned and come short of the glory of God.

And how did he die? Did he pass that crucial test with flying colours? The Rev. Patrick Brontë visited him twice a day and can report that his end was peace. He closed his eyes in tranquillity in entire dependence on the merits of his Saviour. And now the preacher is on ground he has known all his life. Now he is coming into the straight and has steered his discourse where he wanted it to end, on the discussion of the pious death-bed. This young man had died as the saints should. Anyone taught of Wesley knew there must be no fear at the last and Patrick Brontë concludes his funeral oration absolutely true to the standards of the Irish Cabin. He says: "That the followers of Christ should tremble at the last step of their journey which will introduce them into His Presence and His glory can only be accounted for by the weakness of their faith and the remains of sin that would chain them down or keep them back from those unspeakable pleasures which He has reserved for them in the Kingdom of their Heavenly Father."

That old church at Haworth had gathered to itself all sides of the Evangelical Revival of Religion. Here in this pulpit had thundered Grimshaw and Whitefield. Here Wesley had preached with his sweet reasonableness. Here Selina Countess of Huntingdon and kin to all the Shirleys had worshipped. Here Grace Murray had come to prayers with John Wesley at the close of a long summer day. The old place was packed with ghosts. Here people had fallen dead at words of doom. Here souls had been born for eternity. Here men had shouted songs of praise. Here the redeemed had walked. Patrick Brontë was developing all young Weightman's virtues from the same old high pulpit where Wesley had often stood. What did it mean to his son in the pew? The boy had called Weightman his "dearest friend". He had had a fortnight's attendance on his death-bed. His mind was full of Maria mouldering there, in frightful disarray, below the church flagstones for all her child's conquest over death. The young man's heart is almost broken because, for all his new-found scientific outlook on life, culled from railway engineers of Unitarian tendencies, Branwell Brontë would so like to believe the old things true if only he could. It was when you came to this King of Terrors that the rub came. There seemed no way at all to tackle him but Maria's and Weightman's way, than Wesley's way and Grimshaw's—but then they were saints and believed, whereas Branwell knew himself to be a sinner and a castaway. Just then he was feeling so appallingly tired that, in true old Methodist phraseology, in his poems, he confesses that he can neither bear nor avert the Eye of God.

For this young man with his strange background of memories there should be nothing but pity. How could the old heritage fit on young shoulders? How could Papa know everything? Why, he knew nothing of the modern thought of freedom and rebellion which was going about in those hungry forties in England. How could he still continue to make infallible pronouncements with his moth-eaten authority? His mind and his old friend Morgan's only worked clearly now in the past, telling those interminable tales when Thomas Walsh was a reality and Fletcher fell on death. Branwell had always had a sneaking respect for the one villain of that ancient history, the swashbuckling Hastings of the House of Shirley. He must also have had a secret sympathy with that son of Grimshaw's who drank himself to death in spite of all the glories of Heaven and the admonition of the saints. In the guise of the young man Azrael at Methuselah's grave Branwell Brontë would take up the cudgels, silently in the pew, against Papa and all the old brigade.

> "Old man!—a truce to dotard dreams,
> And turn from Heaven thy hazy eyes—
> A thought for Earth far more beseems
> Than childish gazing at the skies.
> 'Tis earth not Heaven shall shortly rise;
> 'Tis man—not God shall soon avenge;
> And if there be a paradise
> We'll bring it in the coming change!"

Those old controls of the Will of God are off and Branwell's critical young mind is putting the whole of Wesley's faith into the pillory.

> "Away with all such phantasies!
> Just trust your reason and your eyes!
> Believe that God exists when I
> Who here—this hour—His name deny
> Shall bear a harder punishment
> Than those whose knees to Him have bent.
> Believe that He can rule above
> When you shall see Him rule below;
> Believe that He's the God of love
> When He shall end His children's woe."

But the Rev. Patrick Brontë was treading his well-worn path through Weightman's funeral sermon with a pitiless reiteration on all the old realities of a loving God and a heavenly home. How would he have faltered could he have read the unseen commentary then going forward, line by line, in his son's bespectacled head in its decorous pew! It was a commentary, but not that of his old standby and favourite Adam Clarke—that other Irishman that Wesley had brought to fame. Branwell's was rather a critical survey of man's mind awaking in a new scientific world. He reasons shrewdly that our hopes of heaven are really earth inspired, for our pride forbids us to consider that pile of meagre dust at the end of the journey as the end of all things. Human life is in revolt against death and hates the thought that "It ever stands on nothing's brink". In self defence it must manufacture life immortal and a future happy hunting ground for all disembodied spirits. What would the saintly Fletcher have made of Branwell's running commentary?

> "So—when the sick man lies to die
> He gasps for Hope in Agony;
> And as the Earth yields none to save
> He makes a hope beyond the grave!
> Thus Heaven is but an earthly dream:
> 'Tis Man makes God—not God makes him!"

But it was sealed from Papa's eyes that October day in the year of grace 1842. The preacher is on familiar and heart-cheering ground. The pious death-bed is all his own. So sweetly homely it is that Wesley's own words come almost of themselves to Patrick Brontë's tongue. He is just now pronouncing the fact that William Weightman was in his life what Wesley said every Methodist should be—the friend of all, the enemy of none.

CHAPTER XV

AUNT'S DEATH

THE EPIC of Haworth Parsonage would be attenuated and fleeting without the presence of the monster Death. He had a way of striking down his victims unexpectedly, as though he were envious of them and experienced downright pleasure in keeping the lych gate on the latch. The death of Mrs. Brontë had sobered her gay saucy Patrick and Maria's translation had profoundly influenced her nurslings, yet now, once again, death was to take a hand in their family fortunes. William Weightman was scarcely cold before Miss Branwell developed the same symptoms and died. Branwell Brontë attended on both death-beds and of Miss Branwell's he says that he had "been waking two nights, witnessing such agonising suffering as I would not wish my worst enemy to endure, and I have now lost the guide and director of all the happy days connected with my childhood."

Charlotte and Emily were away in Brussels and Anne, at Thorp Green, seems only to have got home after her aunt's death. The boy confesses, in a letter to his friend, that he has much on his mind as head nurse in the sick room as "my sisters are far from home." His heart was wrung with pity for the dying woman and he realised this to be one of those experiences of life which tear at its very roots for he knew her to have been: "for twenty years as my mother." She had been very kind to him always, for she was ever ready to save him from the consequences of his own shortcomings. She was, in fact, the linchpin of his parsonage existence. She represented authority in that house and she was on his side. Now she was gone and, in passing, had removed her ready purse quite beyond his reach. Miss Branwell left the whole of her small fortune to her nieces and nothing but a suitcase to her beloved nephew. That was a blow, for it placed Branwell, for the first time in his life, at a disadvantage with his sisters. From that moment they began to assume a shy independence, from the eminence of Aunt's legacy, whilst Branwell, the darling of the Gods, found himself without a penny in his manly pocket. Although Charlotte writes to Ellen Nussey: "Do not fear to find us melancholy or depressed. We are all much as usual. You will see no difference from our former demeanour", the fact remained that Miss

Branwell's death materially affected the whole Brontë saga. Everything begins to happen from that date in the family history which befell at the end of 1842.

The Brontë girls had always stood in awe of Aunt Branwell. Even her favourite Anne would make haste to lift her feet from the fender when Aunt swept into the room unexpectedly and asked: "Where are your feet, Anne?" "On the floor," writes the observant Emily, enjoying the comically swift movement of instinctive obedience. Charlotte too always felt that Aunt was a presence to be reckoned with. She might get round Papa but Aunt was stubborn. She had a way of upsetting all her darling plans. She more than once frustrated her dreams of a holiday alone with Ellen Nussey. She was a stickler for the proprieties and always kept duty well before the eyes of the girls of Haworth Parsonage. But with Aunt on your side dreams might come true, for she was the real power behind the throne. There is one letter which Charlotte wrote to Miss Branwell which shows the aunt and the niece in their true colours at the close of their long and uneasy acquaintance. Aunt was the grand arbiter of the Brussels adventure and Charlotte knew that she must herself be deeply cunning if she was to work that oracle. She must use all Aunt's pet arguments and she must say all the right things. Charlotte was desperately anxious to go to Brussels, for she had mystic sensations at the very prospect of such an adventure but Aunt threatened to be more in her way than God Himself, so Charlotte played her on the end of her fine line of appeal, thus: "I feel certain, while I am writing, that you will see the propriety of what I say; you always like to use your money to the best advantage; you are not fond of making shabby purchases; when you do confer a favour, it is often done in style; and depend upon it £50 or £100 thus laid out would be well employed. Of course I know no other friend in the world to whom I could apply on this subject except yourself. I feel an absolute conviction that if this advantage were allowed us, it would be the making of us for life—I want us *all* to get on. I know we have talents, and I want them to be turned to account. I look to you Aunt to help us. I think you will not refuse. I know, if you consent, it shall not be my fault if you ever repent your kindness."

Charlotte carried her point and worked a further miracle in contriving Aunt's assistance to dislodge Emily once more from Haworth. There must have been something like iron will and authority about Aunt Branwell for her to be able to get her second niece transplanted across the Channel into Romanist soil. Well Charlotte knew that it was only Aunt who could do that. "I fixed on Emily" she says. Then she threw herself on the only possible leverage and continues: "In extreme excitement I wrote a letter home which carried the day. I made an appeal to my Aunt for assistance which was answered by consent." The removal of such a personage from Haworth Parsonage was bound to have far-reaching consequences. The next time Charlotte wanted to go to Brussels she would not have to ask Aunt's permission and she had the old lady's money now in her own pocket to pay her passage there. She might piously exclaim "Aunt, Martha Taylor and Mr. Weightman are now all gone; how dreary and void everything seems", but she really did not mean it for, in that first Brussels sojourn, she had discovered the secret of life. Brussels now meant M. Héger and that tingling vital emotion which men call love. In after years Charlotte shuddered to remember the intensity of that passion which had moved her so powerfully to recross the sea, even clamouring on the shore for a boat to take her out to the ship in the darkness of night. She says "I returned to Brussels after Aunt's death, against my conscience, prompted by what then seemed an irresistible impulse. I was punished for my selfish folly by a withdrawal for more than two years of happiness and peace of mind."

If Aunt's death made possible for Charlotte that fruitful experience of crucified love, it was no less significant for her sister Emily. It meant that, in Charlotte's absence, Emily Brontë stepped straight into Aunt's place in Haworth Parsonage. With the faithful Tabby and the brisk Martha behind her, she shouldered the burden of domestic responsibility. She baked, she ironed, she sewed and pursued the whole blissful routine of her departed aunt. She made out a regularity table for herself and rejoiced that she was not now as idle as formerly. That year of purposeful domestic activity, of kindly kitchen companionship and of Papa's ancient solemnities of the parlour was invaluable for Emily Brontë. It fixed the mould in which her strange angular character was set. She became the one to be reckoned with, for, in every household, the Martha of the family crystallises for herself a centre of strength. She receives the freedom of the city of home and so did Emily Brontë, for she became just that capable, silent, quickly working and invaluable member of her circumscribed community.

In a disciplined energetic silence Emily thought out a philosophy

CONSTANTINE HÉGER

of life. It owed much to her father's old background and yet was all her own. She did not see, if Papa's heroes could live such peculiar yet thrilling lives, why she could not do so, too. His conversation was all of immortal saints who were acquainted with the life of God in the soul. He was never tired of saying with Charles Wesley that this "weary world" should be cast behind. What if Emily did not talk, but discovered for herself the breath-taking reality of it all? Life would become strangely exciting. It would appear that it was everlasting also. Death, the monster Death, was only an incident for you could walk through it. You found no inch of room for it if you were brought up on Thomas Walsh and the saintly Fletchers.

Ellen Nussey said it was Emily who was most influenced by her father's old tales and now she received the full impact of them. There was no one else to listen, for Anne had shouldered the responsibility of Branwell and had obtained a post for him at Thorp Green. Charlotte was sitting at the feet of M. Héger and Emily was for once her very own mistress. Her hands were but employed in earthly matters whilst her strong mind wrestled with the saints of God. She justified the ways of God to man as she turned the heel of a sock. She refuted Calvin and all his works over the making of her own delicious home-made bread. It was no wonder that Charlotte, weighed down with her dearly bought Brussels education, should say that Emily was stronger than a man and simpler than a child. She had herself outgrown Papa's enthusiasms and now, perhaps, she had even stopped dreaming of Maria, since M. Héger had her heart. She had grown a little ashamed, of late, of "Mad Methodist Magazines", for Heaven and Hell were becoming more decently veiled for Charlotte Brontë, whilst Emily was still straying on their confines in a sort of ecstasy. The old heroic traces of her father's upbringing were still good enough for her. This is how Emily herself describes her experience after that year at Haworth alone with Patrick Brontë:—

> "So stood I in Heaven's glorious sun
> And in the glare of Hell.
> My spirit drank a mingled tone
> Of seraph's song and demon's moan—
> What my soul bore, my soul alone
> Within itself may tell."

The death of Aunt Branwell gave Emily Brontë her freedom.

K

Charlotte, in thinking of her sister, long afterwards, knew that she could then be rebuked no more for turning back towards this strange life of the soul which was her inheritance. It has been shown that it is Charlotte's poem about Emily which gives that picture of her sister as "Often rebuked but always backward turning to those first feelings that were born in me." Aunt had insisted on practical Methodism and regularity tables and common sense. Emily would do all that but now, more and more, she would come to realise the fact of her own pilgrim soul. All was now emphatically right with Emily Brontë, for she was mistress of her own house and at home in its ancient background. Its inheritance had become one with her very being for she was even now living as the saints lived, easily, without the strain of imitation. Papa might copy Wesley's hymns to eke out his own poor verses but Emily knew what they meant in actual fact. When Wesley wrote:

> "The invisible appears in sight
> And God is seen by mortal eye"

Emily Brontë followed fast on his heels, not in his words, but in the strength of their meaning. With her they became:

> "Then dawns the invisible
> The unseen its truth reveals,
> My outward sense is dumb
> My inward essence feels."

The old ceaseless talk of mansions in the sky and poor little Maria's naive way of taking a literal Heaven by storm became with Emily a mystical longing for a sight of God here and now. Charles Wesley had said:

> "I cannot see Thy face and live,
> Then let me see Thy face and die"

and Emily Brontë handles the same ecstatic dilemma when, in stretching out after the unseen, she is jerked back to earth by the chain of the flesh. It is as one gasping out her life when she writes:

> "Oh dreadful is the check—intense the agony
> When the ear begins to hear and the eye begins to see,
> When the pulse begins to throb, the brain to think again,
> The soul to feel the flesh and the flesh to feel the chain."

Listen again to the nursery rhymes of this girl's strange upbringing when her father's heroes were wont to sing:

> "Our heart strings groan with deep complaint,
> Our flesh lies panting Lord for Thee,
> And every limb and every joint
> Stretches for immortality."

The death of Miss Branwell seems to have launched every one of her children on a quest for love. Each went about the discovery in his or her own way. Emily for God only. Anne for God in Weightman. There is no more significant contrast than the difference between the religious experience of these two girls. Anne's soul stretches for immortality as does Emily's, but Anne demands a recognised human form as her advocate with God. Enter her innocent little closet and when you have shut the door, listen, in her poems, to her secret prayer. She lies on an alien bed, far away at Thorp Green and Weightman lies buried under the cold flagstones of Haworth Church, but breathless now with adoration, she expects an angel guest. Listen:

> "For ever gone, for I, by night
> Have prayed, within my silent room,
> That Heaven would grant a burst of light
> Its cheerless darkness to illume.
>
> And give thee to my longing eyes
> A moment, as thou shinest now,
> Fresh from thy mansion in the skies,
> With all its glory on thy brow.
>
> Wild was the wish, intense the gaze
> I fixed upon the murky air,
> Expecting, half, a kindling blaze
> Would strike my raptured vision there—
>
> A shape these human nerves would thrill,
> A majesty that might appal,
> Did not thy earthly likeness still
> Gleam softly, gladly through it all."

Was it heart-break? No, rather a sort of religious ecstasy that linked this weary world with those same mansions in the sky which appear to be quite inescapable in all Brontë literature.

Maria had made them real for Branwell and now Anne possessed them through the apotheosis of William Weightman. Strangely enough she could enjoy him so much better in Heaven that ever she could upon earth. Before, she had had to share him with one Alice Walton and with Ellen Nussey and even with Haworth Parsonage. Now he belonged to no one else besides God and Anne Brontë. No more jokes now from Charlotte about his fickleness and unclerical behaviour. There was nothing now to jar on sensitive nerves. Weightman had gone into a world of light and Anne was content, for she loved him better as a pilgrim of eternity. In fact, through him and fortified by his ghostly presence, she had solved the two great problems of life—love and religion. Now she was free to dream of him and write poems to his memory. Now she could keep company with him and yet observe the strictest of propriety as she wrote about him in her innocent little tales of the life of a governess. Now, midst the garish surroundings of those flamboyant Robinsons of Thorp Green, she could look forward to a heavenly reunion with William Weightman. Now she was loved with an everlasting love. God smiled behind the clouds of wrath, for she would hold to Weightman's form of religion through thick and thin and would even print her Arminian All in capital letters like Wesley and according to the pattern shown her from Weightman's pulpit. Strengthened by her immortal friendship with Weightman, Anne Brontë can shake a fist at those hateful Calvinists who appear to have been the bug-bear of the entire Brontë family with what Charlotte calls their "ghastly doctrines" of retrobation and election. Here is Anne's challenge in that first wistful spring after Weightman's death:—

> "And wherefore should your hearts more grateful prove
> Because for All the Saviour did not die?
> Is yours the God of justice and of love?
> And are your bosoms warm with charity?"

Her champion may have risen and gone from her side but he had triumphantly proved his doctrines of the love of God by the charm of his own gracious personality. There is no trace of heartbreak about this girl's serenade of her angel lover. She writes:—

> "Yet though I cannot see thee more,
> 'Tis still a comfort to have seen;
> And though thy transient life is o'er,
> 'Tis sweet to think that thou has been.

To think a soul so near divine,
Within a form so angel fair,
United to a heart like thine,
Has gladdened once our humble sphere."

This spiritual love was really the only kind that these children of Haworth Parsonage could understand or desire. The danger came when they met real living men and women and fixed on them this Methodistical love which in Mrs. Fletcher's case had been content to live on dreams for the whole of 25 years and in Anne Brontë's to worship at the shrine of William Weightman in Heaven. It was a pity that M. Héger had not also seen fit to transform his too masculine person into an angel of light. Instead he existed, just across the Channel, as the father of a large and growing family, and nearly caused the shipwreck of his poor young devotee. And, for Branwell at Thorp Green, the same fate befell him with that large and vivacious Mrs. Robinson who had the misfortune to be named Lydia and so, at the very start, approached the young man Branwell under false pretences. All his life he had known of Henry Martyn's martyred love for his Lydia and the very name had music in it, but there was danger too when a young man is down and out and has just lost one who for 20 years was as his mother.

All the elements of heartbreak and a very pretty comedy were here for Charlotte and for Branwell, for both M. Héger and Mrs. Robinson were at a loss to understand the quality of the heart worship which these two young Brontës unhesitatingly laid at their feet. Mrs. Robinson would have been surprised to know that her son's tutor was preparing to die of a broken heart for her and that he was writing tragic verses, all coloured by and bound up with the hopeless despair of Cowper's Castaway. These were the wild strains which he signed Northangerland and believed that if his Lydia saw them she must understand. The truth was that if she had known anything at all about it, she would only have been intensely amused. But the trouble with Mde. Héger was that she, like Queen Victoria, was not amused at all, and Charlotte was, in consequence, downright puzzled to know why she resented the passionate letters which her English governess wrote to her schoolmaster husband. Charlotte thought that Mde. Héger had not a nice mind, for she must have confused spiritual love with the murky smoke ascending from Tophet. Charlotte knew that the quality of her devotion to M. Héger was nearer akin to heavenly

love, and, in the last analysis, it was dictated, as was Emily's and
Anne's by the overmastering supremacy of the love of God. Here
is Charlotte's prayer in the midst of her tragedy:—

> "Now Heaven heal the wound which I still deeply feel;
> Thy glorious hosts look not in scorn on our poor race;
> The King Eternal doth no iron judgment deal
> On suffering worms who seek forgiveness, comfort, grace.
>
> He gave our hearts to love. He will not love despise,
> Even if the gift be lost as mine was long ago;
> He will forgive the fault, will bid the offender rise
> Wash out with dews of bliss the fiery brand of woe.
>
> And give a sheltered place beneath the unsullied Throne
> Where the soul redeemed may mark time's fleeting course
>   round earth,
> And know its trials over past, its sufferings gone,
> And feel the peril past of Death's immortal birth."

Charlotte and Branwell at the mature ages of 30 and 29 were
no more fit to tackle real life than was the child Maria. They had
been biased too early towards divine love and they believed that
when they lisped in childhood, with Charles Wesley:—

> "O Thou who camest from above
> The pure celestial fire to impart,
> Kindle a flame of sacred love
> On the mean altar of my heart."

they could experience the same thing, in kind, for a great school-
master or a charming motherly woman whom you chanced to meet
when you were very far away from home. When Charlotte speaks
of love she calls it quite naturally "Living fire, seraph brought
from a divine altar" and she had no idea that she was handling
high explosive. This trick of hers of Methodising love would in
the end make history, for it would introduce passion, for the first
time, into the English novel. But something went so wrong with
her brother's identical inheritance.

It was Branwell's fate only to achieve literary distinction in a
roundabout way, for it was his hard hap to fall amongst liars
who fooled him to the top of his bent. They wove about him and
his Lydia a more than Malvolio plot until the lad honestly believed
that Mrs. Robinson was only waiting for her husband's death to

throw herself and her fortune in Branwell's loving arms. In his case the plotters of Twelfth Night were represented by the coachman and the lady's maid of Thorp Green. They must have beguiled many a dull hour by bringing Branwell every tit-bit of gossip about their master and mistress along with the invention of Mrs. Robinson's affection for her shock-headed little tutor whose eye was ever above his station. There was every opportunity for this "below stairs" gossip as Branwell lived out at a nearby farm and could thrive on dreams to his heart's content, at a safe distance from reality.

At Luddenden Foot Branwell had still been able to hear Maria's voice from Heaven, but now it was silenced by that thumping in his ears of his own passionate heart. He would come to confuse Maria and Lydia in his boiling brain, for like Malvolio he also was sick of self-love. He was demanding attention in an unkind world and it was good now to believe that, if the heavenly mansions had failed, those of the mammon of unrighteousness were preparing to take him in to their everlasting habitations. Branwell could then have snapped his fingers at Aunt's legacy, if Lydia Robinson did all that the plotters told him she was eager to do for him. This boy has always been a pitiable little figure, but he is nowhere more pitiable than in this season at Thorp Green when he struts and preens his ruffled feathers in the supposed sunshine of his Lydia's smiles. He had always thrilled to Tabby's kitchen tales of great houses, but now it was vastly more exciting to hear such stories in which he himself sustained the title role. Gossip is the poor man's library for it is akin to romance and it went to Branwell's head like wine. He reacted to the plotters' tales with such alarming enthusiasm that what had been begun as a joke soon threatened to ruin them all.

Charlotte, at the feet of M. Héger, was saved because she had no one to whom to talk, but she would still have languished on in Brussels had not Mary Taylor ordered her to fly for her life and her reason. In after years Charlotte sent her friend the whole of £10 as a thank offering for the service which she had then rendered, but she still had to face "the withdrawal for more than 2 years of happiness and peace of mind." The letters which she wrote to M. Héger during that time would make angels weep. They show an intensity of feeling, as she waits for an answering sign from Brussels, which equals anything Mary Bosanquet knew as she watched for the postman in Birstall Parish that June before the Lord turned the captivity of Zion. The fact that she had put the sea between herself and her idol did not ease the intolerable burden at all, for now M. Héger assumed, in absence, almost angelic proportions like unto Anne's William Weightman in Heaven.

In that lonely bedroom at Haworth Charlotte Brontë was pouring on to sheets of notepaper words of such intense beseeching that they amounted to the strength of a Methodist at prayer. But the only answer she got was an epistle which sounded like a school-master correcting his pupils' essays, in some fantastic correspondence course, and adding a note that the style of previous compositions must be toned down at all costs. Charlotte must write only at infrequent intervals and confine herself to her family's health as a subject for her raptures. Was it cruel or was it sane? At any rate it is certain that M. Héger was completely out of his pedagogic depths now that he had fathered such a pupil as Charlotte Brontë amongst the phlegmatic young ladies of his Brussels Academy. What could he do but tear up the letters in little pieces and throw them away? It was his wife who pieced them together again, for she was a careful soul and desired no scandal in her decorous school, and believed that proof of her husband's innocence should not be cast away so lightly. To do M. Héger justice he really never could decide if Charlotte's heart was fundamentally sick or merely wounded. Years afterwards his pen still hesitated between his fine French adjectives. In a letter to Ellen Nussey he wrote "blessé" twice but crossed out that milder impeachment to confirm his wife's more realistic view of the love-sick state of their late English governess.

CHAPTER XVI

THE CASTAWAY

IT WAS an evening in July and Charlotte Brontë was walking home from Keighley station. It was now the whole of eighteen months since she had torn herself away from Brussels, but still her mind was busy going over all the old ground, again and again, with eager iteration. She had been visiting Ellen Nussey at Hathersage and had enjoyed the change from Haworth and the interest of new surroundings. There had been a healthy bustle over getting the new vicarage ready for Ellen's brother Henry and his bride, but now Charlotte was facing that walk home, in the late evening, alone, and memory had been painfully jolted by a chance meeting in a railway carriage. As the train had toiled along from Derbyshire into Yorkshire, Charlotte had been talking French again. She had noticed a Frenchman in her carriage and had been so carried off her decorous feet that she had gone straight to the point with this remark: "Monsieur est Francais, n'est-ce pas?" The man was so startled that he replied in his own language, accent and all, and to Charlotte's ears it was like the sweetest music, for the stranger had reproduced the French-German intonation of M. Héger himself. It was a bitter sweet experience, and, as Charlotte walked home, she knew she must write once more to Brussels and tell her master of this encounter and how it had been as manna in the wilderness to the hungry of soul.

It was ten o'clock when Charlotte reached Haworth and the warm lamp-light of home embraced her with its gentle welcome. All the family was there and that perfect reunion used once to be so good to these Brontë children, but Charlotte had now to confess that Haworth was only a dull place to her. As she drew near the Parsonage, it threatened to choke her with a sense of utter frustration and it was so difficult to adjust herself to its sober régime with M. Héger's speech so lately in her ears. She had felt that she was going back to sorrow and a glance at Anne's face confirmed the truth of that nervous presentiment which had clung about her all day as she travelled homewards. Branwell was ill—that then was the news. Well, if that was all it might have been much worse, for he was often ill owing to his own incapacity of making his drink sit comfortably on his nervous stomach. No, said Anne, it was worse than that. Branwell had once more been dismissed in disgrace from his job. His employer, Mr. Robinson of Thorp Green, had written to him that week to say he need not return from his holiday and that he considered his conduct as very bad indeed.

It looks as though the lady's maid had told her mistress of Branwell's infatuation, in his absence, lest a difficult situation should develop for the Twelfth Night plotters on his return. A word in the ear of authority would be enough, for it was certain that the young tutor was out of his wits with his poetry making and his foolishly susceptible heart. Mr. Robinson had always detested him and did not believe any of his fine stories or any of his claims to authorship. His sister Anne had given in her notice to leave and had retired, amidst universal regret, so that there remained no reason why a decorous household should tolerate this tedious fellow longer, who, in any case, was far too familiar with the coachman and grooms of the establishment. Mrs. Robinson had only lost a school-boy admirer who had beguiled the somewhat arid waste of her middle-aged matrimony, and Mr. Robinson was rid of a fool, so what was the harm in that? Thorp Green went on much as usual, but it was the beginning of the end for Haworth Parsonage. To Branwell the incredible had happened. He had been torn from the idol of his heart without a moment's warning and he had lost his creature comforts at the same time. He had lived in luxury at Thorp Green, and here he was back again, for good, at that wretched Haworth, with a household of sedate spinsters who offered him toast water for his sorrows as though he had been one of their insufferable tame cats. Those sisters of his did not know the beginnings of feminine charm, and Tabby still treated him as a child, admonishing him always in Grimshaw terms about his desire of going to Hell with his eyes open. He turned in rebellion against them all and against their ancient hells and heavens. He raved like a lunatic and drank every penny of the money he could lay his hands on. For eleven nights he never slept and cried like a child in the darkness, loathing that staid figure of his father in the bed, and torn with agony at the sound of the wind shrieking round the chimneys of Haworth Parsonage.

In times of deep distress Branwell always went back to Maria. This was again like the nights of horror, after her death, when he had called aloud for her and no one had answered but her voice on the storm and that unearthly light behind his eyes of that terrible charnel house where they had crushed down his dearest love. Maria had called him again in the driving rain of Luddenden Foot station, but now her voice had become confused with the tones of his lost Lydia. A man's passion and a little brother's love were uneasy bed-fellows and it looked like the oversetting of reason when Branwell raved of Mrs. Robinson in terms of the child of the storm outside his bedroom window. Charlotte called it "frantic folly," Emily said he was without God and so without hope in the world—"a hopeless being." Anne blamed the shortcomings of human nature in general and of Mrs. Robinson in particular. His father hid his beloved pistols and gave his son money to drink away his sorrows. Did Tabby think there was nothing much out of the way in all this hubbub, if you remembered Grimshaw and his loves and his visions and had kept your eyes open to see how they looked in the chapel when they prayed about crucified love?

There is no stranger story in literature than this of Branwell Brontë posting down to the grave, to join his beloved, with all the abandon of strong drink and religious ecstasy. It was the child Maria who gave the obsession its own peculiar turn of style and conviction. There is no mistake about that if we compare Branwell's poem of Maria, as portrayed in his Caroline, with the last poems of his bewildered brain. He could sustain the similitude between the dead Maria and the dying Lydia the better because that fool of a coachman, coming from Thorp Green with Branwell's left luggage, had told him the outrageous lie that Mrs. Robinson was stricken down at his loss and was not likely to recover. In fact, it was her husband who died and so left her conveniently free to marry an old friend, almost at once, but how could Branwell guess that with his eyes all bemused by self-love?

Branwell writes of this time of agony: "I wildly raised my hands in prayer, that Death would come and take me now; then stopped to hear an answer given—so much had madness warped my mind—When sudden, through the midnight heaven, With long howl woke the winter's wind."

And ten years before he had written:—

"So sobbing as my heart would break
And blind with gushing eyes,
Hours seemed whole nights to me awake
And day as t'would not rise.
I almost prayed that I might die—
But then the thought would come

That if I did my corpse must lie
In yonder dismal tomb.
Until methought I saw its stone
By moonshine glistening clear
While Caroline's bright form alone
Kept silent watching here.
All white with angel's wings she seemed
And indistinct to see,
But when the unclouded moonlight beamed
I saw her beckon me,
And fade, thus beckoning, while the wind
Around that midnight wall,
To me, now lingering years behind—
Seemed then my sister's call."

Branwell makes Mrs. Robinson say, in his mature grief, the words
that Maria said when she beckoned him to heaven as a boy, thus:—

"The all-unnoticed time flew o'er me
While my breast bent above her bed,
And that drear life which loomed before me
Choked up my voice—bowed down my head.
Sweet holy words to me she said,
Of that bright heaven which shone so near,
And oft and fervently she prayed
That I might sometime meet her there."

Charlotte Brontë at least saw nothing pathetic in these grown up
raptures, for all the assurance of Lydia Robinson's "sweet holy
words." As she stood over this pitiable brother of hers, on that
night of her return to Haworth, she spoke scathingly of his emotions
and was blind to the similarity between her own sufferings and
those of Branwell, so lately torn from his idol. She was self-
righteously aware that she had never told her love, whilst here was
Branwell throwing the whole house into commotion with the
vociferation of his woes. But may be, the smell of drink stuck in'
her Puritan throat and scorched the pity from her heart. Once
these two had been everything to each other, but, from this moment,
Charlotte had nothing but scorn for this frail brother who could
carry neither his love nor his liquor like a man.

Anne, white faced and trembling, did better, for she dared to
hope that even Branwell might be saved. She felt the missionary

zeal rise in her breast and later she would write a tract-like novel to stress the new unpopular doctrine of total abstinence, but she never turned Branwell out of doors from the love of her own faithful heart. And Emily kept all these things and pondered them deeply. She had domesticated divine passion and had thus got her bearings for life and was better poised than any of the others to take an impartial view of the things of sense. She could take the gin drinking and the thousand creeds of men equally in her stride, but she knew that love was of God for all its strange manifestations. Yet, with her own firm stance she was puzzled to know how the lad of such fine promise could run his own barque onto the rocks, fumbling over the rudder and deaf to all warnings of disaster. A fragment of her writing has survived from this very July month of tragedy and it is refreshing in its vigour and its commonsense. Emily writes "We are all in decent health, only that Papa has a complaint in his eyes and with the exception of Branwell who I hope will be better and do better hereafter. I am quite content for myself, not as idle as formerly, altogether as hearty, seldom or ever troubled with nothing to do, and merely desiring that everybody could be as comfortable as myself, as undesponding, and then we should have a very tolerable world of it."

To most people Branwell's infatuation would have been a nine days' wonder, but Patrick Brontë seemed also to share his daughter Emily's preternatural calm. It is clear that he was surprised at nothing. Impregnably entrenched in the Will of God, it was all just one more divine dispensation in his pilgrimage through this world. He sat "with the complaint in his eyes" shutting him in with his long, long thoughts, and the old pictures of Irish Cabin and Mourne Mountains were surely more vivid than ever behind those dulling eyes. Did not all his world know of the tribulation that that saint of saints, Thomas Walsh, had gone through over a married woman? And did he not contend that there was no sin in that as the whole experience was purged in the fire of sacrifice? Charles Wesley even had not been able to convince him to the contrary opinion, in spite of walking him up and down for hours in the cold wind on Bristol's quayside, with the lover at his side dying of consumption. Thomas Walsh had won through, in the end, in more than Methodistical triumph, and Patrick Brontë was content to leave Branwell in God's hands and know that no soul was lost as long as the mercy of God held good and that would be until death's judgment divided sheep and goats.

How much of the responsibility for Branwell's tragedy can be laid at the study door of the Rev. Patrick Brontë is a matter of opinion. There had clearly been too much of this go-as-you-please régime with this boy of splendid dreams. The will of God might be strength to the father where it would prove but numbing despair to the son. It seems to have been in that light that he regarded the immutability of his fate when he was presently sent off on a holiday, with his father's sexton, to see what change of scene would do for a broken heart. Through eyes blinded with tears he saw himself as a spiritual castaway and imagined a real corpse floating hither and thither on the waters with whom he longed to change places, for though it was "launched in voyage for eternity" it was quite past thinking "upon what is to be." That was always the dread thought that fetched the spiritual castaway up sharply in the end—Death and after that the Judgment. In his present broken state he was quite unable to swagger under his load of apostasy. Having turned his back upon The Rock of Ages he beseeches the bleak outline of Penmaenmawr to make his heart as stone-like as itself, amidst the storm.

Branwell's distress was no whit less real because it was occasioned by unreality. If he could have made his way back to Thorp Green reality might have shocked him into sanity. He would have seen his Lydia busy about all her own concerns and just then in high good spirits because she had arranged an admirable match for one of her lovely daughters. He would have recognised that his "angel's gentle breast," of which he writes, really belonged to a matron of 45, who, because of her healthy benevolence and good temper, was a woman who loved comfort and would avoid every dangerous corner of acute feeling. The whole household there enjoyed a more than lotus eating existence. Anne always complained that nobody there wanted hard lessons, but that the Misses Robinson must be made to glide along the road of learning, like smiling images, pushed from behind. Meals in that delightful house came at just any time, and, if the children liked, they could get through all "the plaguey business" of their schooling before breakfast and have all the rest of the day free for their own enjoyment.

It was really this indulgent motherliness of Mrs. Robinson which had been Branwell's undoing, for she was as ready to listen to his jingles and his stories as she was to understand the points of her daughters' beloved pony. She never contradicted him when he told her of all the fine people who thought well of his poetry, and, when her husband lost his temper and talked of swelled heads, she soothed Branwell down just in the same way as she treated her other spoiled children. This sense of ease, of comfort, of kindliness quite unstrung him and he retaliated with clamant love. It might all be a little hysterical and Brontësque but that was not Mrs. Robinson's fault. She was a shrewd woman and had made one good match for herself and would make another when the time came, but her knowledge was of this world and not of the kind to understand the background of Branwell Brontë. She would soon be moving, with her second husband, in circles of fashionable benevolence, and it seems preposterous that Branwell could have believed her coachman's cock and bull story of a will having been made which forbade her remarriage on pain of losing her first husband's fortune.

It is incredible that anyone could have believed such a tale, yet Haworth Parsonage accepted it in its entirety. It also accepted the responsibility of Branwell and his shattered wreck of manhood for the whole of three long years. Its ancient peace was bundled out of doors for ever and Branwell abandoned himself to despair. He gave up all thought of further work and never stopped drinking. He never went to church and railed upon his father's gods, whilst he slouched round his parish like a wreck of his former self, with a distraught and dishevelled look about him as though his clothes no longer fitted upon his scarecrow figure. Thus wrapped about in his own inept misery, he lost all track of family affairs and knew nothing of the way that things were developing in his sisters' sitting-room after 9 o'clock at night.

CHAPTER XVII

CURRER, ELLIS AND ACTON BELL

THERE IS a self righteousness about Charlotte Brontë which is sometimes hard to bear. She writes: "My unhappy brother never knew what his sisters had done in literature—he was not aware that they had ever published a line. We could not tell him of our efforts for fear of causing him too deep a pang of remorse for his own time misspent and talents misapplied." It would seem a hundred pities that she was so tender of his feelings and did not remember how near she herself had come to the very precipice of Branwell's destruction. She was still writing impassioned letters to M. Héger right into the November of her brother's year of tragedy, and the tone of her last one speaks of the unabated agony of her mind in separation. The words must have scorched parsonic paper as she wrote: "To forbid me to write to you, to refuse to answer me, would be to tear from me my only joy on earth, to deprive me of my last privilege—a privilege I never shall consent willingly to surrender. Believe me, my master, in writing to me it is a good deed that you will do. So long as I believe you are pleased with me, so long as I have hope of receiving news from you, I can be at rest and not too sad! But when a prolonged and gloomy silence seems to threaten me with the estrangement of my master— when day by day I await a letter, and when day by day disappointment comes to fling me back into overwhelming sorrow, and the sweet delight of seeing your handwriting and reading your counsel escapes me as a vision that is vain, then fever claims me— I lose appetite and sleep—I pine away." And then, still struggling with the French idiom, of which she feels she is fast losing grip, she hurls herself headlong into English, in this postscript: "I must say one word to you in English—I wish I could write to you more cheerful letters for when I read this over, I find it to be somewhat gloomy—but forgive me my dear master—do not be irritated at my sadness—according to the words of the Bible "Out of the fulness of the heart the mouth speaketh" and truly I find it difficult to be cheerful so long as I think I shall never see you more. You will perceive by the defects in this letter that I am forgetting the French language—yet I read all the French books I can get and learn daily portions by heart—but I have never heard French

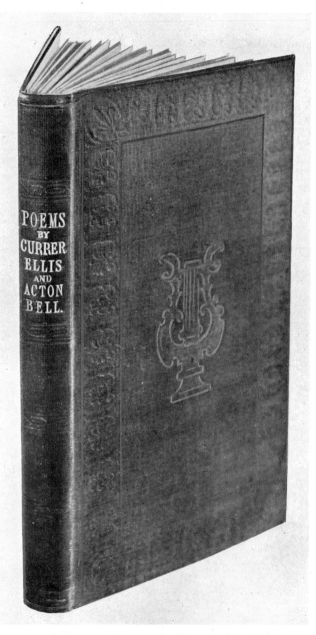

"I only stipulate
for *clear* type—
not too small—
and good paper"
C. Brontë

FIRST EDITION OF THE "POEMS," 1846

In the possession of Brotherton Library, Leeds

spoken but once since I left Brussels—and then it sounded like music in my ears—every word was most precious to me because it reminded me of you—I love French for your sake with all my heart and soul. Farewell my dear master—may God protect you with special care and crown you with peculiar blessings."

It would be interesting to know what M. Héger made of that adjective "peculiar," used like that with the word "blessings." It would take all his English dictionaries that day to find out what ever it meant and then he would be left guessing. It was in reality a positive shibboleth from that Parsonage past against which Charlotte Brontë is thrown up, in such strange relief, as she steps out of it into the outside world. It was an echo of her father's speech, heard how many times at family prayers, and used here, in a gush of religious emotion, winged to light on the un-suspecting head of that correct Romanist, Charlotte's dear master, across the Channel. For all her hard won education, in a wider world, her speech throughout has a way of betraying her. Patrick Brontë insists on speaking and preaching amongst his daughter's words, with the strangest results for the cultured flow of English literature.

It seems likely that there would have been no lasting memorial of Patrick Brontë's past, nor record, for the world to read, of this wild turmoil of mind and heart in Haworth Parsonage, had not Charlotte one day lighted upon a penny exercise book full of Emily's manuscript poems. The discovery checked the current of her fever and turned it into another channel. It just prevented her from being swept over Branwell's Niagara into the eddying whirlpool of his despair, for it saved her from becoming, what she told M. Héger she was fast developing into, "the slave of a regret, of a memory, the slave of a fixed and dominant idea which lords it over the mind."

The world would never have heard of Haworth Parsonage had not Charlotte Brontë been arrested on the brink of despair, for M. Héger thought so little of her rhapsodies that he scribbled a note on this, her last tragic letter, to remind him to call for his boots at the family boot maker. So shod, he could trample at his ease on the broken heart of a mad governess. But had he only known it, for all his master-teaching, the world would also never have heard of him, had it not been for this deluded little letter-writer whose missives were only useful for dotting down domestic chores, or to save a match when lighting his fragrant cigar.

The peculiar blessings of Charlotte's prayer took the law into their own hands and descended on Brontë heads rather than on those of the House of Héger, in that well known boomerang working of a whimsical Providence.

The story is well known. Charlotte had no business at all to read Emily's poems and very well she knew it. She says herself that she did it "alone and in secret" and that it was only the realisation of their unexpected power that forced from her the confession of her eavesdropping, for that was in the light that Emily viewed her sister's meddling theft of the secrets of her heart. She was very angry and the scene in the Parsonage that day must have resembled Vesuvius in eruption. Charlotte with great temerity stood her ground, but it took hours to reconcile her outraged sister. It took days to persuade her that the verses were worth publication, for Emily developed a fine scorn of them now that they were just anyone's property. Finally, she threw them in the face of the public with a sardonic rattle of contempt, calling them nothing more than "rhymes" and implying that they might be called nursery rhymes into the bargain. And so perhaps they were, but according to the pattern shown to her little family by Maria as she posted determinedly towards her heavenly home. They might take the world by surprise but to Emily Brontë and to her father the more fool the world. There was nothing but well worn fustian about a desire to get through this world with as few entanglements as possible and to keep your soul free and "chainless," at all costs, for the joy of everlasting life.

Emily Brontë had but paraphrased the spirit of her father's old pilgrims when they sang:—

> "On all the Kings of earth
> With pity we look down,
> And claim in virtue of our birth
> A never fading crown."

When she wrote:—

> "Riches I hold in light esteem
> And love I laugh to scorn
> And lust of fame was but a dream
> That vanished with the morn.

Yes, as my swift days near their goal
'Tis all that I implore
In life and death a chainless soul,
With courage to endure."

That was really Maria grown-up. It was in fact Maria's very own hymn which Charlotte would put later, in prose, into the mouth of her Helen Burns. But the point was that Charlotte never knew that Emily, amidst her pots and pans, had come by the spirit of Maria and tempered it with steel. She had in fact hammered it into poetry.

That famous phrase of "courage to endure" was nothing but Maria's temerity in lisping with Charles Wesley:—

Bold I approach the Eternal Throne,
And claim the crown through Christ my own."

There is courage demanded for immortality and well Emily Brontë knew it. Later generations, with Heaven swept completely from their vocabularies, have toned down Emily's meaning into a stoical endurance of the evils of this world, when she was only concerned with the chances of the soul enduring into the next. Charlotte herself must not escape blame in this for she named this poem of her sister's "The Old Stoic," but then she knew well enough that no one outside could possibly understand Emily. She always needed an interpreter, Charlotte said, to stand between her and the world. There is no soulless stoicism about Emily Brontë, for the glad confidence of the pilgrim of eternity runs through all her work, and as Charlotte said, on first reading that precious little notebook, it was as though a clarion trumpet sounded in her ears.

There are other characteristics about Emily's poems which have misled the unwary. She had the power of absorbing other people's experiences and of seeing the significance of them. She lived like a nun in a convent, but, as Charlotte again says, in her role of interpreter: "She knew their ways, their language, their family histories; she could hear of them with interest and talk of them with detail, minute, graphic and accurate." So it comes about that Emily gets nearer to Branwell's love for his sister Maria than anyone else could have done. Her poem on this theme, called Remembrance, is a gem of interpretation, and yet the world has twisted its "wild Decembers" just every way to find out some nefarious secret in Emily's own life. It is really as clear as crystal and the fifteen years take the reader back quite surely to that time of Maria's death. Branwell might be saying the whole thing, for it was even what he had said, how many times at home, when wild December melted once again into the tender spring of Maria's translation. Emily loved the constancy of the boy and her heart was full of divine pity for him as she wrote of Maria, dead in her grave, and of young Branwell still mourning for her, after all those long years of separation.

> "Cold in the earth—and fifteen wild Decembers
> From those brown hills, have melted into Spring.
> Faithful indeed, is the spirit that remembers
> After such years of change and suffering!
>
> Sweet love of youth, forgive if I forget thee,
> While the world's tide is bearing me along,
> Other desires and other hopes beset me,
> Hopes which obscure but cannot do thee wrong.
>
> No later light has lightened up my heaven,
> No second morn has ever shone for me;
> All my life's bliss from thy dear life was given,
> All my life's bliss is in the grave with thee.
>
> But when the days of golden dreams have perished,
> And even despair was powerless to destroy;
> Then did I learn how existence could be cherished
> Strengthened and fed without the aid of joy.
>
> Then did I check the tears of useless passion—
> Weaned my young soul from yearning after thine,
> Sternly denied its burning wish to hasten
> Down to that tomb already more than mine.
>
> And even yet, I dare not let it languish,
> Dare not indulge in memory's rapturous pain,
> Once drinking deep of that divinest anguish,
> How could I seek the empty world again?"

As Charlotte turned the leaves of that little note-book the innocent beauty of those old home days must have settled on her poor fevered brain like balm of hurt minds. She seemed to arise whole again and to claim a new interest in life. That perilous fixed idea began to give up its tyranny and the ghost of M. Héger withdrew into a better perspective. The new pleasure of discovery filled the place of old regrets. Now, sleepless heads on pillows could begin arranging poems and filling out the scanty stock for publication, instead of going over and over again the barren wilderness of blighted love. Life began to have the same feel about it again as when the little authors sat round Tabby's kitchen table and dreamed of fame. It was a different partnership now, for Branwell was quite left out, but Anne came shyly in and wondered if Charlotte would like to see her poems as those of Emily had given her so much pleasure. They might not be so full of the rustle of angels' wings but Charlotte in her new found enthusiasm for the dear things of home believed that they had "a sweet, sincere pathos of their own." In fact, they had in them many an echo of home-like, familiar hymns, but whereas Charles Wesley sang "My God! I know, I feel Thee mine," Anne Brontë adopted the prayer of humble access, thus: "My God! If I may call Thee mine."

The three girls settled down to the new project with zest, and now the former melancholy evenings, when Papa wound the clock at nine and said "Now children don't stay up late," were transfigured with light from Parnassus. The girls held an inquest on all their poems, as they walked about the dining-room and the fire leaped in warm friendliness upon the walls amongst their moving shadows. Charlotte submitted 23 poems, Emily 22 and Anne 21, and they chose new names for themselves with which to face the world. Charlotte was Currer Bell; Emily, Ellis Bell; and Anne, Acton Bell. They did not like to be so untruthful as to choose men's names outright, but enjoyed this compromise and the thrill of harmless mystery. They had determined to pay for the publication of their verses out of Aunt Branwell's legacy and there was that sweet feeling of power about them as they launched their book upon the world, at their own expense. It cost them nearly £50 and, although they sold but two copies, the adventure was very well worth while. They had taken the plunge and got over that first intimidating hurdle of approaching publishers. They could try more easily the second time, and who knew if a novel or two might not be floated off the stocks by means of this newly discovered channel? Meanwhile they had forged a bond of union, a three fold cord, which one day might make the world wonder. Currer, Ellis and Acton Bell had come to stay.

The tragedy of Branwell Brontë is no more significantly displayed than in the omission of his name from that famous trio. Why did the girls not ask Northangerland to look up a few of his old poems to strengthen their slender volume? It might have cost more, but after all the girls had inherited Aunt's money and it would have made some little amends for his disappointment over that strange vagary of fortune. He could have brought them quite a respectable handful of poems for their inspection and they could have gathered a little sober nosegay from his writings which would have suited their upright minds and methodistic taste. Even among the poems of the Thorp Green period Branwell begins one, quite inevitably, thus:—

> "I saw a picture yesterday
> Of Him who died for me
> Which vainly struggled to display
> His mortal agony."

Branwell could have brought his poem of Maria and the radiant cross which he had called Caroline and remembered to the end of his life. It would not have been poetry like Emily's version but it was surely up to the standard of Charlotte's rhapsody over a missionary's farewell and her description of the dream of Pilate's wife. There was his poem on Nelson, almost a family ancestor as Duke of Brontë, which Miss Martineau and Leigh Hunt were reputed to have admired. It is according to the pattern of Haworth Parsonage and is Emily and her divine yearning for untrammelled immortality turned pedestrain and strongly tinctured with the Rev. Patrick Brontë himself. It ends in a prayer, thus:—

> "Give me great God! give all who own thy sway
> Soul to command and body to obey:
> When dangers frown—a heart to beat more high,
> When doubts confuse—a more observant eye;
> When fortunes change—a power to bear their blight;
> When death arrives—to life a calm "good-night."
> We are Thy likeness—give us on to go
> Through life's long march of restlessness and woe,
> Resolved Thy image shall be sanctified
> By holy confidence, not human pride.
> We have our task set—let us do it well,
> Nor barter ease on earth with pain in Hell.
> We have our talents from Thy treasury given—
> Let us return Thee good account in Heaven."

But Branwell was not asked to try his fortune with the Bells.

The chance went by for ever and with it the hope of his restoration to the old sane things of home. It so happened that the poems of Currer, Ellis and Acton Bell were published in 1846, in the very month of Maria's May Time memory, and almost with their appearance Branwell heard of the death of Mr. Robinson of Thorp Green. It brought back all the old misery in more violent form than ever and robbed him again of sleep and of appetitte. The girls, wrapped up in the warmth of hidden authorship, seemed to the lonely Branwell more unsympathetic than ever, and it is only from his letters to his friend Leyland that we get a glimpse of the castaway amidst the pleasurable activities of Currer, Ellis and Acton Bell. He writes: "My appetite is lost, my nights are dreadful and having nothing to do makes me dwell on past scenes—on her own self, her voice, her person, her thoughts, till I could be glad if God would take me. In the next world I could not be worse than I am in this."

The lad was writing under the same roof which sheltered the Bells and was as ignorant of what they were doing as they were of his poetical efforts, for he had, in truth, just been struggling with a poem on Morley Hall for Leyland and had also got him to take the Northangerland poem of Penmaenmawr to the Editor of "The Halifax Guardian." He was dreaming of a voyage abroad, as the quiet of his home was unbearable with the inner turmoil of his pent-up emotions. He confesses that the inability of his family to realise the nature of his suffering made it much worse for him with his long memory of what it once was like in Haworth Parsonage, and then he has to put the thought into his constant old jingles as he says:—

> "Home thoughts are not, for me,
>   Bright as of yore."

The news of Mr. Robinson's death had been brought to Branwell by the coachman again, and, with it, another chapter of the book of lies, but it all seemed true to this deluded, lonely, empty hearted boy and he cried out: "What I shall *do* I know not—I am too hard to die and too wretched to live." Of course what he did was to drink more and more until he could not write at all, and there is surely an irony about his history that his increasing degradation kept pace with his sisters' rising triumph.

Branwell Brontë was scrawling pictures of himself hung by the neck or dragged off the stage of life by little black devils, whilst

Charlotte's novel of *Jane Eyre* was reaching a third edition. She was receiving letters from Thackeray and from G. H. Lewes and sustaining a literary correspondence with her publishers, whilst Branwell was being put to bed drunk in a Halifax inn and cadging about for money to pay his drinking debts. Charlotte was pocketing a cheque for a cool £100, whilst Branwell was leaving his last literary composition to posterity in this form: "To John Brown, Sexton, Sunday, Noon. Dear John, I shall feel very much obliged to you if you can contrive to get me five pence worth of gin in a proper measure. Should it be speedily got I could perhaps take it from you or Billy at the lane top, or what would be quite as well, sent out for to you. I anxiously ask the favour because I know the good it will do me. *Punctually* at half past nine in the morning you will be paid the five pence out of a shilling given to me then. Yrs. P.B.B.

POEMS

BY

CURRER, ELLIS, AND ACTON

BELL.

LONDON:
AYLOTT AND JONES, 8, PATERNOSTER-ROW.

———

1846.

CHAPTER XVIII

JANE EYRE

IT WAS time for Patrick Brontë to make one of his periodic incursions into family history. Like Virgil's picture of Neptune, rearing his old head amidst the storm, so the Rev. Patrick suddenly surfaced amongst the secret excitements of Currer, Ellis and Acton Bell. For some long time past he had remained quiet in his study, where, as Charlotte said, he "sat all day long in darkness and inertion." Now, he suddenly sallied forth into the open and declared that the time had come to do something about his eyes, and that Charlotte and Emily must go to Manchester and find out a specialist and a plan of action.

The little book of poems had been published but two months and the prose tales of *The Professor*, *Wuthering Heights* and *Agnes Grey* were going the rounds of the London publishers, seeking acceptance there. The girls' own publisher, Mr. Aylott, did not like novels, being of Patrick Brontë's strait-laced school of the Evangelicals, but he had advised other places where they might find favour and hope springs eternal in the author's breast. The girls in this month of July had been greatly cheered by one review of their poems which really said the right thing in this sentence in the "Critic." "They in whose hearts are chords strung by nature to sympathise with the beautiful and the true will recognise in these compositions the presence of more genius than it was supposed this utilitarian age had devoted to the loftier exercise of the intellect." Now Currer and Ellis Bell had to pack their bags and traipse off to Manchester and face up to the teasing anxieties of home and affliction, with the best grace they could.

They managed well, for they were able to fix up a consultation for their father with Mr. Wilson who was Hon. Surgeon of the Manchester Infirmary and founder of the Manchester Institution for Curing Diseases of the Eye. Presently, Patrick Brontë himself would be picking his way over those cobbled, rainswept streets of Manchester to take up his abode at 83, Mount Pleasant, Boundary Street, just off the Oxford Road. He remained there for five weeks and underwent the operation on his eyes, with all his old reliance on the will of God and the patience which he had learned from his inheritance of the Irish Cabin. Whenever these strange Brontës came out into the open, the ordinary people of the world always expressed surprise at their archaic style of deportment. Not knowing all the vagaries of divine assistance that lay behind their queer faces, they were at a loss to assess their value, as Charlotte writes to Ellen Nussey: "Papa displayed extraordinary patience and firmness—the surgeons seemed surprised. I was in the room all the time, as it was his wish that I should be there—of course I neither spoke nor moved till the thing was done—and then I felt that the less I said either to Papa or the surgeons, the better—Papa is now confined to his bed in a dark room and is not to be stirred for four days—he is to speak and to be spoken to as little as possible."

Patrick Brontë could thus observe the silent amenities of his Haworth study in his Manchester sojourn, but it was Charlotte who had to contend with reality in the shape of a too real nurse and the ever present urgency of her demands to be decently fed. She confesses, to Ellen Nussey, to a feeling of strangeness "in this big town" and that "I can't think what the deuce to order in the way of meat." Papa was easier to cope with in his monastic retreat, just mutton, beef, bread and butter and a cup of tea supplied his every need. But that nurse! Charlotte began to wish her speedily at Jericho and got rid of her as soon as she possibly could. She did not trust her, with her "obsequious ways," which to the world would only have meant the rendering of the attention for which it was willing to pay, but to a Brontë smacked of insincerity. Charlotte damned her liberally with faint praise as "not the worst of her class," and heaved a sigh of relief when she saw her depart.

In such a household it can have been no joke for the nurse, either with that monument of old world piety for her patient or Charlotte Brontë for her only light relief. And it was with Charlotte in the birth pangs of authorship with whom she had to deal, for this month at Manchester marked the arrival of *Jane Eyre*. That poor, unwitting monthly nurse had never before delivered a child like that, and it was a miracle that the beef and mutton were ordered at all. Charlotte had to put up with a sick father and an obsequious nurse, but she well knew how to outwit them both. She could escape into her own kingdom for long hours of pure creative pleasure and discovered that she had never before had such a time of leisure in which to dream and to write. She had never had such a time when her mind was so forward to the business. In fact she had never written as she wrote at Manchester, in her life before, and she would never write quite like that ever again. In the heart of the Manchester of the Industrial Revolution, of Mrs. Gaskell's Manchester of Mary Barton and the slaughter of the innocents, Charlotte Brontë spilled the secret of her heart on to the paper before her in a stream of molten lava. She was blind and deaf to all around her and as one caught up in the Delphic ecstasy of the Pythia delivering oracles.

Stand in Boundary Street to-day with the modern University and the old Manchester High School close at hand and ask how it happened, for happen it did. The birth of *Jane Eyre* meant a revolution in English literature, as shattering and as fruitful as the publication of the Lyrical Ballads. Somewhere behind both is the link of the same ancestry, for Charles Lamb, himself a connoisseur of that old intensive religion, knew what he was saying when he called Wordsworth's new art "natural Methodism." Charlotte Brontë's new writing might be called erotic Methodism, but that would be too ugly a word for something beautiful which went back, instinctively, to Maria and embraced M. Héger himself in the same blameless fraternity of enthusiastic love. It is positively eerie the way that child Maria haunts all Brontë literature. Like some wandering ghost she calls outside the windows of Luddenden Foot and Haworth Parsonage, and here, in Manchester, she is at her old tricks again—creeping in to lie close to Charlotte, on her hired bed, and to die again in the crook of her arm.

Jane Eyre is a transcript of the life of Charlotte Brontë. It begins where Charlotte's memory began, in a dim time of frustration, with an uncompromising aunt too prone to punish faults of temper in the good old fashioned way. That memory of the room where death had been so lately and that picture of the little devotee of the dungeon, seeing lights, and hammering the door down to escape from terror, were forever buried deep in Charlotte's consciousness as the first things of memory. Then on went her mind to Cowan Bridge, and here Maria held the centre of the stage, and Charlotte watched her die again as some martyred saint of early Christian history. What a death was that, for Maria had been so eager to go and had said she was so happy. She had fluted her tender swan song in words that Charlotte could never forget, and there was the lilt of them again in a child's pathetic treble sustaining their imponderable weight of theology—"And God himself our Father is and Jesus is our friend."

Onward went Charlotte's pen, hardly able to keep pace with the memories and the story-writing and she is now in Ellen Nussey's

house when she describes Thornfield. Now she is telling of her
experience, as lonely governess, and the hard way her employers
treated her when she always felt left out of everything. But she
has reached M. Héger at last, and here is his shadowy separating
wife, in the background, and here a vindication of the purity of
her love. All has gone at white heat in the book until now, but
memory has stopped painfully at the loss of her master, and
Charlotte has to make Jane tear herself away from Rochester in
the same agony of mind and heart. It is significant how this tale
of *Jane Eyre* falls in two just at this point. Charlotte moves her
scene to Hathersage, collects Emily and Anne and Tabby into
her story, and even falls back on Henry Martyn to eke out life,
robbed of M. Héger. But the fire has gone out.

How shall it be rekindled? Memory knows there was no return,
but the book must have one and Jane must somehow get back
to Rochester. It is at that realisation of difficulty that memory
goes further back than Brussels and finds that tale of old love
between the saints that thrilled Charlotte in old days, standing
by open windows in Haworth long ago. How did Mary Bosanquet
drag John Fletcher to her side, over miles of sea and land, and
after fifteen years of absence? A voice on the wind, a prayer, a
longing, the viewless urgency of love. That shall be Charlotte's
method and she will see no strangeness in it for it is the deepest,
oldest memory of all. So as her Jane talks with St. John Rivers,
"Eye and ear waited while the flesh quivered on my bones—I heard
a voice somewhere cry Jane! Jane! Jane! Nothing more. And it
was the voice of a human being—a known, loved, well-remembered
voice—that of Edward Fairfax Rochester; and it spoke in pain
and woe, wildly eerily, urgently."

Charlotte Brontë ends her famous book in the old home atmosphere, safe again with the saints and with every twist and turn of
that old world known to a nicety. That really was her salvation
and the significance of that strange ending of *Jane Eyre* which does
not close with Rochester, alias M. Héger, but with St. John Rivers,
alias Henry Martyn. It might be Martyn's Lydia and not Charlotte
Brontë bringing the tale to its incongruous close thus: "St. John
is unmarried; he never will marry now. Himself has hitherto
sufficed to the toil; and the toil draws near its close: his glorious
sun hastens to its setting. The last letter I received from him drew
from my eyes human tears, and yet filled my heart with Divine
joy: he anticipated his sure reward, his incorruptible crown. I

know that a stranger's hand will write to me next, to say that the good and faithful servant has been called at length into the joy of his Lord. And why weep for this? No fear of death will darken St. John's last hours: his mind will be unclouded; his heart will be undaunted; his hope will be sure; his faith steadfast. His own words are a pledge of this: "My Master" he says, "has forewarned me. Daily He announces more distinctly—'Surely I come quickly°' and hourly I more eagerly respond—Amen; even so come, Lord Jesus!"

William Makepeace Thackeray might weep over the passion of Charlotte Brontë's famous book, but he confessed to a certain difficulty which he experienced in swallowing Henry Martyn after the rhapsodies which were inseparable from Fairfax Rochester. He writes "The Missionary is a failure I think," but then, how could Thackeray know how successful that failure had really been to Charlotte Brontë herself. It was by his means that she had neatly propelled love back to where she always believed it to belong—in heavenly places. The Missionary was worth his weight in gold, in India, loving greatly yet untrammelled of the flesh, for when he put in an appearance at the end of Charlotte's writing he was a sure indication that she had regained her ancient poise. That terrible "fixed idea" no longer lorded it over her mind.

Charlotte Brontë had written the whole perilous stuff of her love for M. Héger right out of her heart into her book of Jane Eyre and Fairfax Rochester. Her freedom from her old obsession is nowhere more clearly pronounced than when she tries to get Jane and Rochester into the reality of wedded bliss. She is helpless to handle anything approaching such a relationship, and there can be no more inadequate phrase, after all Charlotte had written of the whirlwind of bleak emotion, than her famous banality: "Reader, I married him." When Charlotte writes again of M. Héger she will be her own master and do it so much better in his own setting of Brussels, or Villette as she calls it, and with emotion remembered only in tranquillity. At last here is a real man, and Charlotte writes vividly of him and of Mde. Héger with a woman's detailed trick, of memory and character drawing, which is done with relish.

Paul Emanuel of *Villette* is an irascible, enthusiastic French professor. Rochester of *Jane Eyre* is an atom bomb. Charlotte Brontë could never have got that deadly charge of miasmic love out of her system without the writing of Jane Eyre. It is significant that when she writes in *Villette* of those precious letters for which she waited, in agony at Haworth, after her separation from M. Héger, she transfers them safely to Dr. John as their author and not at all to Paul Emanuel. She could never have done that in *Jane Eyre*, for it was impossible that she could have made anyone else then responsible for that old anguish and ecstasy, except the one and only hero. Here is her description of the receipt of one such harmless epistle: "A letter! The shape of a letter similar to that had haunted my brain in its very core for seven days past. I had dreamed of a letter last night—the letter whose face of enamelled white and single Cyclop's-eye of vermilion red had printed themselves so clear and perfect on the retina of my inward vision. I knew it. I felt it to be the letter of my hope, the fruition of my wish, the release from my doubt, the ransom from my terror. It was what the old dying patriarch demanded of his son Esau, promising in requital the blessing of his last breath. It was a godsend, and I inwardly thanked the God who had vouchsafed it. Outwardly I only thanked man, crying 'Thank you, Thank you, Monsieur'."

There could be no other book like *Jane Eyre*, for it was written to the relentless throbbing of a crucified heart. When Charlotte writes again, as in *Villette*, she will be writing freely as an artist, using her old stores of memory, just as she likes, and without the urgency of sorrow, but it was *Jane Eyre* that made the name of Currer Bell famous. It appeared on October 16th, 1847, and its success was instantaneous. "The Westminster Review" declared it to be the best novel of the season, and the second edition contained no less than seven pages of the eulogistic opinions of the Press. Charlotte Brontë knowing so well all that had gone to its birth, was slow to believe her good fortune. She began a long correspondence with Mr. Williams of Smith Elder and Co., a tranquil and delightful pastime, and only gradually grew into that expansive feeling of the successful authoress to which her two sisters continued strangers all their lives.

Although *Wuthering Heights* and *Agnes Grey* were both accepted for publication by Mr. Newby before *Jane Eyre* saw the light, it was Currer Bell's success that really brought them into prominence and propped their tottering footsteps in the world of books. The Trade was given to understand that there was a pleasurable confusion in the names of Currer, Ellis and Acton Bell and that, for conditions of best sellers, it were better to believe that all three novels sprang from Currer Bell's magic pen. It meant endless confusion and much searching of heart for the three sisters, and caused so fine a burst of speculation and gossip that it has scarcely been cleared up to this very day. It is the whole of one hundred years since the publication of *Jane Eyre* and the world is still asking for a clue to what it is pleased to call the mystery of Haworth.

M

CHAPTER XIX

WUTHERING HEIGHTS

OLD HOUSES have a way of losing their front door keys, and, for a hundred years, that of *Wuthering Heights* has been mislaid. Charlotte might have helped in the search by replying simply that it was in Papa's pocket, but she was not going to give Emily away as easily as all that. She rather felt it was a juvenile performance and that Ellis Bell would be better at essay writing, but she really could not understand that, when the Bells wrote at all, the world considered their efforts "unfeminine". Charlotte could not understand how *Wuthering Heights* produced its horrifying effect on its readers, for she knew so well what had gone to its writing and from what a homely background it had sprung. She says "*Wuthering Heights* was hewn in a wild workshop, with simple tools, out of homely material", and she but speaks the truth. But she could not see that the monsters in the old home story-telling cupboard would spring out on the world in an atmosphere of brimstone and fireworks. Homely indeed, but the world still goes on asking how the girl did it and thinking that Branwell would be a far more suitable parent for such an offspring.

Branwell's friends declared, when they read the book, that they had heard it all before at Luddenden Foot in those wild tales the lad told them of Ewood and Grimshaw and graves and passion, all well spiced with market language. But that did not alter the fact that it was Emily who had written the book, for, from nursery days in Haworth Parsonage, it had always been anybody's tale. They had all read the very beginnings of the plot in that letter which Grimshaw wrote to John Wesley from the old Parsonage at Haworth, and all those old letters of Parson Grimshaw which Wesley had printed in the Methodist magazines and which went with a swing, when the writer professed himself hearty and happy in the Lord. Had not his old parsonage, just across the graveyard, always belonged to them all and had it not been a game since childhood's days to fit the young people, who figured in Grimshaw's letters, into the pattern of that sheltering house? Grimshaw was always befriending waifs and strays and tells Wesley of the work of grace he hoped to perform on their young hearts. This letter might almost match the Heathcliffe, the Nelly Dean and the Catherine of

THE SETTING OF "WUTHERING HEIGHTS"

the book in its: "Two under my own roof are just now under true conviction; one a girl about eighteen years old, and the other a boy about fourteen, and I hope my own little girl between ten and eleven years old."

The names of the people in *Wuthering Heights* are those which Wesley knew and faithfully transcribed in his Journal, so that Emily Brontë has only to alter Grimshaw to Earnshaw and Sutcliffe to Heathcliffe to give a verisimilitude to the tale and its old memory, and she does not even trouble to alter the name of Lockwood at all. She wrote down her story just like that, in the guise of an oft heard tale and she threw it in the face of the public as contemptuously as she threw her poems. If they were nursery rhymes then *Wuthering Heights* was a bed-time nursery story. If Charlotte said they should all write books, after the publication of their poems, Emily would not stand out and spoil her sisters' pleasure, but the public should only have the easy old stuff lying about in her memory and told as Tabby and her father always told it. She herself, Emily Brontë, would not be put out of her way foɪ any public that existed. She could toss off the old childhood's tale as though she were still listening to it, and she could talk like Tabby talked as she remembered the dear home words and phrases. She could use Grimshaw's very own words in the telling, for Emily's Joseph's remark about "the sound of the gospel still in yer lugs" comes straight from Grimshaw, under the dying sinner's bedroom window in Haworth, shouting in stentorian tones "If ye perish, ye shall perish with the sound of the gospel still in yer lugs."

The difficulty is, in this sort of writing, that a little has to be made to go a very long way. Memory is active to lay hold on all sorts of homely material to build the full-sized tale. The character which loomed the largest, in that old store cupboard of memory, was undoubtedly that monster of a man Shirley, Lord Ferrers, and Emily had had a warm admiration for the cut of his coat with her liking for something fierce, trimmed close for action. She could handle Heathcliffe as very small beer after her life-long acquaintance with him. Shirley had done all that Emily made Heathcliffe do, but whereas Heathcliffe merely tormented his victims Shirley really killed them. He even made assurance doubly sure by tearing off those healing bandages which had been applied to save their lives. That was something like a villain. He did more than go to hell with his eyes open, for he positively exulted in the transit. His figure stood out upon the scaffold silhouetted in eternal flame.

There were other milder monsters of Papa's acquaintance who had to be pressed into the service to fill a few of Emily's gaps in her story telling. Jabez Bunting even managed to find a boisterous corner for himself. He had always been an unseen guest in Haworth Parsonage, for Patrick Brontë had not forgiven him for turning Uncle Fennell out of Woodhouse Grove in order to install one of his own relations in the position of headmaster. His own old patron and Wesley's friend Crosse of Bradford had had to come to the rescue to get him a living in the Church of England, in that well-known way of his of providing for the casualties of the older order which the newer Methodism of Jabez Bunting was throwing overboard. In Uncle Fennell's downfall, Patrick Brontë had also lost the amenities of that institution of the gentleman's mansion which had once been dear to his young and ambitious heart.

Emily, that loyal daughter of an outraged father, had the satisfaction of putting this Jabez into the pillory and of making him look ridiculous in his pulpit antics and his swelling pomposity. Such a scene as she describes in Lockwood's dream of Jabez Branderham had taken place in real life at the opening of the new school chapel at Woodhouse Grove. The building had been packed full, but other pilgrims had come a little late and forced an entrance, to the confusion of the righteous and for the death of decorum. Jabez Bunting had to take a hand himself to quell this unseemly riot, by thumping vigorously on the pulpit book-board and demanding silence in stentorian tones. It had been a scene never to be forgotten by the schoolboys and must have atoned for much which they had been made to suffer. Emily takes it all to make it the background dream work of that bough which kept rapping on Lockwood's window, after he had fallen into that ghost-haunted slumber, in Catherine's room at Wuthering Heights.

Homely material indeed! But how strangely it all reads to people who have never so much as heard of a Jabez Bunting or of that guardian spirit of Maria which comes inevitably to Emily's mind as she thinks of Branderham's rappings and of Catherine's voice on the storm about the casement. She writes: "Presently the whole chapel resounded with rappings and counter rappings: every man's hand was against his neighbour; and Branderham, unwilling to remain idle, poured forth his zeal in a shower of loud taps on the boards of the pulpit, which responded so smartly that, at

last, to my unspeakable relief they woke me. And what was it that
had suggested the tremendous tumult? What had played Jabez's
part in the row? Merely the branch of a fir tree that touched my
lattice, as the blast wailed by, and rattled its dry cones against
the panes. 'I must stop it, nevertheless°' I muttered, knocking
my knuckles through the glass, and stretching an arm out to seize
the importunate branch, instead of which my fingers closed on the
fingers of an ice-cold hand."

That visitation of the child at the window with the wailing
refrain of "Twenty years—twenty years. I've been a waif for
twenty years," is the high place of tragedy in the whole book. Emily
Brontë has such a disconcerting way of sticking close to the truth
and yet of placing it in such a setting, with her splashes of Hell and
Heaven, that it seems like the truth of another world. The ghost
of Maria had always haunted the casements of Haworth Parsonage
and there is a strange little bit of mental arithmetic here which
makes Emily advance her "fifteen wild Decembers" to twenty
years for the haunting Catherine, for it was so long ago since
Maria left them in the spring of 1825, and the year 1846 saw the
beginning of *Wuthering Heights*.

It is that picture of the ghostly little hand and the broken
window which has held the imagination of men and women
all over the world. It assumes epic proportions, but it owes its
creation to Branwell's life-long devotion to his ghostly and angelic
sister Maria and to her propensity for haunting the windows of
Haworth Parsonage. It owes something too to Branwell's devotion
to his Lydia, confused and brain fevered, and yet linked with his
Maria obsession and made capable as a vehicle of passion. It also
owes something to Grimshaw, in the throes of conversion, when he
fasted night and day and saw visions of torn flesh in the hands of his
Saviour, forcing their way through to his chamber, as he agonised
in the priest's house. Emily Brontë, with all her old memories and
her present knowledge of her poor brother's pitiable ravings, found
her masterpiece ready to her hand. Branwell could not have written
the book for he was beyond writing then and was the victim of his
own tragedy and not its wise spectator. How often lately had Emily
heard him muttering at the windows of his home—his voice of
anguish, strangled in his throat.

There was another improvisation for the making of stories which
this strange girl had to make, for what did she know, from

experience, of this heady, tempestuous thing called love? Knowing nothing of earthly passion, but being a connoisseur of the divine, she must needs use the thing she did know for the description of the love of which she was ignorant. That is the invertion which gives *Wuthering Heights* the significance which no other novel can have. It stands alone in English literature, for it is Methodist passion of the old school employed as the means of expression for the love of a man and a maid. It was this sort of writing which startled the world when, at the time of Catherine's death, Emily Brontë writes of Heathcliffe: "Whether the angels have fed him or his kin beneath I cannot tell; but he has just come home at dawn and gone upstairs to his chamber, locking himself in—as if anybody dreamt of coveting his company! There he has continued praying like a Methodist: only the deity he implored in senseless dust and ashes, and God, when addressed, was curiously confounded with his own black father! After concluding these precious orisons, and they lasted generally till he grew hoarse and his voice was strangled in his throat—he would be off again; always straight down to the grave."

In the whole of this burning book there is not one hint of sex. Heathcliffe and Catherine conform to the pattern of Grimshaw and to his startling experience that "To me to live is Christ", for, listen to Catherine speaking thus of Heathcliffe, the lover of her soul: "He's more myself than I am. Whatever our souls are made of, his and mine are the same; and Linton's is as different as a moonbeam from lightning or frost from fire. My great thought in living is himself. If all else perished and *he* remained, *I* should still continue to be; and if all else remained and he were annihilated, the universe would turn to a mighty stranger: I should not seem part of it. My love for Linton is like the foliage of the woods: time will change it, I'm well aware, as winter changes the trees. My love for Heathcliffe resembles the eternal rocks beneath, a source of little visible delight but necessary. Nelly, I *am* Heathcliffe. He's always, always in my mind, not as a pleasure, any more than I am always a pleasure to myself, but as my own being."

All the Brontës understood that quality of religious passion as the legacy of their father's and mother's own inheritance, but it is only in Emily that the thing stalks as itself, pure and untrammelled of the flesh. She had no earthly idols to confuse the issue as had Charlotte and Branwell and even gentle Anne, so that *Wuthering Heights* reads as a scrap of history torn from the communion of the

saints of old and flung in the face of the modern world, out of its
context, to startle its dainty self-restraint. No one in Haworth
Parsonage could have done that but Emily, for she had made that
religious experience her very own and was own twin sister to her
father's saints. She had seen for herself "heaven's glories shine"
and knew of her God that "every existence must exist in Thee".
For her the Rock of Ages was necessary to her very being in the
very same way that Catherine declares her need of the eternal rock
of her love for Heathcliffe. In her desk was a crumpled poem which
no other Brontë could have written but which says in verse about
God what Catherine says in prose about Heathcliffe. It is this
invocation:

> "O God within my breast,
> Almighty, ever-present Deity!
> Life—that in me has rest,
> As I—undying life—have power in Thee!
>
> Vain are the thousand creeds
> That moved men's hearts: unutterably vain;
> Worthless as withered weeds,
> Or idlest froth, amid the boundless main,
>
> To waken doubt in one
> Holding so fast by Thine infinity;
> So surely anchored on
> The steadfast rock of immortality.
> With wide-embracing love
> Thy spirit animates eternal years,
> Pervades and broods above,
> Changes, sustains, dissolves, creates and rears.
>
> Though earth and men were gone,
> And suns and universes ceased to be,
> And Thou were left alone,
> Every existence would exist in Thee.
>
> There is not room for death,
> Nor atom that his might could render void:
> Thou—Thou art Being and Breath
> And what Thou art may never be destroyed."

To breed such divine passion in a slip of a girl and to set her
down to contemplate, on every Sunday of her life in Haworth
Church, ever since she could read, those deep words of Pauline

experience that "To me to live is Christ", and then to go still further than that and to shut her in with God on a Yorkshire moor were surely stages in a soul's evolution which made Emily Brontë what she was and created *Wuthering Heights* into the bargain. In that willowy figure of the girl, whom Charlotte said only left her home to go to church or to walk on the moors, was confined the very essence of the passion of Redeeming Love. It was as though the whole of that divine pageantry on which the Methodist revival of religion was built had been forced through the channels of her heart, in its pristine vigour, and purged from the sophistication of sect or man-made creed. For years now Emily had taken up the tale where Maria laid it down and had so cherished it, in the silence of her constant heart, that in Haworth Parsonage in the midst of the 19th century it were as though Thomas Walsh himself had become incarnate. For both such devotees it would seem that the sword of the spirit was in danger of wearing out the scabbard of the flesh. But Emily Brontë still baked good bread and ironed Papa's nightshirts and tossed off *Wuthering Heights* and so far managed to keep her feet in the cart ruts of earth. Managed so far, but for how long?

Emily Brontë could write of all that went forward in Heathcliffe's bedroom when "praying like a Methodist" he agonised for Catherine, for she knew to write just like that from what went forward in her own chamber of secret strength. She had been brought up with Wesley's Traveller Unknown and all that went to His mystic Presence. The words were ever lilting in her heart or blown about the chimneys on the wings of the wind on Haworth Hill—words like a Methodist at prayer in their beseeching:

"Come Oh! Thou Traveller Unknown,
Whom I still hold, but cannot see,
My company before is gone
And I am left alone with Thee,
With Thee all night I mean to stay
And wrestle till the break of day."

Is there not an echo of the same insistence in Emily's nightly encounter with her Visitant of air, after she has outmanoeuvred the unwelcome and prying eyes of sire and dame:

"Burn then, little lamp, glimmer straight and clear—
Hush! a rustling wind stirs, methinks, the air;
He for whom I wait, thus ever comes to me;
Strange Power! I trust thy might; trust thou my constancy."

CHAPTER XX

TRILOGY OF DEATH

EVENTS in Haworth Parsonage were to prove that the Almighty could repose his uttermost confidence in the constancy of Emily Brontë. She would presently go all the way and walk unflinchingly through death itself in the steadfast confidence of a Methodist of the old school. Like Thomas Walsh and like their Master Himself, Emily Brontë refused all opiates which might dull the fine edge of that glimpse of glory which the saints expected—on tiptoe for immortality. Both Thomas Walsh and Emily Brontë refused "poisoning doctors" on the brink of the grave, but, before Emily's translation, Branwell must first set out on that last perilous journey which had held the imagination captive of all Maria's children, ever since her own triumphant entrance into Heaven. What sort of a hand could he make of it, devilled and damned, weak maudlin and hopeless as he was?

It has been the lot of Branwell Brontë to be left out of everything in his sisters' world of fame and yet to be responsible, by proxy, for so much of it himself. It was the same in his death which so profoundly influenced his two younger sisters that it sent them posting after him with incredible speed. That epic chapter of swift death has had so much to do with the interest and appeal of the whole of the Brontë saga, but Branwell, the chief actor in it, has received the scantiest applause. Who could have thought that it should be he, the castaway, who managed, on the very brink of hell, to back-somersault into heaven? Who of late years would have dared to hope that Branwell, in his death, should emulate his father's old heroes and spring forward into eternity with their abandon of hope and with the darkness of despair quite sloughed from his mind? The little world of Thomas Walsh, in Ireland, had waited round his death-bed to see him go away into eternal night—that youth who had once been their epic saint—all for the love of a woman. But what they saw was a saint still, flinging up his hands in loyal salute to his divine Master and struggling to rise from his death-bed, in joyous greeting, as he cried: "My Beloved—He is mine and I am His." And so even with Branwell Brontë, as his father and his sisters stood round him, at the last, they marvelled to hear him pray and to see him struggle up to greet all that angel host which had once carried Maria's soul away to the heavenly mansions of bliss. At least Charlotte marvelled. She was the only one that day who was out of sympathy with that drama of life and death, for all the rest were to the same manner born themselves. She stood a little apart, in thought, from that group round the dying Branwell, for she felt herself superior to them all in that warm, yet secret, knowledge of the famous authoress who knew herself to have grown away from their fusty background. She would presently be writing to her publishers no heartbroken letter about this pitiable brother of hers but one fit to come from the creator of *Jane Eyre*.

Yet even Charlotte, in spite of herself, was too fast bound to the old tradition to escape either its spirit or its jargon, for, if she sets herself to describe the coming of dawn or sunset, it is inevitably with her "terribly glorious", which is but the way the saints described the coming of their Lord in that awful moment of dawning eternity as "so terribly glorious His coming shall be". She was about to slip into her next book, which even now had her fast in its toils, there by Branwell's death-bed, that old phrase of her father's youth about "the sovereign balm" for every wound. Was it possible that the old man was using it even now, as he commended Branwell's soul to his all forgiving Saviour? It was a phrase which owed its existence to that Shirley of old who, purloining one of Isaac Watts's hymns, produced the verse:

> "Salvation, oh! The joyful sound,
> What pleasure to our ears,
> A sovereign balm for every wound
> A cordial for our fears."

There was surely something steadying and noble about Patrick Brontë's voice that day as he prayed, with the unction of Tighe and Fletcher, for the soul of a sinner and besought a merciful God for the eternal life of his only son. As the well worn phrases came through the darkness to Branwell they were surely balm and cordial to his wounded spirit, and so did he lay hold on them, as one who lays hold on life. The unreal realities of his strange childhood were still the only real things to Branwell Brontë and, in the article of death, they were all his own once more. Charlotte writes to her publishers: "The remembrance of this strange change now comforts my poor father greatly. I myself, with painful mournful joy, heard him praying softly in his dying moments; and to the last prayer which my father offered up at his bedside he added 'Amen'. How unusual that word appeared from his lips, of course you who did not know him cannot conceive. Akin to this alteration was that in his feelings towards his relations—all bitterness seemed gone."

For two days before his death Branwell had become as one reborn into the old home borderland of Heaven. Eternity was drawing near and it was embracing Haworth Parsonage in celestial light, so that the warm core of love of the old home was seen again as something spiritual and one with Everlasting Mercy. The young man's face in death assumed the beauty of love's satisfaction and instinctively Charlotte thought of Grimshaw and of his funeral text which said: "He was a burning and a shining light." That, she told Mr. Williams of Smith Elder and Co., was what she had always thought Branwell would be, instead of this unhappy wreck of humanity which he had become. But in death he seemed to be just that burning and shining light, as the sight of him tore at Charlotte's heart in a rush of old memory and emotion.

It was the first "death scene" which the author of *Jane Eyre* said she had witnessed and it was inevitable that, for her, it should be overwhelming, lighted as it was by ancient household words and memories and darkened by regret and confusion of mind. On that Sunday evening of Branwell's death his sister Charlotte collapsed. Headache and sickness and the prostration of migraine kept her in bed for a week after her brother's death. Her father too had been shaken, but with the tears of natural affection, sobbing out "My son, my son" even as David wept for the young man Absolem. But Patrick Brontë was not the man to dispute the will of God, for he had bent to it too long, and he was also thankful to know that the Lord had tempered judgment with mercy and saved a soul from death. That was so enheartening a confirmation of his old beliefs that he rejoiced over it as does one who achieves a second pious death-bed amongst his own children, so as by a miracle. It was the ambition of every saint to get the whole family to Heaven by hook or by crook.

Emily and Anne, strong in their integrity of faith, came through the crisis well, so that Charlotte lamented that she was the only one who had failed, in that important hour, and lay on her bed feeling very sorry for herself. That "pale corpse" of her brother seemed always behind her eyes, and, haunted like that, she was vaguely apprehensive that she would never be able to finish her second book and despatch it to her good friends in Cornhill. She did not like to remember that she had frankly not believed in Branwell's illness until he had laid up and died of it, and that he had been confined to bed but one day before he was gone. The contrast was too painful in the attention which she was receiving from her devoted sisters who were waiting on her hand and foot and emptying her slops, in a cutting east wind, when she was only suffering from a headache and an unacknowledged twinge of conscience.

For a long time now Charlotte Brontë had been under a considerable strain. She had been living a double life, in letters and reviews, and drinking the heady wine of literary success, as the famous Currer Bell, when all the time she knew only too well the homeliness of Charlotte Brontë of Haworth Parsonage. She had had that one wild journey to London with Anne to disclose her identity to her publishers, but there was a constant fear that the secret would come to light at home and yet a growing passion to go still further in the world outside, as Currer Bell. It would be easier with Branwell out of the way and Papa let into the secret, but it was all provokingly difficult for a successful authoress who had to pluck up her courage to beard her father in his den and try to explain how matters stood with her. Patrick Brontë felt sure it would mean that a lot of the copies of her book would be left on her hands, as his own Cottage Poems must have been, but, when he heard that *Jane Eyre* had actually sold well, he hurried across the passage to tell Emily and Anne that "Girls, what do you think, Charlotte has written a book, and it is much better than likely."

History does not say what Patrick Brontë thought of *Wuthering Heights*, but it is clear that Emily and her sister Anne were encumbered with none of Charlotte's ambition of worldly success in their own determined race to Heaven. Branwell's death found them heart whole and eager to follow him and seemed to slip them the more easily from their earthly moorings. Emily could feel the pull of her divine destiny through the very walls of her heart and that pressure had been intensified by seeing the way the reality of the unseen was acknowledged by Branwell, at the very edge of his loss of consciousness. From that very moment Emily made haste to be gone. She caught cold at Branwell's funeral, but took not the slightest notice of tight chest and obstructed breathing, and in ten weeks was in her grave. Anne lagged a little tardily behind her, as she was ever patient and lacked Emily's impetuosity, but she got there at last by Maria's kindly May time and met the monster death as heroically as ever Emily did, but in her own quiet way. So noiselessly did she negotiate the awful steeps of eternity that her landlady put her head round the sitting-room door to tell her that dinner was served, in the very crisis of her fate.

John Wesley, who was surprised at nothing, used to say that his people died well, and he would have passed the same verdict on both Emily and Anne, in spite of the fact that the manner of their death has always made mere worldlings wonder. Patrick Brontë, as a dutiful son in the gospel, seems to have shared Wesley's complacency and to have made no protest when Emily set about carrying out the method of one of his ancient heroes to the letter. Anne, who understood, said nothing, but the sight of Emily's grim encounter broke Charlotte's heart. From her position, now a little outside the old home background, she saw it, as it would appear to an outsider, as a terrible mistake, but she also saw it, as heir to all the holy Fletchers. That made the spectacle pathetic as well as terrible.

Charlotte Brontë, in her role of interpreter and always mindful never to give away any secrets, could only state it to the world in terms which said that her sister was stronger than a man and simpler than a child. That indeed was the sober truth, for it takes strength to conquer death without yielding an inch to his crushing importunity and only a child or an old Methodist would dream that it could ever be done. It really can't be done, but John Fletcher and Emily Brontë did it, and to the spectators the signs of visible collapse were made the more obvious and the more heart-rending by the indomitable spirit that never acknowledged them. Mrs. Fletcher, in her pew, seeing her dying husband celebrate the Sacrament and knowing herself powerless to stop him, endured the same agony as did Charlotte Brontë when she watched her sister tottering out into the cold winter, with a plate of scraps for her dog's supper, and allowing no one to prevent her fulfilment of Wesley's command "to cease at once to work and live". Charlotte writes of the death of Emily as deep branded on her memory. She says: "Yet while physically she perished, mentally she grew stronger than we had yet known her. Day by day, when I saw with what a front she met suffering, I looked on her with an anguish of wonder and love. I have seen nothing like it; but, indeed, I have never seen her parallel in anything. Stronger than a man, simpler than a child, her nature stood alone. The awful point was that while full of ruth for others, on herself she had no pity; the spirit was inexorable to the flesh; from the trembling hand, the unnerved limbs, the faded eye, the same service was exacted as they had rendered in health. To stand by and witness this and not dare to remonstrate was a pain no words can render."

The climax was reached on the day of her death when, rising at seven in the morning, Emily dressed herself and came downstairs as usual, to refuse all help and entreaties to return to bed, and then, dying, to struggle to her feet with piteous dignity for the final count. All her life she had known of Grimshaw, just over the way there at Sowden's Farm, who at his own last day had said: "I have suffered last night what the blessed martyrs did: my flesh has been as it were roasting before a hot fire. But I have nothing to do but step out of my bed into Heaven. I have my foot upon the threshold already." Emily Brontë would do even better than that, for, with that raging fever in her lungs, she would take the actual step itself in the split second between time and eternity. It was as literally true to her as to Maria and to that dying preacher from Birstall who had said "I have endeavoured for above thirty years to keep the hour of death constantly in view that it might be as easy as going out of one room into another, and blessed be God I find it now as easy."

To Emily Brontë, in her thirty-first year of life, it was as easy as that and easier, after her intensive schooling amongst her father's veterans and with her own intimate knowledge of what Grimshaw called "the fire of God in the soul". That energy has a way of rolling up the poor tawdry things of this world, as a scroll, and of burning its way through the frail wall of flesh until existence exists only in God.

When Charlotte later tried to explain Emily and her great book to the world she thought instinctively in terms of that divine fire, but, knowing no modern could understand that inheritance and the "peculiar character" of her sister, she coined a phrase for its description. She called it "moral electricity" which was a thing she believed well within the vocabulary of the world. That was Charlotte's way of explaining something of that incandescent flame which had been brought from the altar of God by Patrick Brontë's old hero John Wesley and called by his brother Charles "pure celestial fire". It is impossible to understand either the Brontës or the Romantic Revival of literature, or, indeed, all the social upheaval of the 19th century apart from it, for as Charlotte

THE DINING ROOM IN HAWORTH PARSONAGE
with the sofa on which Emily Brontë died

Brontë's own reviewer said, as interpreter of this new style of authorship: "The tone of mind and thought which fostered Chartism and rebellion at home is the same which has written *Jane Eyre*."

The world is still incredulous or indeed frankly forgetful of old glory, for now it has but the ashes of the thing in its disillusioned heart. Under cover of the black-out it did indeed permit the Brontë sisters to steal into Westminster Abbey and to find a little niche there for themselves, but it chose a text for them which it believed to represent the type of grim stoicism appropriate to Haworth Parsonage. The memorial is in Poet's Corner and bears the names of Charlotte, Emily and Anne and the legend: "With courage to endure." But what Emily Brontë meant, when she wrote her own epitaph, was not what the world meant but what Grimshaw meant and Fletcher meant and Thomas Walsh, when they flung the world away and sprang forward into eternity. What this strange girl was trying to say was what Wesley said when he talked of: "A soul out of prison released and freed from its bodily chain" for the world should have quoted her more fully, thus:

> "In life and death a chainless soul
> With courage to endure."

In her sister Anne was found the same fortitude, at her own last day. Indeed, the tender light of a dawning Heaven played upon her face and transfigured it with a strange joy. Here was nothing terrible, as in Emily's heroic stride forward, but rather it were as though a friend supported her in the deep waters of death. Charlotte could write more clearly here and not speak in parables of Anne as of Emily, for she writes: "I have said that she was religious, and it was by leaning on those Christian doctrines in which she firmly believed that she found support through her most painful journey. I witnessed their efficacy in her latest hour and greatest trial, and must bear my testimony to the calm triumph with which they brought her through." Ellen Nussey amplifies the direction, whither she was carried triumphant, in her description of that farewell scene. She says: "Her faith never failed, and her eye never dimmed till about two o'clock, when she calmly, and without a sigh, passed from the temporal to the eternal. So still and so hallowed were her last hours and moments. There was no thought of assistance or of dread."

Anne Brontë endured Emily's passing in a still quiet grief, but she began to sink before her sister was buried and in two weeks' time was showing unmistakable signs that she would follow after her as soon as God permitted her discharge. She had a great longing to go to Scarborough and to see again all those old scenes of her own *Agnes Grey* where she had made Weightman walk and talk, near the old castle and within sight of that great sweep of the sea. How she got there must remain a miracle of courage, for Ellen Nussey, who travelled with her, said: "Through the trials and fatigues of the journey she evinced the pious courage and fortitude of a martyr". She was no whit behind Emily in the way she encountered death. When she tottered from one room to another, at their sea-side lodgings, she would give God thanks for enabling her still to walk, and, before she sank exhausted on her bed, would kneel in perfect submission at the throne of grace and beg a blessing on them all.

The only reason that a doctor seems to have been called in at Scarborough was to give Anne Brontë the information how long he thought she had to live, and, whoever the man was, he was startled by this unexpected and alarming question and declared that he had never seen before a deathbed upon this fashion. The textbooks of his medical religion had never embraced this "fixed tranquillity of spirit and settled longing to be gone." Anne Brontë was only twenty-eight years old but as Charlotte watched her, there by the open window at Scarborough, she believed that from her childhood she had been preparing for so early a death. She must have thought of Maria and of her happiness at her own departure with that quality of sorrow which tears at the very heart. It is certain that it was to Maria's Heaven that Anne believed she was now going and it was bright with its familiar realities and its promise of reunion—as bright as that glorious sunset which shone on her haggard face.

The first little hostage of fortune, over that bright border, had been the angel child Maria. She had bidden everyone of the little pilgrim band meet her in Heaven and who was Charlotte to hold them back, Branwell, Emily and Anne, as she closed their eyes in this world that they might, the better, see in glory. Charlotte says: "I let Anne go to God and felt He had a right to her." So it is but fitting to pipe that gallant trio aloft to the plaintive treble of Maria's own swan song, for they were the last of their kind and the end of one dispensation of the grace of God. It is certain that the creator of Jane Eyre and of Helen Burns would remember:

"Angels our servants are
And keep in all our ways,
And in their watchful hands they bear
The sacred sons of grace.

Unto that heavenly bliss
They all our steps attend;
And God Himself our Father is,
And Jesus is our Friend."

N

CHAPTER XXI

SHIRLEY

THE PAGEANT of death found Patrick Brontë still impregnably grounded in the conviction of the Will of God. He sustained that overwhelming tragedy well. To one brought up in his old school, such affliction had the hallmark upon it of God's continued interest in his affairs. After all, as he told Charlotte, it but made him "feel and know" that with Wesley "the world was not his place." He said that there was but a remnant left now of the race, for the others had contended only too successfully for "their native Heaven." The larger part of his little family had now gone home to God. His habits for thirty years had been, as Charlotte says, those of a recluse, and he but the more found comfort in a quiet house through which the ticking of the clock was the only sound to check or to assist his meditations.

Charlotte Brontë sustained this triple blow of fate for quite other reasons. She was writing another book and was all sharp set that its merits should not fall below *Jane Eyre*. True it is that the home-coming nearly broke her heart and that she sat and cried like a child in that sitting room of hers where she had seen Emily die and known the first glad thrill of successful authorship. But it is also true that she had taken the manuscript of her new book to Scarborough and had gone on afterwards to Filey and to Easton, near Bridlington, and had kept on writing all the time. She had almost finished her second volume when Branwell died and the whole of the book was in the hands of her publishers by the end of August 1849, just three months after her sister Anne's death.

The new book had first been called Hollow's Mill and had formed itself in her mind round Papa's tales of the Frame Breakers in the parts about Birstall. It came to be known as *Shirley* as the character of her heroine developed and the presence of Emily, her sister, seemed so insistently at her elbow. It is full of significance in its title for that was how Charlotte remembered her best, standing forward a little as a "gallant cavalier" and loving something fierce and trimmed close for action. As Charlotte thought of Grimshaw, as she looked at her dead brother and remembered his old enthusiasms that he too should be a "burning and a shining light," so she thought of the familiar name of Shirley, as she drew Emily's likeness, and remembered all that had gone to the making of family history in that boisterous name. It is the kind of thing which is done, in the amateur authorship of which Charlotte Brontë was mistress, to give a friend a secret talisman and to exhult in the knowledge that only she will understand. It would surely have appealed to the sardonic humour of the Brontë clansmen if, in following years, they could have seen film stars masquerading in that name which had brought forth Fletcher's *Checks to Antinomianism* and made Horace Walpole laugh at a handful of pious Methodists.

Yet, the picture of Shirley, in this so tragically environed book, is certainly not all Emily Brontë. So much of that character is unlike her, but Charlotte elaborates from living memory to put in pictures and incidents which were all Emily's own. She sees her kneeling before the fire making the family toast, again she catches sight of her soul in a moonlit night of snow on Haworth Hill, and again she remembers that time of terror and of heroism when Emily was bitten by a mad dog and cauterised the wound herself with a glowing iron. Charlotte's publishers complained of that incident, for they said it was unlike the Shirley of the brace of pistols and the defence of Hollow's Mill to be scared of an imaginary idea of going mad from the dog's bite. Would Charlotte alter it, as not in keeping? But Charlotte knew her Emily better than that and stuck to her guns as obstinately as she had to her picture of Helen Burns who had wanted to go to Heaven and scandalised her publishers again with her precocious piety.

Charlottee Brontë, in both these criticisms of her old memories, refused to alter either, for that same reason, because, she said, they were true. And true they were, however incomprehensible to the world they might be. Indeed, Charlotte said the half had not been told of Maria, as forerunner of Helen, for the wonder of her happy death-bed, and she was not going to give more away of Emily's faith either. Who were the rude public to understand that Emily's horror of going mad was no physical terror but a spiritual one, close woven with her upbringing and those very revels on the confines of Heaven and of Hell? If the mind was distraught with madness how could it see the dawn of the Invisible? There was the rub. It was sheer horror to rob Emily of her dearest hope on earth when she looked forward confidently to walking into heaven over Grimshaw's threshold, with her eyes open. Who was Charlotte to alter truth? Had she not once seen Emily's soul and was it not indeed Shirley's too: "Like a shrine—for it was

holy; like snow—for it was pure; like flame—for it was warm;
like death—for it was strong." Charlotte could also remember
Emily's gusts of anger when anyone encroached upon that citadel
of her integrity and Shirley inherited her very look of mystic
passion in that moment when "she rose—she grew tall—she
expanded and refined almost to flame: there was a trembling all
through her, as in live coal when its vivid vermilion is hottest."

Charlotte Brontë's friends also complained that the pictures
of the masculine characters in *Shirley* were weak and not to be
compared with Rochester of *Jane Eyre*. How could she help that
either? She had written the perilous stuff of her love for M. Héger
right out of her bosom then and could never afterwards recapture
that same fervent heat to do duty for any hero whatsoever after
Rochester. In her second book she is drawing from her memory
of real people and fitting them in to a real historical background
of Orders in Council and Peninsular Wars and rebel Luddites,
but she is not writing with passion any more. The sorrows which
Caroline endures for Moore are Charlotte's sorrows for M. Héger,
but they have now become something to use for the sake of art
and are emotion recollected in tranquility. Indeed the whole
book bears witness to the fact that Charlotte has become too
conscious of her reading public and of her reviewers and cannot
shake them off her mind at all.

In *Shirley* the writer seems perplexed how to pick her way between
a first or third person narrative. Charlotte keeps on apostrophising
the reader but does not maintain her first person singular approach
after the beginning of her tale and then but fitfully afterwards.
The result is that the book loses unity and swing in its texture
and brings with it a sense of irregularity and hotch potch which
is sometimes very trying. Towards the end of the book indeed
Charlotte, as she looks out from the windows of Haworth Parsonage
on that uncompromising church tower and remembers the havoc
that death has made amongst her dear acquaintances, allows herself
a word in the first person. It is a lament for little Martha Taylor
of the Red House but it is really a cry from the heart for all those
dear joys of youth which have fled away for ever and seem to lie
buried in that grave. Here is her strangest of all literary asides:
"But Jessy I will write about you no more. This is an autumn
evening, wet and wild. There is only one cloud in the sky, but it
curtains it from pole to pole. The wind cannot rest: it hurries
sobbing over hills of sullen outline, colourless with twilight and

mist. Rain has beat all day on that church tower: it rises dark from the stony enclosure of its graveyard: the nettles, the long grass and the tombs all drip with wet. This evening reminds me too forcibly of another evening some years ago—when certain who had that day performed a pilgrimage to a grave new made in a heretic cemetery—knew they had lost something whose absence could never be atoned for as long as they lived—the fire warmed, life and friendship yet blessed them but Jessy lay cold, coffined, solitary—only the sod screening her from the storm."

Charlotte Brontë can never manage her Yorke family in her book *Shirley* without slipping into this confusion of authoress and friend. She writes of each member of the Taylor clan in her description of the Yorkes of Briarmains and shows herself immensely at home. Her memory is here word perfect. Mr. Yorke is the embodiment of that old Methodist inheritance which has gone fearlessly forward, away from Mother Church, away from Tory politics, to make that great contribution of protest on behalf of all God's children lost, downtrodden and starving beneath the scrambling selfishness of the Industrial Revolution. Charlotte draws him cleverly against the foil of her mill-owners and throws in whole hymns of apocalypse from his schism shop and a whirl of "antinomian" agitators and ragamuffin preachers to show the strange composition of the ranks collected against starvation and oppression.

In *Shirley* the rabble attend services, sing and rebel. They declare themselves "joined Methody," threaten their foes with God's judgment and quote fluently from the Bible. Hiram Yorke gives his friend good advice for his sins and exhorts him to "confess lad: smooth naught down: be candid as a convicted, justified, sanctified Methody at an experience meeting. Make yourself as wicked as Beelzebub: it will ease your mind." There were all the old shibboleths and in their right order, and, in this strange turmoil, Charlotte's memory flashes truth which will read more decorously, in years to come, when Halévy, one of her own beloved Frenchmen, as an outsider seeing more of the game, will write of this same epoch: "The majority of the leaders of the great Trade Union Movement that would arise in England within a few years of 1815 will belong to the Noncomformist sects. They will often be local preachers, that is, practically speaking, ministers. Their spiritual ancestors were the founders of Methodism. In the vast work of social organisation

N*

which is one of the dominant characteristics of nineteenth-century England it would be difficult to over-estimate the part played by the Wesleyan Revival."

There are other protagonists in *Shirley* besides those in the industrial field and again Charlotte flashes onto her pages hints of reality of which she is perhaps not wholly conscious. Her publishers much disliked her savage attack upon the new clergy in the persons of the curates of the story, but again she was unrepentant and for the same old reason that—it was the truth. And truth it was, but so garbled as to seem falsehood, were her animosity not explained by the fact that she was striking out at something, from the fastness of Haworth Parsonage, which she instinctively knew as an enemy to the immutable background of her childhood. She threw in Mr. Hall, her pious clergyman, as a foil to the worthless curates and in that action revealed the centre of the trouble, for he was a picture of Mr. Heald of Birstall, the descendant of Wesley's friend of Dewsbury, who believed in sentimental feeling and not at all in rubrics, surplices and Apostolic succession.

The wheel had, in fact, come full circle, and the time of reaction to the Wesleyan Revival had arrived. The Anglo-Catholic movement, derided by Charlotte Brontë, was the protest against too much feeling and introspection and also against the enormous success of the rebel ranks of Wesley's followers. In all but name they had become almost the established church of England, and, in this year of the publication of *Shirley*, had lost 100,000 members on the rock of rebellion and reform, and yet survived. On this stricken field the curates of Charlotte's acquaintance were not slow to follow up their advantage. They represented a movement of Counter Reformation to Evangelicalism, and, like its namesake of the 16th century, stopped the drift and arranged the forces, both inside the Church of England and without, in deadly combat.

Charlotte Brontë saw the start and hit out against it in the person of her curates, lately fallen in showers in faithful Yorkshire. She believed that these fatuous young men could not hold a candle to the evangelical Weightmans and Healds of her own inheritance and was outraged to know that they had the nerve to declare themselves apostles. She sat down to write her second masterpiece with every intention of giving their arrogant backs to the smiters of her reading public and vigorously she warmed to her subject. She showed the curates scuttling about to each other's lodgings, giving their landladies endless trouble and eating all their spiced cakes, whilst they "settled the Dissenters." If words could have killed, Charlotte Brontë would dearly have liked to settle the curates too in her mordent: "The present successors of the apostles, disciples of Dr. Pusey and tools of the Propaganda, were at that time being hatched under cradle-blankets, or undergoing regeneration by nursery-baptism in wash-hand basins. You could not have guessed by looking at any one of them that the Italian-ironed double frills of its net-cap surrounded the brows of a pre-ordained, specially sanctified successor of St. Paul, St. Peter or St. John; nor could you have foreseen in the folds of its long night-gown the white surplice in which it was hereafter cruelly to exercise the souls of its parishioners, and strangely to nonplus its old-fashioned vicar by flourishing aloft in a pulpit the shirt-like raiment which had never before waved higher than the reading-desk."

In this antagonism Charlotte Brontë was her father's daughter. Ten years later, when this alien tide had risen so steadily as to threaten the precious legacy of his Irish Cabin, Patrick Brontë wrote to an old friend: "The newspaper account of the idle and ostentatious pageantry got up in the church, where the gospel was once faithfully preached, grieves me. But, my dear madam, a bad spirit, some call it the spirit of the age (I fear it might rather be called the spirit of revolution, vanity, scepticism and Romish idolatry), this ominous spirit of the age is actuating numbers; and the young, thoughtless and vain have looked upon, loved, and greedily embraced the delusion. But Christ, who conquers death and hell, will give His followers the victory, and make all things work together for good to those who enlist in His service, and fight the good fight of Faith, in His name, and by His wisdom and power. All things work together for good to those who love God. Yes, for good, in reference to *both* the worlds."

It was the publication of *Shirley*, with its pen portraits of curates and friends, which gave away the secret of the identity of Currer Bell. Charlotte was wonderingly surprised to discover that people in Yorkshire read her books and also recognised themselves in their pages. The Rev. Wm. Heald was quick to see it and good humouredly was full of interest and friendly chuckles. He had known Charlotte from a child and aptly quoted the appropriate lines:—

"A child's among you taking notes,
    And faith he'll print it."

The curates were not quite so pleased, as was to be expected, but the one amongst them, Arthur Nicholls, who had come off best, shouted with laughter at their discomfiture.

Now began a new life for Charlotte Brontë, as, in her own right, she was invited to stay with her publishers in London and to lionise and be lionised for a season. She was a shy little lion it is true, rather more of a sprite Mrs. Gaskell thought, and she was ever under the extremity of putting her headache "in her pocket" and contending against overwhelming nervous prostration. Yet she bearded Thackeray and had the satisfaction of giving him a sermon on his sins, whilst she really enjoyed living with Mrs. Smith and her tall, pleasing son George, who was very much at her service with delightful expeditions to places of interest and even to far away Scotland. There was Matthew Arnold to be visited and Miss Martineaux, and an overpowering visit to be paid to Burnley and to the Kay Shuttleworth's mansion there. And in the background there was always Papa, who had to be regaled with only very mild accounts of Charlotte's success and who mentioned her books perhaps once a month and kept religiously to his cloister. It was a new, restless, torturing life but it had its moments. Charlotte could not tell if *Shirley* was better than *Jane Eyre*, but if it was *Jane Eyre* who made Currer Bell famous it was *Shirley* who brought to Charlotte Brontë the harvest of renown. The sprite had fluttered the dovecotes of the literary world and the name of Brontë was now on every tongue. Charlotte wished she could have told Emily and Anne about it, but contented herself by writing home about the spring-cleaning.

CHAPTER XXII

LOVE AND DEATH

THE FAME of Charlotte Brontë was established and her name might be in every mouth, but the sober truth was that the authoress herself was the more conscious now of her own terrible load of solitude. Her loneliness hung on her heart imponderably and turned her mind faint and her body sick, just when she most wanted to harvest her laurels and to give the world another book to do it good and to shake its smug complacency. The arrest of effort had something to do with the loss of the dauntless three from Haworth Parsonage, but it also had much to do with her friends' and her father's heavy jokes about her approaching lover. In reality Charlotte had none, but, in that gaunt world of her present life and in the reaction from eminence, she turned over two possibilities in her restless mind until they seemed true. She asked herself would it be George Smith or James Taylor of the firm of Smith Elder and Company who would ask her to be their lawful wedded wife?

Charlotte Brontë, who had taken all love for her literary province, was really being starved into inanition by its absence in her own life. She therefore rather relished the jokes and the dreams and talked of them to her friend Ellen Nussey until she believed them true. Was it not good of Papa to say, as Charlotte set out for a visit to the Smiths, that he would gladly go into lodgings when she returned married? All things were possible with God. Yet Charlotte was a little puzzled when Taylor went out to Bombay without declaring his love and the lingering defection of his chief, George Smith, made Charlotte nervously ill and froze her pen.

The mischief with Charlotte Brontë's temperament was that she was set up with so fatal a bump of enthusiasm that all her geese inevitably became swans. It had been the same with M. Héger and now again with George Smith, her beloved publisher, who had actually taken her to have that ponderous bump explored by a real phrenologist who confirmed the fact, without knowing who she was, of her "enthusiastic glow." She could not see that M. Héger's interest in his clever pupil and George Smith's joy in his discovery of a best seller were things concerned with the disciple and the authoress and not at all with Charlotte Brontë herself. What a startling dose of reality she would have received could she have read George Smith's estimate of her character in his forthright avowal that the woman would have given all her brains for a chance of that beauty which she had so sadly missed. Indeed the descriptions of Charlotte Brontë at this period of fame are far from complimentary with their unvarnished tale of "large mouth, many teeth gone—very plain."

It was surely the fault of that silent Parsonage to throw things into so wrong a perspective to Charlotte Brontë, sitting there alone with her thoughts. She began to dread the old signs of dependence on the post and to sigh over the longing for that one handwriting and the London postmark. There followed headache and sickness, and, if she tried to cast off depression in writing, she found a pain in her chest which robbed her of all effort and left her with nothing else to do but to brood for hours, in desolate evening after desolate evening, and far into hopeless night. She writes to Ellen Nussey: "You will recommend me I dare say to go from home—but that does no good—even could I again leave Papa with an easy mind (thank God he is still better). I cannot describe what a time of it I had after my return from London-Scotland etc. There was a reaction that sunk me to the earth—the deadly silence, solitude, desolation were awful—the craving for companionship—the hopelessness of relief—were what I should dread to feel again."

Cornhill began to get restive and to press their famous authoress for her next masterpeice, to keep their coffers nicely filled, but they made no headway at all with Charlotte in this mood. She dashes Mr. Williams's hopes with her letter of October 1850 in which she explains how he must expect nothing from her just yet, for she says: "I feel to my deep sorrow—to my humiliation—that it is not in my power to bear the canker of solitude—I had calculated that when shut out from every enjoyment—from every stimulus but what could be derived from intellectual exertion—my mind would rouse itself perforce—It is not so: even intellect—even imagination—will not dispense with the ray of domestic cheerfulness—with the gentle spur of family discussion—late in the evenings and all through the nights—I fall into a condition of mind which turns entirely to the past, to memory, and memory is both sad and relentless. This will never do and will produce no good—I tell you this that you may check false anticipations. You cannot help me—and must not trouble yourself in any shape to sympathize with me. It is my cup—I must drink it as others drink theirs."

Was it the irrevocable loss of George Smith, in the information given to Charlotte that the man was himself engaged, that got *Villette* finished in the end? It seems more than likely, for the book had hung fire long and yet all at once Charlotte goes off to Filey "utterly" alone with a secret distress of which she cannot tell Ellen. But she comes home to finish the book at a canter. After all she had her pride and that will act as well as anything else as stimulus, for she would show them what brains could do and beauty could not. In her new book she lets Dr. John go his own sweet way and pursues Paul Emanuel again in the very gait of M. Héger. She puts in a word about those letters and confesses that when she reads them over again they do not seem so fervent as once she thought them. The snapshots of the Smith household, as the Brettons of the novel, and the way *Villette* falls in two, with one set of characters left behind for other interests, rather baffled Cornhill. But Charlotte was in this complaint as obstinate as ever and said simply that it became necessary and could not be altered because it was true.

There is this thread of personal history and vehemence in each of Charlotte Brontë's books, and deep woven in all is the stain of tears. But now salvation was just round the next corner and was to come, as is its way, from a wholly unexpected quarter. *Villette* was only just in the hands of her publishers when Patrick Bronte's own £100 a year curate Arthur Nicholls proposed, in very truth, for the hand of Charlotte, his daughter. It did not matter that Charlotte did not love him, that she thought him dull, narrow minded and rude to Papa, for the fact remained that he had loved her for seven years and said nothing about it and that, when she had refused him, he could neither eat nor sleep. He lost weight. He pined away. Now, Charlotte had always wanted to be loved like that. Here at last was the real thing and it had nothing to do with Currer Bell but all to do with little Charlotte Brontë. In spite of her dislike, that was the lovely thing about Nicholls, for Charlotte now knew that she was "the first object" with somebody at last.

Haworth Parsonage, distraught, agitated as it now was, in reality, was quick with vivid life again. There were scenes, suppressed excitement and the veins standing out on Papa's forehead like whipcord. Charlotte must promise never to see "the unmanly driveller" again. She writes to Ellen Nussey that she sent Mr. Nicholls her instant refusal and adds significantly that the incipient inflammation in her father's eye has begun to abate. But of course it could never end there, for Charlotte's lonely heart was captured although she did not know it, for how could she resist that sight of a strong man broken to pieces for the love of a woman and positively kneeling at her feet? She tries to tell Ellen Nussey what a man really in love looks like, after all their maiden dreams of the experience which had been so hopelessly wide of the mark.

That dream's reality arrested Charlotte Brontë and filled her mind to the exclusion of all other considerations. She writes of Nicholls tapping on her lonely door and adds: "He entered—he stood before me. What his words were you can guess; his manner—you can hardly realise—never can I forget it. Shaking from head to foot, looking deadly pale, speaking low, vehemently yet with difficulty—he made me for the first time feel what it costs a man to declare affection where he doubts response. The spectacle of one ordinarily so statue-like, thus trembling, stirred and over-come, gave me a kind of strange shock. He spoke of sufferings he had borne for months, of sufferings he could endure no longer, and craved leave for some hope." Charlotte goes on to tell Ellen Nussey that she never had any attachment before to Mr. Nicholls but that now her heart feels for him "poignant pity" and, in that confession, her fate was sealed. There could be but one result for Charlotte Brontë before the spectacle of love's distress.

At first there was nothing for it but that Mr. Nicholls should resign his curacy, for Patrick Brontë was greatly enraged at his presumption in looking so high as the hand of his famous daughter. The fact that the man was "a Puseyite" only the more added to his sin. There was one terrible scene in Haworth Church when Nicholls tried to administer to Charlotte Brontë the broken Body and Blood of his Lord but could find no words, even in that sacred moment, and stood white faced and trembling before her, struggling to speak with tongue struck dumb with the sorrow of broken earthly love. There was one memorable parting when, as life always arranges these moments of doom, the sitting room was being turned out and its paint so well washed that Charlotte's farewell had to be said in the garden. Ellen again hears all about it with Charlotte's growing pity for the wretched swain, as she writes: "I would not go into the parlour to speak to him in Papa's presence. He went out thinking he was not to see me, and indeed, till the very last moment, I thought it best not. But perceiving that he stayed long before going out of the gate, and remembering his long grief, I took courage and went out trembling and miserable. I found him leaning against the garden door in a paroxysm of anguish, sobbing as women never do. Of course I went straight to him. Very few words were interchanged, those barely articulate. Several things I should have liked to ask him were swept entirely from my memory— Poor Fellow!"

There was but a step from such a moment as this to a regular correspondence, and soon Papa had to be told of it and at last gave in and accepted the inevitable. It is true that Nicholls had to accept Papa also with the hand of his daughter, for if Charlotte, like Mrs. Fletcher, had to marry Nicholls and his parish, the unfortunate clergyman had to shoulder Patrick Brontë for the rest of his natural life. At one neat blow Charlotte had undone the Gordian knot of Haworth Parsonage, at least as far as sharing the puzzle.

The incubus of Papa's inexorable presence had been strangely lightened with the advent of Nicholls, for they all lived together in Haworth Parsonage and Charlotte could rejoice because her marriage had turned out so well for Patrick Brontë. Now he would always have at hand a son-in-law and a perpetual curate ready to don gown or surplice, for Patrick's benefit, when that omnipotence felt that, under Providence, it was better for him to nurse his delicate health and neither preach nor pray in Haworth Church. It was strange how the old man, entombed in his study, and bending so constantly beneath the will of God, should yet exercise such unbounded temporal power. Charlotte Brontë might make merry over the pretensions of the Pope of Rome, but she never seems to have questioned the infallibility of Papa.

It was a sober marriage which the creator of Rochester had in contemplation and she did not disguise that fact either to herself or to her friends. She writes to Ellen Nussey, as the wedding day approaches: "What I taste of happiness is of the soberest order. I trust to love my husband—I am grateful for his tender love to me. I believe him to be an affectionate, a conscientious, a high principled man; and if, with all this, I should yield to regrets, that fine talents, congenial tastes and thoughts are not added, it seems to me I should be most presumptuous and thankless. Providence offers me this destiny. Doubtless then it is the best for me." To Mrs. Gaskell she writes: "My destiny will not be brilliant certainly, but Mr. Nicholls is conscientious, affectionate, pure in heart and life. He offers a most constant and tried attachment—I am very grateful to him. I mean to try and make him happy, and Papa too . . ." And to George Smith, in answer to his letter of congratulation, she writes: "Thank you for your congratulations and good wishes, if these last are realised but in part I shall be very thankful. It gave me also sincere pleasure to be assured of your happiness though of that I never doubted. I have faith also in its permanent character—provided Mrs. George Smith is—what it pleases me to fancy her to be. You never told me any particulars about her, though I should have liked them much, but did not like to ask questions knowing how much your mind and time would be engaged. What I have to say is soon told— My future husband is a clergyman—I believe I do right in marrying him. I mean to try to make him a good wife—my expectations however are very subdued—very different, I dare say, to what *yours* were before you were married. Care and fear stand so close to hope, I sometimes scarcely can see her for the shadows they cast—on one feature in the marriage I can dwell with unmingled satisfaction, with a *certainty* of being right. It takes nothing from the attention I owe my father. I am not to leave him—my future husband consents to come here—thus Papa secures by the step a devoted and reliable assistant in his old age. I hardly know in what form of greeting to include your wife's name, as I have never seen her. Say to her whatever may seem to you most appropriate and most expressive of goodwill."

The Rubicon, as Charlotte says, was now passed, and she cancels a promised visit to London and stops for all time that delicious box of books which had been forwarded to her from Cornhill ever since she began her friendship there with her publishers. The glory had departed and Charlotte was determined, however sober her dreams of wedded bliss might be, never to pass another winter in Haworth Parsonage like that one of doom, before *Villette* was written, which had come near to oversetting her reason as nearly as the loss of M. Héger had unstrung all her fortitude "after Aunt's death." Her friends were puzzled over her future and the Gaskell clan a little rebellious. A Puseyite and very stiff, as they heard, would surely sever the friendship with the saintly and unblameable William Gaskell who had the misfortune to hold Unitarian views in this storm-tossed sphere. Why had she done it? Charlotte confessed to them that what she dreaded was Nicholls's dullness and lack of any intellectual gleams of mind. One young friend was sure Charlotte must have been crossed in love and that this was a decision taken hastily on the rebound. They puzzled and puzzled and then perhaps came somewhere near the truth in their declaration to one another: "If only he is not altogether too narrow for her, one can fancy her much more really happy with such a man than with one who might have made her more in love, and I am sure she will be really good to him. But I *guess* the true love was Paul Emanuel after all, and is dead; but I don't know."

The wedding was arranged for June 29th, 1854, and was to be solemnised in Haworth Church, very early in the morning. Charlotte had insisted that it must be very quiet and no one in the town was to know it. At the last that immortal, invisible man, in his parsonage study, refused to attend and so neatly saved his face and his conscience over giving one of his own children away to a Puseyite and betraying every memory of his Irish Cabin. That was so like Patrick Brontë with his inveterate desire to make the best of both worlds, but it caused no little consternation in the room across the passage from the hermit's study, on the night before the wedding service was to be performed. Patrick was not to be argued with and help came from that quarter where help has so often issued in the history of great moments—a good school-mistress with her head screwed on tightly for all emergencies. Miss Wooler went straight to the Prayer Book and found that a friend there might give the bride away and mercifully the friend might be of the masculine or feminine gender, so what more simple than that Charlotte's old school-mistress should come to the rescue when her own father had thrown in his hand?

The honeymoon was spent in Ireland and the bride was not without courage when she set out on that long journey from the brow of Haworth Hill on that quiet misty morning of the month of June. She had always thought that Ireland was a wild place, but to her delight she found it full of delightful people of such charming courtesy and gentleness that her heart was won by her husband's home and country. Also she found that now travel had become transformed by Arthur's presence, so that the cankering anxiety of tickets, berths and railway coaches was all lifted from her shoulders in the delight of discovering the efficiency and tender care of her good husband. She visited Glen Gariffe and Killarney and made the acquaintance of those great Irish houses of faded grandeur but of warm welcome, with the smell of their turf fires lingering in the air.

The crossing from Dublin to Holyhead was mercifully calm and the travellers returned to Haworth on August 1st, climbing the steep hill together with the hope of a good Yorkshire tea before them. Charlotte had written early to Martha to have "a little cold meat or ham as well," for by this time she had developed a thoughtful care, not for the title of her new book, but for Arthur's healthy appetite. Gone were the days of his sad fasting, for he was very happy and had gained twelve pounds in weight during his Irish journey. Of course, in the gladness of the home-coming, Papa managed to be ill and rather took the fine edge off the warmth of welcome, but then as Charlotte said there was never a cup prepared, in this world, of unmixed happiness. Papa might fade into the background a little, for the important and vital thing in Haworth Parsonage just now was the fact of Arthur's stimulating companionship.

That this unexciting marriage was happy there can be no doubt, for Charlotte was better than she had ever been in her life. She had no headache and no old enemy of migraine, and she found just heaps to do and no time to think. Arthur was always needing her help or insisting on taking her for a walk on the moors. He would rush her off, out of doors, in the middle of her sedate letter writing and demand her full attention when they came to rest again by their sitting-room fire at the end of the day. Her husband was a tower of strength to Charlotte, to shoulder all her misgivings in life and to take away all that old nervous dread of visitors and ceremonies which before had dogged the footsteps of the parson's daughter. The newly wedded couple actually gave a reception in the schoolroom to all Haworth and managed to enjoy it, whilst something of Irish hospitality began to creep into that old starved solitary parsonage.

Of course this glad state could not last, for, sooner or later, reality was bound to break through. It would have been impossible for a woman of Charlotte's background to accept the physical implications of this gift of love without some qualms of silent criticism. She and her kind were too spiritually minded for it to be otherwise, and she confesses to Ellen Nussey something of this discovery after those first weeks of married life were over. She says: "Dear Nell—during the last six weeks—the colour of my thoughts is a good deal changed: I know more of the realities of life than I once did. I think many false ideas are propagated perhaps unintentionally. I think those married women who indiscriminately urge their acquaintance to marry—much to blame. For my part—I can only say with deeper sincerity and fuller significance—what I always said in theory—wait God's will. Indeed—indeed Nell— it is a solemn and strange and perilous thing for a woman to become a wife. Man's lot is far—far different."

It was there in a nutshell—the clash of dream and reality and the questioning of the order of life which meant satisfaction for the sons of Adam but distress for the daughters of Eve—and when reality was at last conceived Charlotte laid down and died of it. Fellowship was delightful, but not this crude fact of the body's demands with its tangible, terrifying results of pregnancy. That Charlotte Nicholls did not want to give house room to that unknown visitant is proved by the course of her illness. She died from the exhaustion of nervous sickness, after living for nine months as the wife of Arthur Nicholls. All her life Charlotte Brontë had believed that love was a dream of celestial bliss. It was the potent, earthly reality of marriage that killed her.

CHAPTER XXIII

MRS. GASKELL

IT WAS on the morning of Saturday, March 31st, in the year 1855, that the inevitable bell, that had so often tolled for others, tolled now for Charlotte Nicholls. The world never called her by that name, but, at the news, sent up a cry of grief for the loss of Currer Bell. In the Parsonage itself the little body of Charlotte Brontë lay very still and very cold—all passion spent. Her husband had watched beside her with more than a mother's care and, at the last, some ray of comfort must have crept into her dying brain, to know that love was there close to her at last and that it had become incarnate in human form—the white face and straggling whiskers of Arthur Nicholls not withstanding.

As Charlotte Brontë slipped away from this world, in drowning seas of sheer exhaustion, she rambled in her talk and must have kept company with Maria and visited Brussels again, but her passing was not like unto her brethren. They had been on tiptoe for their translation, alive to Heaven only, whereas Charlotte had never taken kindly to a departure from this vain, illusive world. It had always held her captive and she had lamented the fact that, unlike her father, she could not *feel* it was only "a place of probation." It was Maria the dead child she remembered, not Maria the angel's voice on the storm. It was a real incarnation of love in the volcanic person of M. Héger that she knew, with a scent of a cigar for incense, so that it is likely that she found the drawn face and the whiskers of Arthur more than reassuring in that last hour. She had, she said, a horror of dying alone and had never been able to rid her mind of Calvin's terrible creed. But at the last it was very simple with Arthur there. Charlotte returned, from fearful dreams, to hear his broken, pious voice praying God for her life—not for her eternal life as Patrick Brontë would have asked—but life now, full of laughter and tears and bread and butter and love. She turned in struggling consciousness to her husband then and cried aghast "Oh. I'm not going to die am I? God will not separate us, we have been so happy." In that dim borderland of death Charlotte was still conscious of the supremacy of God and of His ways with the saintly Fletchers of life and with more humble folk. She knew that His arbitrament was the final word on life or she would have been false to all her background. Where her creed had been softened and made more human was in her now believing that happiness too was part of God himself and that He could love it in His children. She had never believed that before, when life had shut her in alone with Patrick Brontë. Then experience had meant the draining of a cup of sorrow to the dregs and life had been a thing ordained for suffering. Arthur Nicholls, for all his prosaic appearance and his lack of sparkle, had yet proved an angel of Heaven in disguise to open up for Charlotte Brontë a realm in which happiness also, as well as affliction, might be a mark of God's interest in His lost world.

The death of Charlotte condemned her husband to six long years of lonely life in Haworth Parsonage. He was not the man to go back on his word and he had given his wife a promise that he would see her father through, to the very end. But the death of Charlotte, for Patrick Brontë himself, meant a temporary release from that permanent silence and solitude in which he had walled himself in, ever since his own wife's death. Now, with a shock of pleasure, he realised that he had come into his own again. The success of his daughter, as he saw it, was really his own success. Now, by proxy, he could enjoy the fruits of it as he had dreamed of enjoying the laurels of fame which a grateful world was to place on his brows after their reception of his Cottage Poems and his Wesley jingles. It was only after Charlotte's death that her father began to realise the extent of the fame which she had brought to the name of Brontë. It had always been her aim to give him a very sober account of her achievement and she had well succeeded in her moderation.

Now Patrick Brontë begins to take a real interest and to sun himself in those borrowed rays of authorship. He picks up a hint from Ellen Nussey and declares that a life of his daughter must be written and that none other than the famous Mrs. Gaskell must write it. Arthur Nicholls, strong in his love for Charlotte herself and hating publicity, did not want such a book at all, for all the world to read, but against Papa's vehemence he knew, for the sake of peace and whipcord veins, he must give in and help the gruesome project forward as best he could. His attitude throughout did him the greatest credit, for, as he had always been disinterested in his love of Charlotte, so was he to the end. The mantle of Currer Bell was a drapery with which he had no patience and the world's gossiping tongues and inquisitive fingers, griping amongst his very heart strings, made him too furious to be polite or to appreciate the fact that his wife had belonged to the world of letters before she belonged to him.

Mrs. Gaskell's Life of Charlotte Brontë was a masterpiece for it was written as such a tale should be, with earnest care and with a heart of love. She went on pious pilgrimage to almost all the places where Charlotte had been and she talked to anyone who had known her. It is true that her warm heart led her astray in over-emphasis and that the fact that she knew how to write made her sometimes sacrifice truth to the fine effect, but how could the transformer of the Cheshire village of Knutsford into Miss Mattie's Cranford do anything less? She had that flair of the artist about her which Charlotte Bronte never achieved in her pen pictures of places or people. Mrs. Gaskell must make a literary whole or perish. Charlotte was content with a series of the loose ends of truth. Mrs. Gaskell's biography was written as a woman writes history, from intuition in a framework of fact, and it fell into the pitfalls inseparable from that method. But that it drew the character of her friend for the world to read, and placed her firmly on her pinnacle of fame for ever, can never be denied.

It is certain that Mrs. Gaskell was responsible for that mantle of gloom which ever afterwards has hung round the world's view of Haworth Parsonage. It was she who gave out, to this same greedy gaping world, that unpleasant character of Patrick Brontë and left to posterity that likeness of his only son as the profligate and the villain of the piece. Also, as Ellen Nussey said, she missed the significance of the religion of her subject, but how could it be otherwise in a book written by an enfranchised Unitarian who knew not one shred of that palpitating, crude, glowing and terrible legacy of the Irish Cabin? Mrs. Gaskell had caught a look in Patrick's eye which she quite misread but was enough to make her declare that she knew her man. Never afterwards did she spare him from the venom of her pen, for she hated his well meant platitudes and his heavy old time courtesy too poignantly ever to let the old sinner rest in peace.

Amongst her papers, Mrs. Gaskell cherished a gem of Patrick Brontë's literary style which would have told her volumes, if only she could have read it with eyes to see. It is in the form of an invitation to Haworth which he issued to her, during Charlotte's lifetime, when it had evidently dawned upon the old man that

his daughter might want sometimes another companion than her
father in the Parsonage. It reads: "My dear Madam—From what
my daughter has told me and from my perusal of your able, moral
and interesting literary works, I think that you and she are congenial spirits, and that a little intercourse between you might,
under the strange vicissitudes and frequent trials of this mortal
life and under Providence be productive of pleasure and profit
to you both. We are gregarious beings and cannot always be
comfortable if alone, and a faithful and intellectual friend—"
and there Mrs. Gaskell tore the precious note in two and lost for
herself and the world the further wisdom of the disciple of Tighe
and Fletcher and the old time flavour of their contemporary
language.

Patrick Brontë thought he was doing very well, but of course
his pious flourishes only served to make a humanitarian of Unitarian
creed very angry indeed. "We cannot always be comfortable
if alone—" now did anyone ever hear the like of that? Mrs. Gaskell
would show the whole world what loneliness could be, shut up
on Haworth Hill with that "half mad father" of her heroine,
and she would show how Charlotte could rise above even that
terrible environment. She pours the gloom on to her picture and
sacrifices all the warm hearted inhabitants of Haworth into the
bargain. She goes astray in fury when in sober thought she should
have known better, for she had stayed with Patrick Brontë and
Charlotte and her letters then are full of sprightly grace and of
twinkling fires in every room of Haworth Parsonage. There is
no gloom about those days and the picture is full of life and quiet
methodical enjoyment. Mrs. Gaskell herself rather upset the ordered
routine by leaving her chair out of place and her sewing on the
dining table. She also hurried Martha out to show her the Brontë
tombs when Charlotte was busy with household chores, but she
knew her own limitations and did not then cavil at the Parsonage
life or find its method irksome.

Martha in these letters comes into her own as that vigorous,
neat, talkative worker who could enjoy Mr. Nicholls's "flaysome
looks" and knew and loved all the Parsonage family. She told
the tale so artlessly to Mrs. Gaskell and it goes with a swing of
reality still. There is a touch of thrilling sorrow about the triple
tragedy of the place, but no hint of that imponderable gloom
with which Mrs. Gaskell invested it. Martha's words fall over
themselves in those brief moments when her pleasant guest talks

with this good hearted woman behind Charlotte Brontë's back. "Yes! They were all well when Mr. Branwell was buried; but Miss Emily broke down the next week. We saw she was ill but she never would own it, never would have a doctor near her, never would breakfast in bed—the last morning she got up, and she dying all the time—the rattle in her throat while she would dress herself; and neither Miss Brontë nor I dared offer to help her. She died just before Christmas and we all went to her funeral. Master and Keeper, her dog, walking first side by side, and then Miss Brontë and Miss Anne, and then Tabby and me. Next day Miss Anne took ill just in the same way—and it was "Oh if it was but spring and I could go to the sea—" "Oh if it was but spring." And at last spring came and Miss Brontë took her to Scarborough—they got there on the Saturday and on the Monday she died. She is buried in the old church at Scarborough. For as long as I can remember—Tabby says since they were little bairns—Miss Brontë and Miss Emily and Miss Anne used to put away their sewing after prayers and walk all three one after the other round the table in the parlour till near eleven o'clock. Miss Emily walked as long as she could, and when she died Miss Anne and Miss Brontë took it up—and now my heart aches to hear Miss Brontë walking, walking on alone."

What artist could resist that last picture? Mrs. Gaskell certainly could not, for she is in a hurry to say that Charlotte must hear the feet of those dead sisters following her every night in her lonely vigil. But what Charlotte was really hearing and seeing just then were pictures and sounds of George Smith's voice to his newly married wife and of Arthur Nicholls's dejection and of Papa's wrath. What she was debating, during Mrs. Gaskell's visit, was whether she should cross the Rubicon and brave the tantrums or continue to walk alone. The turmoil in her mind left no room for ghostly footfalls.

The days of Mrs. Gaskell's sojourn in Haworth Parsonage went like clockwork, but very pleasantly for all that. She was positively electrified to find herself at prayers with Patrick Brontë, kneeling down demurely alongside his loaded pistol or rising to discuss her breakfast with him and this deadly little weapon at full cock. Breakfast was at nine o'clock in the study, dinner at two o'clock in the parlour, and Papa had his sent in to him across the passage, then tea at six and prayers at half past eight with talk by the fire

HAWORTH PARSONAGE

The wing on the right was added after the time of the Brontës

after nine o'clock at night. There were walks on the moors inter-
spersed in this delightful programme—those moors so beloved
of the Brontës but which to Mrs. Gaskell's Manchester eyes seemed
to be stretching sombrely towards the North Pole. It was in those
evening confidences, rather than in the daytime walks, that Mrs.
Gaskell found out so much, and yet, from the nature of the case
of chat over the dying fire, she got her details and impressions
just a little confused in her mind and just a little distorted.

Mrs. Gaskell during her visit heard much about Emily who
was Shirley, she understood, and much about Maria who was
Helen Burns. She heard the tale of Branwell's downfall from the
Parsonage view of the tragedy and as the victim had told it to
his believing sisters. She heard about that will which forbade his
marriage to Mrs. Robinson and all the rest of the below-stairs
gossip. It made Mrs. Gaskell's blood boil, without a shred of real
evidence, to think that a woman could be so wicked, and, being
quite ignorant of Branwell's real character, she saw him as a
profligate as well as a drunkard and laid the blame at the woman's
door. How she came to embellish that tale, in her Life of Charlotte
Brontë, is well known, and how a libel action was threatened on
behalf of the outraged Mrs. Robinson who had been to so much
trouble to get her Malvolio dismissed from Thorp Green without
hurting his sister Anne's feelings. That the Robinsons knew little
of what Branwell was fabricating in the bosom of his own family is
proved by the fact that the Robinson girls continued to visit
their old governess Anne Brontë in the most friendly way, coming
all the way to Haworth for that purpose.

It was the fault of Mrs. Gaskell's virtues that she wrote as she
did, for she wanted everything brought into the service of her
heroine who should rise superior to all difficulties. She also
demanded an outlet for her own feelings of love and pity. She
was puzzled at the outcry over her book, for she had tried so
very hard to make it perfect and could not understand how she
had managed to stir up a nest of hornets. She had to tone the
third edition of her book down considerably and bow before the
storm, but she could not see at all why her victims were so un-
reasonable. She could not see that she had a way of writing down
Charlotte Brontë's fireside confidences as though they were gospel
truth and that she would, by this method, come to heap praise
or blame on the wrong shoulders. A case of this sort is seen when,
in her efforts to make Mrs. Robinson's sins more lurid, she says

that the woman ought to have known better because the leaders of piety in England had once congregated under her ancestral roof. Now this statement was wrong and was a clear case of Mrs. Gaskell having transferred what Charlotte Brontë had told her of Anne's first employers on to the innocent shoulders of her second ones. It was a true statement when applied to the Inghams of Mirfield, where Anne went first as governess, but quite untrue of the Robinsons of Thorp Green. The Inghams fitted Mrs. Gaskell's description, but then they had never known Branwell Brontë. They were the descendants of Benjamin Ingham, of the Holy Club of Wesley's Oxford days, who had married that paragon of virtue Lady Margaret Hastings of the boisterous Shirley clan. How often indeed had the leaders of piety met under Ingham's roof, for Wesley and Whitefield were wont to stay there on their Yorkshire journeys and well the Brontës knew it. Anne herself, in *Agnes Grey*, says that the choice of her situations was governed by those at home who insisted on just those pious credentials from the past.

It was the same with Mrs. Gaskell's description of Cowan Bridge and the sins of its founder, the Rev. Carus Wilson. All his pious following rose in their wrath against her and started to prove what a wonder the man was and how God-fearing. And so indeed he might have been had not Mrs. Gaskell been writing in the light of that flash of anger in Charlotte Brontë's eye, seen in the firelight at Haworth, that night she told her the tale of Maria and her martyr sufferings. Who was Mrs. Gaskell to sift evidence and doubt a sister's love? It was the same propensity for collecting a good story which brought those tales of Patrick Brontë's wild fury forth for all the world to see. They came from an old woman who had nursed Mrs. Brontë in her last illness and were mediated to Mrs. Gaskell through the gossip of the Shuttleworths of Burnley, where the nurse was reputed to be living. Any stick was good enough with which to belabour Patrick Brontë and Mrs. Gaskell lays it across his broad shoulders without mercy, along with his reputed habit of dismissing good servants for wastefulness.

Patrick Brontë did not seem to mind Mrs. Gaskell's tempestuous methods in the least, now that the literary fame of his name had been established for all time. He was kept pleasantly busy writing certificates of merit for the Garr sisters who declared they had had their characters ruined by Mrs. Gaskell, and he writes to that

lady herself in his most characteristic vein and without a trace
of resentment, thus: "Why should you disturb yourself concerning
what has been, is, and ever will be the lot of eminent writers?
But here as in other cases, according to the old adage 'the more
cost the more honour.' Above three thousand years since Solomon
said, 'He that increaseth knowledge increaseth sorrow.' 'Much
study is weariness to the flesh.' So you may find it, and so my
daughter Charlotte found it, and so thousands may find it till the
end of the world, should this sinful perverse world last so long as
to produce so many authors like you and my daughter Charlotte.
You have had and will have much praise with a little blame.
Then drink the mixed cup with thankfulness to the great Physician
of souls. It will be far more salutary to you in the end and even
in the beginning, than if it were all unmixed sweetness."

CHAPTER XXIV

SOLE SURVIVOR

It was in the year 1860 and the Rev. Patrick Brontë was in bed again. This time he intended to stay there. For one thing, it saved him from taking his meals with Mr. Nicholls, and, after all, it was his eighty-third year in the land of probation and surely he might now be allowed to insert his pillows permanently between himself and the few remaining rough corners of life. His old face was crumpled into pleasure at the glowing thought that the whole world had heard of this his last home, in spite of its strange deafness to his youthful pipings in praise of his first one: "The Cabin of Mourne." He had no more need to compose his jingles, nor indeed had he any time for them, for just now Martha was bundling a clean night-shirt over his head of silver bristles and ancient poetic muse.

The Rev. Patrick Brontë was expecting visitors. Martha had put his room to rights with her cheerful morning bustle. She had made his bed and given him a good wash. Mercifully the old man had given up shaving and had allowed an inverted halo of snowy down to appear under his chin, so that Martha had only to comb his hair, to find his spectacles and to spread, on her spotless sheet, one of her equally immaculate hand-towels for the old fingers of her patient to play upon. When she had finished her work everything in the room had "a white look," from the clean boards of the floor to the bright windows and to Patrick Brontë, all freshly groomed and now sitting up alert and radiant in his bed. At that glad moment, as the brisk Martha whisked round the room with her finishing touches, the visitors were actually in the Parsonage. They were sitting waiting in Charlotte Brontë's old parlour, in a fever of excitement and with a considerable load of trepidation upon their hearts.

Mrs. Gaskell, greatly daring, with her daughter Meta, had climbed the hill that day because the young girl was consumed with curiosity to see Mama's monster. They had talked as they journeyed of their possible reception. Mrs. Gaskell, looking for some hope in a bleak world, had told her daughter, between her gasps of terror at their horse's slipping feet on those stones of Haworth, that for all his short-comings she did believe that Patrick

Brontë did what he thought was right. This was cold comfort, for Mrs. Gaskell's courage nearly failed and she asked if Meta would go alone to beard the righteous lion in his den. They decided to face it out together, and here they were, on the edge of their chairs and greatly apprehensive of approaching doom. They had that morning scurried through their breakfast, just caught the train to Keighley and had reached Haworth about 11 o'clock. Now Meta's eyes were taking in every object that could in any way link her to her mother's heroine, and she was listening to a running commentary on her surroundings and life in this very place.

Mrs. Gaskell explained that the room had been done up since Charlotte Brontë's success as an authoress had given her a little money. Until she was nineteen her father could not see what need women had of bank balances or even of a penny a week for their pocket. The prevailing colour of the room was a warm red and Mrs. Gaskell thought it looked cosy and bright with the contrast of the landscape outside and the view of the grey church tower, through the window, and those aggressive tombstones, just over the wall. The few pictures were presents from George Smith and had once brought gladness with them. Now they looked a little friendless, hanging there with the sampler about sin and serpents, for after all they were strangers from an outside world, and Thackeray and Wellington had their work cut out for them, to look at home in this hermit's retreat.

After about half an hour of time had gone by, in the contemplation of that strange assortment of pictures together with the formidable church tower and graves, Martha broke in on these meditations and all at once brought with her welcome, happiness and courage. Meta Gaskell was reassured at once and loved her on sight, declaring her to be "such a blooming, bright, clean young woman." After that, and with Martha as escort, it was easy to climb the stairs to the gorgon's bed-room, and Meta, at least, was so excited at the prospect that she really did not care if she were petrified or not. She need not have felt any alarm, but she had taken her mother's view of Patrick Brontë for gospel and in spite of Mrs. Gaskell's stout declaration about knowing her man she really did not understand him in the very least. Now she went straight to the point that was rankling in her biographer's heart and told her host she feared her visit would give him pain after what she had written in that book. To which remark

Meta appends the amazing discovery that: "It never seemed to have entered his head."

Patrick Brontë did make the couple hold their breaths, just as they were settling down to enjoy themselves, and that was when he said there was one thing in which Mrs. Gaskell was wrong. Meta was sure that Mrs. Robinson was now to be discussed, but not a bit of it. It was just this, that Patrick had never forbidden his children to eat animal food and in that erroneous statement of Mrs. Gaskell a weapon had been put into the enemy's hands, in that the Carus Wilson crowd had said that was the reason of the Brontë pupils' delicacy and not at all the hardships encountered at Cowan Bridge. But would Patrick Brontë dream of giving Mrs. Gaskell away? Never in this world. Meta reports that "He had chosen not to defend himself at the expense of proving Mama inaccurate and so giving a handle to those who accused her of misstatements." Could magnanimity go further? The man must have been greatly forgiving, for Mrs. Gaskell had made him a figure of volcanic bad temper and spiced the picture with a woman's ridicule. Now he rallied her, in his old pompous manner, like unto one with literary discernment from the pedestal of his own authorship, when he said: "As I told you in my first letter the Memoir is a book which will hand your name down to posterity."

It was this pontifical manner of Patrick Brontë which had always troubled Mrs. Gaskell. Now in old age and bed-ridden, as he was, he shot at her just that same stilted phrase of welcome which was his habitual form of greeting. He asked "in half grandiloquent style" as Meta reports "how she had passed through this weary and varied world" since last they had met. Mrs. Gaskell called that sort of talk pompous, and said that Patrick Brontë mingled "moral remarks and somewhat stale sentiments with his conversation on ordinary subjects." But she never stopped to ask herself how that style had originated, and, if she had meditated upon it, she would have been none the wiser. Patrick Brontë and his language were a survival from the past which was a sealed book to Mrs. Gaskell. How could she know that such pompous questions were the preface to all religious experience meetings amongst the people called Methodists to whom Patrick had once belonged? If Mr. Tighe talked like that who was his dutiful son in the gospel to improve upon it?

The words and the sentiments might well seem stale to Mrs. Gaskell and foreign to her own language of a newer humanism, but once such greetings had been a challenge of hope in those companies of humble, persecuted people who met to sing their pilgrim songs and help each other on to Heaven with rapture on their pinched faces and the weary world upon their backs. No emotion can keep its sweetness or its meaning after so long a lapse of years. True, the Methodists still sometimes use Patrick Brontë's form of words, but many of them know the meaning of the language now as little as Mrs. Gaskell did when they rise to sing:—

"Strangers and pilgrims here below
This earth we know, is not our place,
And hasten through the vale of woe,
And restless to behold Thy face,
Swift to our heavenly country move,
Our everlasting home above.

Patient the appointed race to run,
This weary world we cast behind,
From strength to strength we travel on,
The new Jerusalem to find.
Our labour this, our only aim,
To find the new Jerusalem.

Through Thee Who all our sins hast borne,
Freely and graciously forgiven,
With songs to Zion we return,
Contending for our native Heaven;
That palace of our glorious King,
We find it nearer while we sing."

The miracle of Haworth Parsonage was that in it this tradition had been kept so wonderfully intact. There Patrick Brontë had walled in himself and his family for so long that the isolation had served to hold, as it were, the thing solidified and static, long after its form had vanished in the outside world. That Parsonage wall had fulfilled the same office as the fossilising age which retained its monsters in their entirety centuries after every one of their fellows had perished from the earth. Now as Patrick Brontë is seen, propped up in his bed, he is, as it were, the sole survivor of another age, perfect in detail and in bulk, as is a museum mammoth from the morning of time. Mrs. Gaskell could not see it, but Meta's clear eyes observed something of greatness there.

P

She wondered and gazed and became awestruck in the presence of such a phenomenon. She read an expression on the old face that years of submission to the Will of God had chiselled there and she says it was so different from what she expected. She had looked for "the stiff scarred face above the white walls of cravat" and behold! "such a gentle, quiet, sweet, half-pitiful expression on his mouth."

Meta Gaskell picked her adjectives so well because she was painting in words the picture which she saw before her. In spite of her ignorance of it she revealed the very hall-mark of Patrick Brontë's inheritance. No Methodist could have described better the expression which was once habitual to its saints. It came from years of belief in the love of God, which, in the Passion of Redemption, had found out a way for the recovery of undone sinners. It was not caused by hope of "pie in the sky," but rather by the vivid recollection of something achieved, in past memory, at terrible cost. It reflected the knowledge that straying sheep need the sacrifice of a dying Shepherd, Who, ever after their rounding up, in this world, will set upon them the branding of His own secret sign. With this idea of epic love graven on the heart, the poor temporary habitation of such souls became nothing but a waste howling wilderness. Patrick Brontë and his children came of a people who were restless for a sight of their Redeemer and homesick for Heaven.

The tragedy was that when Patrick's own time came to set out on that last long journey, he would have no one who spoke his language to see him off. No one in Haworth Parsonage now would be able to point him to the Leader of faithful souls and whisper words that were familiar and appropriate for him, in the swellings of Jordan. There would be no voice to reach him, through the darkness, to remind him of that sovereign balm for wounds and of cordial for fears. Everyone who talked like that had gone on before him into the world of light, and even Tabby had up and followed them, just six weeks before Charlotte's own death. She had known all about how a priest of Haworth should live and die, for she talked as Patrick talked, for all it was in broad Yorkshire. This was the penalty of being the sole survivor of a tradition and an age, for the old man had outlived them all in spite of a dispensation, as he supposed, of most indifferent health— under Providence. But it would be safe to guess that Patrick Brontë would not lag behind his own children when the time of his death drew near. He had one well known phrase with which he was wont to exhort his friends when they had to face a difficult new experience and it was this: "No quailing—No drawing back." So Patrick Brontë would know how to swallow his own medicine, for he was a connoisseur of the mixed cup of destiny.

It would have been no good to look to Arthur Nicholls for a guide in the dark valley, for the breach that Charlotte's little person had filled now widened daily. Patrick Brontë could be very trying, in his role of father to the famous authoress, and he seems to have spent his time cutting up Charlotte's letters into strips and sending them to anyone who asked for such coveted relics. To Charlotte's husband this sort of traffic was gall and wormwood, and he was not any the better pleased with the insistence on that name of Brontë. With his views on the importance of baptism he was outraged that so many parents wanted to call their children by that name, not from Christian motives but much in the manner of the naming of modern heathen after popular film stars. There was one such unfortunate small boy whom Nicholls refused to christen altogether until his parents could come to a better mind, and great was his wrath on finding out that Patrick Brontë had had the child up to his bed-room and baptised him there and then in the name of "Brontë Greenwood."

Patrick Brontë told his side of the tale to Mrs. Gaskell and her daughter with many chuckles, for he believed he had been very clever in explaining his sins to his angry son-in-law. He had told him that the child was delicate and that he might have died unchristened and then where would Nicholls have been and what about burying such an infant in consecrated ground? Of course Patrick Brontë had no such scruples, but he enjoyed the joke of belabouring his son-in-law's broad back with a stick of his own High Church manufacture. The two priests had such different views of their office that it was impossible for them to achieve harmony there, whilst Patrick would glory in the name of Brontë to his dying day and Nicholls would go on having his feelings lacerated and doing his level best to hold the old man in check, as Mrs. Gaskell said—by terror.

Even now, in Patrick Brontë's Parsonage bed-room, where he had been enjoying the holding of open court to the Gaskells, he began to get uneasy. All that time Mr. Nicholls had been safely bestowed in the school, but he would be home now at any moment. Patrick could give them but five minutes more and then his guests

must make themselves scarce and not be caught worshipping at the
Brontë shrine. It would be as much as their life or his was worth.
So, amidst laughter, the ladies are bowed out of the presence with
the old man's "verbum sap" ringing in their ears, and leaving
but a narrow margin between their heels and the avenging and
outraged husband of Charlotte Brontë. Perhaps Martha laughed
too as she gave Patrick his dinner and found him more letters to
snip up, for it was her father who had said of this strange couple:
"Aye Mester Brontë and Mr. Nicholls live together, still ever
near but ever separate."

Amidst laughter and tears the story closes. The sightseers came
and went. But what Meta Gaskell could never forget was the way
in which Patrick Brontë had named the name of God, for "there
was something very solemn in the way he said it and in him
altogether." So the old man was ending where he began. That
tall body was now shrunken, the merry eye was darkened, the stalwart frame was entirely confined to bed and the hand, so steady
with a pistol, now trembled over scissors, but the old heart was
loyal to the last. Patrick Brontë had never played fast and loose
with the Holy Name. A compelling reverence and a desire to do
and to suffer the Will of God was the warp and woof of the texture
of Haworth Parsonage.

It was a sly trick of fate to give Patrick Brontë a Unitarian for
his daughter Charlotte's biographer and a Puseyite for that
daughter's husband. Between them they contrived to cover up
the significance of those tracks which Patrick's feet had trodden
all the faithful way from Rathfryland to Haworth. It was a secret,
outmoded way, of which Emily Gaskell had no knowledge and with
which Arthur Nicholls had no sympathy. In oblivion it has therefore languished for a hundred years. Now it seems but justice to
the memory of Patrick Brontë to clear away the heaped rubbish
of legend which has hidden those real footprints so assiduously,
and, in the centenary year of the publication of *Jane Eyre*, of
Wuthering Heights and of *Agnes Grey*, to give the man his undoubted
due. Without all that went to his making and the tradition walled
up in his Parsonage the famous Brontës would have been nothing.
It is certain that Patrick Brontë himself would have been less
than nothing without the glory behind the Mourne Mountains
and the shadow of John Wesley, on his old horse, butting up from
the south towards the Irish Cabin.

REFERENCES

Chapter I

The preface or "Advertisement" to *Cottage Poems* by REV. PATRICK BRONTË, B.A., Minister of Hartshead-cum-Clifton, near Leeds, Yorkshire. 1811.

Life of Charlotte Brontë, by MRS. GASKELL.

The Father of the Brontës, his Life and Work at Dewsbury and Hartshead-cum-Clifton, by W. W. YATES.

Cottage Poems, by REV. PATRICK BRONTË, B.A. From "The Irish Cabin."

Brontëana. The Rev. Patrick Brontë, his Collected Works and Life, edited by HORSFALL TURNER. P. 295: "Miss Shannon and her sister state that their grandfather Walsh Brontë was named after a clergyman."

Journal of John Wesley. Standard Edition. IV 179.

History of Methodism in Ireland, by CROOKSHANK. I 116.

The Lives of Early Methodist Preachers, Vol. III, gives Life and Death of Thomas Walsh and bears John Wesley's introduction thus: "I have carefully read the following account and believe it to be strictly true. I think it will need no other recommendation to the children of God."

Life of Wesley, by ROBERT SOUTHEY.

Journal of John Wesley. Standard Edition. IV 177, 379;
V 202;
VI 68, 201;
VII 92, 289, 510
Do.   Do.   III 334.

Notes on the First Epistle of St. John, by JOHN WESLEY.

Letters of John Wesley. Standard Edition. III 82.

Cottage Poems, by REV. PATRICK BRONTË. Epistle to a Young Clergyman.

Shakespeare Head Brontë : Life and Letters. I 60-68.

Chapter II

I am indebted to F. J. Cole Esq., of Belfast for his research into the Tighe family. Rev. Thomas Tighe was the son of William Tighe of Rosanna, County Wicklow. He was educated at Harrow, admitted St. John's College, Cambridge, 18th January, 1771, B.A., 1775, M.A. Peterhouse 1778. Fellow of Peterhouse 1775. Vicar of Drumgooland from 1778, Vicar of Drumballyroney, 1778-1821. J.P. County Down. His half-brother William Tighe of Rosanna was married to Wesley's friend Sarah Fownes. *History of Methodism in Ireland*, by C. H. CROOKSHANK, M.A., II 129, gives for the year 1798: "Having spent the first fortnight of the year in Dublin, Mr. Averell set out on a tour to the north, which occupied three months. The first places on his plan were Drogheda, Dundalk, Newry, and the Rev. Mr. Tighe's, near Rathfryland, in all of which he sowed the seed of life with hope of fruit."

Journal of John Wesley. Standard Edition. IV 177; VII 289, 39.

Life and Times of the Countess of Huntingdon, by a member of the House of Shirley.

Charlotte Brontë's heroine Shirley, Anne Brontë's character Huntingdon in *The Tenant of Wildfell Hall,* the Poet of Angria, Henry Hasting, in the juvenile writings, given in the *Shakespeare Head Brontë: Miscellaneous and Unpublished Writings* Vol. II.

Letters of Rev. John Fletcher to William Tighe.

Shakespeare Head Brontë: Miscellaneous and Unpublished Writings of Charlotte and P. Branwell Brontë, II 359, 140-143.

Chapter III

Memorials of the Wesley Family, by Stevenson.

Clement Shorter is the authority for the introduction of Patrick Brontë into Yorkshire by Fletcher influence.

Shakespeare Head Brontë: Life and Letters, I 2.

Methodist Recorder (Christmas Number, 1892): Henry Martyn's Links with Methodism.

Life of Henry Martyn, by GEORGE SMITH.

Journal of John Wesley. Standard Edition. VI 380.

The Life of Mrs. Mary Fletcher, compiled from her journal and other authentic documents by HENRY MOORE.

Life of Rev. J. Fletcher, by BENSON.

Works of J. Fletcher. Vol. VII.

Works of John Wesley. VII 434.

Shakespeare Head Brontë: Life and Letters, I 60-68.

Chapter IV

The Early Methodist Preachers. Vol. I. Life of John Nelson.

Letters of John Wesley. Standard Edition. VIII 273.

Journal of John Wesley. Standard Edition. VII 521.

Life of Jabez Bunting, by his son.

Methodist Magazine, 1812. XXXV 395.

Woodhouse Grove School, Memorials and Reminiscences, by J. T. SLUGG.

Journal of John Wesley. Standard Edition. V 149, 373 (note) for Crosse of Bradford.

Chapter V

Shakespeare Head Brontë: Life and Letters, I 9-29.

Chapter VI

The Rural Minstrel, by REV. PATRICK BRONTË, B.A. 1813.

Shakespeare Head Brontë: Life and Letters, I 39-45, for Miss Firth's Diary. She had been a pupil of Miss Richmal Mangnall of *Mangnall's Questions.*

Life of William Grimshaw, by MYLES.

Methodist Heroes of the Great Haworth Round, by LAYCOCK.

Shakespeare Head Brontë: Life and Letters, I 59.

Life of Charlotte Brontë, by MRS. GASKELL

Works of John Wesley. Vol. VII.

Memoir of Crosse of Bradford by W. W. STAMP in *Wesleyan Methodist Magazine,* 1844: "John Crosse was converted under the preaching of Alexander Coates, one of the first race of Methodist preachers.

He joined the Society at West Street (London) and became known to John Wesley. They became life-long friends. At Whitechapel near Birstall where Crosse was incumbent he became a friend of Miss Bosanquet and upon her marriage exchanged clerical duties with John Fletcher for 3 months. He was Vicar of Bradford from 1784 to 1816 and in his own vicarage conducted a class-meeting on the Methodist plan."

Chapter VII
Life of Charlotte Brontë, by MRS. GASKELL.
Jane Eyre.
Shakespeare Head Brontë: Life and Letters, I 110, 158, 60-68.
Life of Mrs. Fletcher gives: "If they love us why do they whip us? A little one, about six years old, replied, 'Why, it is because they love us; and it is to make us remember what a sad thing sin is; and God would be angry with them if they did not do so'."
Shakespeare Head Brontë: Life and Letters, I 72, quotes an anecdote of Carus Wilson thus: "A poor little girl who had been taken into a school was whipped. She asked 'If they love us why do they whip us?' A little girl of six replied: 'It is because they love us, and it is to make us remember what a sad thing sin is. God would be angry with them, if they did not whip us'."
Villette.
Shakespeare Head Brontë: Life and Letters, I 69.
Shakespeare Head Brontë: The Poems of Charlotte and Patrick Branwell Brontë, p. 297.
Poetical Works of John and Charles Wesley (collected and arranged by G. OSBORN, D.D.). Vol. VI 436.
Chapter VIII
Life of Charlotte Brontë, by MRS. GASKELL.
Shakespeare Head Brontë: Life and Letters, I 69, gives Patrick Brontë's statement that Maria "exhibited during her illness many symptoms of a heart under Divine influence."
Shakespeare Head Brontë: The Poems of Charlotte and Patrick Branwell Brontë. P. 326. To Caroline.
Villette.
Jane Eyre.
Life of Mrs. Fletcher.

Chapter IX
Life of Charlotte Brontë, by MRS. GASKELL.
Life of William Grimshaw, by MYLES.
Methodist Heroes of the Great Haworth Round, by LAYCOCK gives contemporary letters, thus: "At last he thought he evidently saw the Lord Jesus put down His hands and feet below the ceiling, and he had time enough to see the nail holes in them, which he observed to be ragged and blueish, and fresh blood streaming from each of them."
Arminian Magazine, 1778. Vol. I 475.
Shirley.

Arminian Magazine, 1785. Vol. VIII 111.
Shakespeare Head Brontë: Life and Letters, I 153.
Works of John Wesley. Sermon on the death of the Rev. John Fletcher.
Shakespeare Head Brontë: Unpublished and Miscellaneous Writings of Charlotte and P. Branwell Brontë. Vol. II 89, 417.
DOROTHY WORDSWORTH: *The Grasmere Journal,* March 1802: "There was something in the air that compelled me to serious thought—I had many very exquisite feelings." Also for September, 1800, at a Lakeland funeral with its open-air singing: "The sun was shining and the prospect looked as divinely beautiful as I ever saw it—it seemed more sacred than I had ever seen it." Cf. "The opening heavens around me shine, With beams of sacred bliss."
Shakespeare Head Bronte: Life and Letters, I 131.
Chapter X
Shakespeare Head Brontë: Life and Letters, I 92-100, 137.
Old Records at Methodist Chapel, Birstall.
Shirley.
Life of Charlotte Brontë, by MRS. GASKELL.
Shakespeare Head Brontë: Life and Letters, I 121, 137, 140, 143, 153.
Methodist Magazine, March 1939. "The Red House, Gomersal" by REV. W. B. HOULT, M.A., B.D.
Letters of John Wesley. Standard Edition. VI 102.
Chapter XI
Shakespeare Head Brontë: Life and Letters, II 261.
Shakespeare Head Brontë: Unpublished and Miscellaneous Writings of Charlotte and P. Branwell Brontë, II 8, 9.
The Brontë Family with special reference to Patrick Branwell Brontë, by LEYLAND.
Brontëana, edited by HORSFALL TURNER. P. 54.
Shakespeare Head Brontë: Life and Letters, I 130, 143.
Shakespeare Head Brontë: Unpublished and Miscellaneous Writings of Charlotte and P. Branwell Brontë, II 182, 184, 60.
Life of Charlotte Brontë, by MRS. GASKELL.
Selections from Poems of ELLIS BELL, published in the 1850 edition of *Wuthering Heights* and *Agnes Grey.*
Chapter XII
Shakespeare Head Brontë: Life and Letters, I 239.
The Poems of THOMAS CHATTERTON from the collection in Bristol City Library.
(The Gospel Magazine of the Calvinistic Methodists is older than Wesley's Arminian Magazine).
Shakespeare Head Brontë: Life and Letters, I 265, 151, 133, 135, 150.
Shakespeare Head Brontë: The Poems of Charlotte and Patrick Branwell Brontë. P. 297, 345.
Poems of SAMUEL TAYLOR COLERIDGE.
Life of Samuel Taylor Coleridge, by LAURENCE HANSON.
Poems of HARTLEY TAYLOR COLERIDGE.
Shakespeare Head Brontë: Life and Letters, I 216.
Pictures of the Past, by FRANCIS GRUNDY.

Chapter XIII
Shakespeare Head Brontë: The Poems of Charlotte and Patrick Branwell Brontë give the Luddenden Foot Notebook poems, pp. 380, 381, 383, 385.
I am indebted to Mr. J. Hodgson of Westminster College for his research amongst the old books which formed the library at the Lord Nelson Inn at Luddenden. On the inside of the cover of the Oxford Magazine for 1769 he found written in Branwell's writing: "P. B. Brontë, sheep stealer." The books contain commentaries by Matthew Henry, 1722, Lowth on the Prophets, 1739, Stachhouse on the Creed, 1747, Art of Preaching, Explanations of the grand mystery of Godliness, History of Infant Baptism, 1707, Whitefield's Letters (3 vols.) 1772, The Enthusiasm of Methodists and Papists Compared, 1749, Life of Thomas Coke (Wesley's friend), Missionary and Slave Tracts, Isaac Watts, Poems, 1770.
Life of William Grimshaw, by MYLES.
Methodist Heroes of the Great Haworth Round, by LAYCOCK.
Journal of John Wesley. V 475. There are eight visits of John Wesley to Ewood, thus, in his Journal: IV 32, 113, 212, 470; V 475; VI 16, 229, 350.
Shakespeare Head Brontë: The Poems of Charlotte and Patrick Branwell Brontë, pp. 357, 382, 373.
Chapter XIV
Shakespeare Head Brontë: Life and Letters, I 167, 168, 169.
Wuthering Heights: gives Joseph's tirade and comment: "He must have need of divine aid to digest his dinner." Cf. Life and Letters, IV 230: "So that by Divine aid his useful life may be spared long."
Brontëana, edited by HORSFALL TURNER. Pp. 243, 244, 245, 235.
Shirley.
History of Woodhouse Grove School, by J. T. SLUGG.
Agnes Grey.
Shakespeare Head Brontë: Life and Letters, I 201, 214, 217, 209, 213, 227.
Shakespeare Head Brontë: The Poems of Charlotte and Patrick Branwell Brontë. Pp. 397, 227.
Brontëana, edited by HORSFALL TURNER gives the funeral sermon of Rev. Patrick Brontë on William Weightman. Pp. 261, 252, 255.
Shakespeare Head Brontë: The Poems of Charlotte and Patrick Branwell Brontë. Pp. 397, 396, 399, 400. (1842).
Journal of John Wesley. Standard Edition. III 293, 369; IV 68, 114, 213.
Brontëana, edited by HORSFALL TURNER: A Funeral Sermon for the late Rev. William Weightman, M.A., preached on Sunday the 2nd of October, 1842. By the Rev. Patrick Brontë, B.A., Incumbent. P. 259: "A friend to many and an enemy to none."
Chapter XV
Shakespeare Head Brontë: Life and Letters, I 273, 277, 242, 124, 282, 283, 287.
The Poems of EMILY BRONTË.
Shakespeare Head Brontë: The Poems of Emily and Anne Brontë. Pp. 229, 273, 282, 220.

Shakespeare Head Brontë: The Poems of Charlotte and Patrick Branwell Brontë. Pp. 240.

Shakespeare Head Brontë: Life and Letters, II 9, 19, 64, 65, 67.

The Footsteps of the Brontës, by MRS. CHADWICK.

Chapter XVI

Shakespeare Head Brontë: Life and Letters, II 43, 64, 51, 84.

Shakespeare Head Brontë: The Poems of Charlotte and Patrick Branwell Brontë. Pp. 326, 429, 417, 410.

Chapter XVII

Shakespeare Head Brontë: Life and Letters, II 262, Charlotte to Mr. Williams, October 2nd, 1848; pp. 68, 69.

Introduction to the 1850 edition of *Wuthering Heights* and *Agnes Grey,* by CHARLOTTE BRONTË.

Shakespeare Head Brontë: Poems of Emily and Anne Brontë. Pp. 30, 7.

Shakespeare Head Brontë: Poems of Charlotte and Patrick Branwell Brontë. Pp. 410, 327, 380.

Shakespeare Head Brontë: Life and Letters, II 72, 91, 95, 99, 113, 124, 125, 223, 224.

ANNE BRONTË's poems give "I knew that my Redeemer lived"; (cf. "I know that my Redeemer lives, by Wesley). Also "My God, oh let me call Thee mine"; (cf. Wesley's "My God! I know, I feel Thee mine").

Chapter XVIII

Shakespeare Head Brontë: Life and Letters, II 105, 106, 107, 108, 109, 110.

Letters of Charles Lamb. Everyman Edition. P. 325. The phrase is in a letter to Dorothy Wordsworth in December 1814.

Jane Eyre.

Chapter XIX

Biographical Introduction by CHARLOTTE BRONTË to *Wuthering Heights.*

Arminian Magazine, I 475.

Methodist Heroes of the Great Haworth Round, by LAYCOCK gives contemporary letter, with this account of Grimshaw's "bedside manner,' from Mrs. Jones, then staying at Haworth.

The Life and Times of the Countess of Huntingdon, by a member of the House of Shirley.

Sidelights on the Conflicts of Methodism, by BENJAMIN GREGORY.

Wuthering Heights.

Shakespeare Head Brontë: Poems of Emily and Anne Brontë. Pp. 158, 178.

Chapter XX

The Lives of the Early Methodist Preachers. Vol. III. The Life and Death of Thomas Walsh.

Shirley.

Shakespeare Head Brontë: Life and Letters, II 261, 263. Venn's funeral sermon for William Grimshaw had for text "He was a burning and a shining light" and Charlotte writes (II 261) that she weeps "for the wreck of talent, the ruin of promise, the untimely dreary extinction of what might have been a burning and a shining light."

Biographical Introduction by CHARLOTTE BRONTË to *Wuthering Heights*. 1850.

Obituary notice of William Sanderson. Minutes of Conference. 1810.

Shakespeare Head Brontë: Life and Letters, II 269, 286, 288, 289, 290, 293, 294, 298, 299, 301, 315, 324, 333, 337, 338, 339, 340.

Life of Charlotte Brontë, by MRS. GASKELL gives Ellen Nussey's account of Anne's death.

Shakespeare Head Brontë: Life and Letters, II 61 gives Branwell's rendering of Grimshaw's phrase thus: "while roasting daily and nightly over a slow fire."

Chapter XXI
Shirley.
Life of Charlotte Brontë, by MRS. GASKELL.
Shakespeare Head Brontë: Life and Letters, II 313, IV 237; III 12, 17, 53, 57, 65.

Chapter XXII
Shakespeare Head Brontë: Life and Letters, III 125, 166, 167, 174, 205, 220, 222, 223, 229, 230, 231, 236, 257, 336. IV 68, 112, 115, 117, 119, 125, 133, 135, 150, 171, 145.

Chapter XXIII
Life of Charlotte Brontë, by MRS. GASKELL.
Shakespeare Head Brontë: Life and Letters, IV 189, 190, 192, 84, 86, 87, 88, 93, 226.

Chapter XXIV
Shakespeare Head Brontë: Life and Letters, IV 239, 240, 241, 243. IV 230: "This state of our probation." 1858. Patrick Brontë's letter to Mrs. Nunn.

INDEX

Weightman, William, 115, 116,
    118, 120, 121, 122, 123, 125,
    126, 127, 128, 130, 133, 134,
    135, 138, 178
Wellington, 20
Wellington, Duke of, 2, 43, 73, 75,
    96, 205
Wesley, Charles, 18, 21, 60, 78,
    90, 102, 105, 131, 136, 143,
    149, 151, 176
Wesley John, 3, 4, 5, 6, 7, 10, 11,
    12, 14, 18, 21, 25, 28, 30, 33,
    40, 46, 50, 51, 52, 53, 64, 68,
    71, 72, 73, 81, 82, 83, 84, 87,
    88, 97, 98, 100, 105, 107, 108,
    109, 117, 119, 125, 126, 127,
    132, 134, 164, 170, 175, 177,
    202, 210
Westminster Abbey, 177
Whitefield, George, 12, 13, 14, 46,
    100, 125, 202
Wilberforce, 18, 77

Williams, of Smith, Elder and
    Company, 162, 173, 188
Wilson, Carus, 59, 61, 67, 202
Wilson, Surgeon, 157
Wolfe, General, 111
Woodhouse Grove, 28, 29, 30, 31
    32, 33, 34, 35, 37, 41, 42, 47,
    53, 117, 122, 166
Wooler, Miss, 80, 81, 83, 193
Wordsworth, Dorothy, 77, 78
Wordsworth, William, 65, 102,
    105, 159
Wright, William, 2
Wuthering Heights, 157, 162, 164,
    165, 166, 167, 168, 170, 174,
    210

Yorke, Hiram, 183
Yorkshire, 2, 5, 18, 20, 21, 22, 23,
    24, 26, 28, 51, 71, 139, 184

Zamorna, 76, 80, 96

MADE AND PRINTED IN GREAT BRITAIN BY
CHARLES BIRCHALL AND SONS, LTD.,
LONDON AND LIVERPOOL